THE
VANISHING AT
PINECREST

Ty Swartz

To Andrew, Tristian, and Dylan, you keep me young and motivated.

ACKNOWLEDGMENT

To my wife, for 20 years of my antics, stories, and adventures,
I bring to our lives. You keep me balanced and loved.

CONTENTS

CHAPTER ONE

PINECREST NEW BEGINNINGS

The rain fell in sheets against the windows of Dr. Olivia Rivera's sedan as she navigated the unfamiliar streets of Chesapeake, Virginia. Her son, Samuel, sat silently in the passenger seat, watching raindrops race down the glass with disinterest. The wipers struggled against the downpour, creating a rhythmic soundtrack to their arrival in this new city.

"We're almost there, Sam," Dr. Rivera said, glancing at her son with a forced cheerfulness that didn't quite reach her eyes. "Pinecrest Middle School is just up ahead. I know starting in April is weird timing, but you'll adjust quickly."

Sam nodded without enthusiasm, his gaze fixed on the imposing brick building that emerged through the rain. Something about the place made his stomach tighten— perhaps it was just new-school anxiety, or maybe it was the way the old east wing jutted out at an odd angle from the main structure, its windows dark despite the gloomy morning.

The school was built in the late 1940s, initially as a segregated high school for African American students. It was renamed in the early 1950s and later converted to a middle school during integration. Its history was precisely why his mother, a historian specializing in educational segregation and integration, had accepted the teaching position.

As they pulled into the visitor parking lot, Sam noticed a stone memorial bench beneath a massive oak tree. Even in the rain, something was solemn about it, as if it were watching over the grounds. Dr. Rivera gathered her folders and new employee paperwork, her excitement palpable.

"Remember, I'm meeting with Principal Fletcher first, then getting set up in my classroom. You'll meet with your guidance counselor, who'll get you sorted out regarding your schedule and locker assignment."

Sam nodded again, shouldering his backpack as they made a dash through the rain to the main entrance.

The school's interior contrasted old and new – original terrazzo floors polished to a high shine, display cases filled with trophies and photographs, and modern bulletin boards announcing spring activities and upcoming testing dates.

The main office was warm and brightly lit, a welcome contrast to the gloomy day outside. A secretary with a kind smile greeted them, and within minutes, Principal Fletcher emerged from his office. He was a tall man with silver-streaked dark hair and intelligent, gifted eyes. He assessed Sam quickly before turning a charming smile toward Dr. Rivera.

"Dr. Rivera, we're so pleased to have someone of your caliber joining our faculty," he said, shaking her hand firmly. "Your work on educational transitions during integration will be especially valuable given Pinecrest's unique history."

Sam's attention wandered to a partly open filing cabinet behind the secretary's desk as the adults exchanged pleasantries. A red folder labeled "INCIDENT REPORTS" caught his eye, and through the gap, he could just make out a date: "April 2013." The secretary noticed his gaze and smoothly closed the drawer with her foot while maintaining her smile.

"Samuel, right?" she asked. "Mrs. Winters, your guidance counselor, is ready for you. First door on the left down that hallway."

Reluctantly, Sam parted from his mother, who gave him an encouraging nod before following Principal Fletcher into his office. Mrs. Winters was a petite woman with curly gray hair and reading glasses that hung from a beaded chain around her neck. Her office walls were covered with college pennants and motivational posters.

"So, Samuel- do you prefer Sam?" she asked, already typing into her computer.

"Sam," he confirmed, settling into the chair across from her desk.

"Well, Sam, we'll get you all set up. Transferring in April is unusual, but we'll make sure the transition is smooth. Pinecrest is a wonderful school with a rich history. We just need to find you the right homeroom..."

She trailed off, squinting at her screen with a slight frown.

"Is something wrong?" Sam asked, noticing her hesitation. Mrs. Winters quickly rearranged her features into a smile.

"Not at all. Just comparing class sizes to find the best fit. Ah, here we go – Ms. Bennett's class in room 127 has an opening. She's one of our best teachers."

She printed his schedule and wrote his locker number and combination on a small card for easy access.

"Your first class starts in twenty minutes. Would you like a student guide to show you around?"

Before Sam could answer, a quick knock on the open door drew their attention. A girl about Sam's age stood in the doorway, her dark hair pulled back into a neat braid, and intelligent eyes assessed him from behind rectangular glasses.

"Mrs. Winters, Principal Fletcher asked me to give our new student a tour," she said, her voice confident but not unfriendly.

Mrs. Winters brightened.

"Perfect timing! Sam, this is Leila Washington. She's on our student welcoming committee and knows the school inside and out. Her grandfather was actually a teacher here when it was still Pinecrest High School."

Leila gave a small smile at this introduction. "My grandfather had a lot of stories about this place," she said, with an emphasis that seemed significant. "I'll ensure Sam knows all the important things about Pinecrest."

Something in her tone made Sam curious, as if "important things" meant more than just where the cafeteria was. As they left the office, Sam glanced back to see Mrs. Winters watching them with an odd expression – concern, perhaps, or worry – before she turned back to her computer, shoulders tense. Leila led him through the main hallway, pointing out the gymnasium, cafeteria, and library with practiced efficiency.

"So your mom's the new history teacher?" she asked as they walked.

"That's what I heard." Sam nodded.

"Yeah, she specializes in educational history, especially segregation and integration. This school's background is exactly what she's been researching."

Leila's pace slowed slightly. "Has she mentioned anything about... incidents in the school's history?"

The way she stressed "incidents" made Sam pause.

"No, not specifically. Why?"

Leila glanced around before lowering her voice. "Nothing. Just curious what kind of history she's interested in." They continued walking, turning into an older corridor with dimmer lighting, and the lockers showed more wear.

"This is the east wing," Leila explained. "It's the original part of the building from when this was a high school. Most classes aren't held here anymore – it's mainly storage and a few special classrooms."

Sam noticed how their footsteps echoed differently there, as if the building itself were listening.

"It feels different," he observed. Leila nodded.

"The east wing has a lot of... history." The first bell rang before Sam could ask what she meant, signaling ten minutes until classes began. Leila quickened her pace.

"That's your locker there, 237. And your homeroom is just around the corner. We have lunch at 12:30. Find me in the cafeteria?"

The question seemed more significant than a casual lunch invitation.

"Sure," Sam agreed, curiosity clearly piqued.

As Leila turned to leave, she hesitated. "One more thing. Be careful about asking too many questions about the school's past. Not everyone appreciates curious new students." With that cryptic warning, she disappeared into the growing crowd of students, leaving Sam staring after her in confusion.

Homeroom with Ms. Bennett was uneventful – routine announcements, a brief introduction as the new student, and curious stares from classmates. Sam took an empty desk near the window, noticing that the seat behind him remained vacant.

During attendance, Ms. Bennett called out, "Aaron Mitchell?" and was met with silence. She frowned slightly, marked something on her tablet, and continued. After homeroom, Sam followed his schedule to English, math, and science, trying to navigate the unfamiliar building. In each class, he noticed the teachers taking attendance with unusual attention, sometimes exchanging glances with students when certain names went unanswered.

By lunchtime, Sam was ready for answers to the strange undercurrent he'd been sensing all morning. The cafeteria buzzed with the typical middle school energy: loud conversations, clattering trays, and occasional bursts of laughter. Sam spotted Leila at a corner table with two other students. She waved him over, her expression serious despite the casual gesture.

"Sam, these are my friends," she said as he set his tray down. "Noah Chen and Mia Patel."

Noah was slim, with spiky black hair and rectangular glasses, and a laptop was open beside his lunch tray. Mia had warm brown skin, curly hair pulled into a high ponytail, and watchful eyes that assessed Sam with cautious interest.

"So you're the history teacher's kid," Noah said, adjusting his glasses. "Interesting time to move here."

Before Sam could respond, Mia cut in. "Noah, be nice. It's not his fault when they arrived." She offered Sam a small smile. "Ignore him. He's just on edge because of Aaron."

Sam recognized the name from homeroom. "Aaron Mitchell? The empty desk in my homeroom?" The three friends exchanged glances. Leila leaned forward. "Aaron didn't come to school yesterday. Or today. His parents called the police because he never came home from robotics club on Monday afternoon."

"That's terrible," Sam said, feeling a chill despite the warm cafeteria. "Do they know what happened to him?"

Noah's fingers tapped a nervous rhythm on his laptop. "Officially? No. But we have a theory."

Mia shot him a warning look. "Noah, we agreed..."

"We agreed to be careful who we talk to," Noah interrupted. "But his mom's researching the school's history. They deserve to know what they've walked into."

Leila sighed, then turned to Sam with a serious expression. "What do you know about Pinecrest's history?"

Sam shrugged. "Just the basics. It was originally a segregated high school for Black students. It was renamed from something else in the early '50s, then converted to a middle school during integration in the '70s. My mom's interested in how the transition affected the educational experience."

"That's the official history," Leila agreed. "But there's more." She glanced around before continuing in a lower voice. "Every twelve years, students disappear from Pinecrest. Always in April. Always four students."

Sam stared at her, waiting for the punchline to what must be a joke played on the new kid. When none came, he asked, "Is this some kind of school legend? Like a haunted bathroom or something?"

Mia shook her head, her expression grave. "I've lived in Chesapeake my whole life. My aunt was a student here in 2001. Four students disappeared then, too. The official story was that they ran away, but no one really believed it."

"And twelve years before that, in 1989," Noah added, turning his laptop so Sam could see a digitized newspaper clipping. "Four students vanished within the same week. And in 1977, and 1965..."

"You're saying this has happened every twelve years since the school was built?" Sam asked incredulously. "And no one's connected the dots or done anything about it?"

Leila pulled a worn leather journal from her backpack. "My grandfather was a teacher here in the 1960s. He documented everything, including the 1965 disappearances. He tried to investigate but was shut down by the administration. After integration, when they converted the school to Pinecrest Middle, he was forced into early retirement."

She opened the journal to a marked page. "April 14, 1965. Four students absent today. Principal says they're all out with spring flu, but office records show no parent calls. Strange coincidence."

She flipped forward a few pages. "April 16, 1965. Still no sign of the four. Called Thomas's home, pretending to deliver homework. His mother had no idea he wasn't in school. Something is very wrong here."

Sam felt a chill run down his spine that had nothing to do with the cafeteria's air conditioning. "So you think Aaron Mitchell is the first of four students who will disappear this month? Because of some... what, curse? Conspiracy?"

Noah closed his laptop with a decisive click. "We don't know if it's supernatural or human, but the pattern is undeniable. Aaron fits the profile – he's brilliant, president of the robotics club, and won the state math Olympiad last year. In previous cycles, the first to disappear is always the scholar."

"Profiles?" Sam echoed. "You mean the disappearances follow a specific pattern?"

Mia nodded solemnly. "From what we've been able to piece together, it's always four specific types of students. The scholar, the artist, the leader, and the healer."

"Aaron's the scholar," Leila explained. "Academic star, brilliant mind. The second is usually someone with artistic talent. The third is a natural leader, like a student council president. And the fourth has a nurturing, healing nature."

The bell signaling the end of lunch interrupted their conversation. As students around them gathered trays and backpacks, Leila quickly scribbled something on a piece of paper and handed it to Sam.

"My phone number. Text me after school. We've been researching this for months since we realized April 2025 would be the next cycle."

As they parted ways, Sam felt disoriented. Part of him wanted to dismiss their story as an elaborate prank or a case of pattern-seeking in random events. But the seriousness in their eyes, the newspaper clippings, the journal entries – and the very real fact that a student named Aaron Mitchell was indeed missing – all gave him pause.

Throughout his afternoon classes, Sam found it difficult to focus. His mind kept returning to the conversation at lunch, analyzing it for any signs that they were messing with him. But why would they? And the empty desk in homeroom was real enough.

When final dismissal came, Sam texted his mother that he was staying after school to get caught up on assignments. In reality, he wanted to explore the building a bit, particularly the east wing that Leila had pointed out. The hallways gradually emptied as students headed home or to after-school activities. Sam wandered toward the east wing, noticing how the building seemed to transition from a modern educational facility to something older, more solemn. The floor here was original terrazzo, worn smooth by decades of footsteps. Display cases contained faded photographs of basketball teams and debate clubs from when Pinecrest was still a high school.

CHAPTER TWO
WHISPERS IN THE HALLS

He stopped at one case containing a 1965 yearbook and opened it to a page showing students in a science laboratory. The caption read: "Science Club earns top state honors." Young faces gazed out confidently, unaware that, according to Leila's grandfather's journal, four students would vanish without explanation within months.

"They were the best in the state," a voice said behind him. Sam jumped, turning to find an elderly man in a custodial uniform leaning on a mop. The man's dark eyes held a depth that suggested he'd seen more than his share of history pass through these halls.

"Sorry," Sam said automatically. "I was just looking at the old photos."

The custodian nodded toward the display case. "I was there when that picture was taken. Senior year, 1967."

Sam's eyes widened. "You went to school here? When it was Pinecrest High?"

"And came back to work here after a stint in the Navy," the man confirmed. "Name's Mr. Thompson. Been watching over this building longer than most folks have been alive."

There was something both reassuring and unsettling about his presence, as if he were both protector and gatekeeper. "I'm Sam. My mom's the new history teacher."

Mr. Thompson studied him for a moment. "Dr. Rivera? I heard we had a historian joining us. Interesting timing." The phrase echoed what Noah had said at lunch.

"What do you mean?" Sam asked, trying to sound casual. The custodian's weathered face remained impassive.

"April's an interesting month at Pinecrest. Lots of history in these walls. Not all of it is written down in books." He gestured toward the east wing corridor stretching beyond them. "This part of the building, especially. They don't use many of these rooms anymore. Say they're for storage, but mostly, they just stay locked."

Sam hesitated, then decided to take a risk. "I heard a student is missing. Aaron Mitchell. Did you know him?"

Something flickered in Mr. Thompson's eyes – recognition, perhaps, or concern. "Bright kid. Always stayed late working on his robots. Asking questions nobody wanted to answer." He studied Sam more intently. "You've been making friends already, I see. Let me guess – Leila Washington and her little investigation crew?"

Sam tried to hide his surprise. "They mentioned something about students disappearing every twelve years."

Mr. Thompson sighed, leaning more heavily on his mop. "This old building's collected a lot of stories over the decades. Not all of them are worth repeating."

"So it's not true?" Sam pressed. The custodian glanced down the empty hallway before speaking. "Listen, young man. Schools like Pinecrest – they hold history in their walls. Some of it is painful. This was one of the county's first high schools for Black students. When they closed it down to make it a middle school, it wasn't just a building that changed. It was a community that got scattered. Teachers lost their jobs. Traditions were erased. History got... rewritten."

His voice had dropped to barely above a whisper. "Sometimes, the past doesn't want to stay buried."

A chill ran down Sam's spine. "What does that have to do with missing students?"

Mr. Thompson straightened up, his demeanor shifting back to that of a school employee. "Nothing but stories, like I said. But since you're new here, let me give you some advice: stay away from the old storage rooms in this wing, especially around sunset. The building settles and makes strange noises. Gives people ideas."

Before Sam could press further, the distinct sound of heels clicking on terrazzo echoed down the hallway. They both turned to see Dr. Rivera approaching, her arms full of folders. "Sam! There you are. I've been looking all over."

She smiled at Mr. Thompson. "I see you've met our custodial staff already."

"Mr. Thompson was just telling me about when he was a student here," Sam explained, watching his mother's expression shift to professional interest.

"Really? I'd love to hear more about that sometime, Mr. Thompson. I'm researching the school's transition during integration, and firsthand accounts are invaluable."

Mr. Thompson gave a noncommittal nod. "Happy to help where I can, Dr. Rivera. But some memories are better left in the past." He nodded to them both. "You two have a good evening now."

As he wheeled his mop bucket away, Dr. Rivera turned to Sam. "Ready to go home? I want to hear all about your first day."

On the drive home, Sam recounted his classes and the students he'd met, carefully omitting the conversation about disappearances. Something held him back – perhaps Mr. Thompson's warning or the intensity with which Leila and her friends had spoken of the cycle.

Their rental house was a small craftsman-style home in a neighborhood of similar houses, most built in the 1950s. As they pulled into the driveway, Dr. Rivera sighed contentedly. "A bit different from our home in Richmond, huh?"

Sam nodded, taking in the modest front yard and covered porch. "It's nice. Quieter."

Inside, while his mother prepared dinner, Sam sat at the kitchen table with his homework spread before him, his mind still churning with questions about Pinecrest.

Unable to concentrate, he pulled out his phone and searched "Pinecrest Middle School disappearances." The results were less illuminating than he'd hoped. Local news articles from 2013 referenced three students who were reported missing within the same week. Still, the follow-up stories suggested they had been runaways and were eventually found – though details were conspicuously absent.

Nothing conclusive about 2001 or earlier years. He was about to give up when one link caught his eye: a forum post from 2014 titled "The Truth About Pinecrest's Missing Kids."

The post had been removed, but Sam could still read it thanks to web archives:

"I was a teacher at Pinecrest when four students vanished in 2001. The official story was that they ran away, but I know better. Two of those kids were straight-A students with plans for the future. One had just been accepted to a prestigious summer program. They didn't run away.

Something happened to them in the school's east wing, in the old storage rooms that used to be science labs. The administration knows more than they're saying. The pattern goes back decades to 1989, 1977, and even earlier. Always in April, always four students. It's no coincidence that the school was built on land where four enslaved people were supposedly executed for attempting to escape in the 1800s. I've collected evidence for years, but now I'm being forced into early retirement. If anything happens to me, know that Pinecrest holds secrets darker than anyone wants to admit."

The post was signed simply, "A Concerned Educator." A chill ran through Sam. Could this have been the librarian Leila had mentioned? He quickly texted Leila's number: "Hi, it's Sam from school. Can we talk more about what you mentioned at lunch?"

Her response came quickly: "Meet us at the public library tomorrow after school. There's a corner table in the local history section. Don't tell anyone."

"Dinner's ready," his mother called, startling him. He quickly closed the browser and joined her at the table. Over spaghetti bolognese, Dr. Rivera chatted enthusiastically about her first day. "The history department has some great resources, but they're woefully disorganized. I found records from the 1960s mixed in with material from the 1990s. I'm going to need to do some serious archival work."

"Mom," Sam said, twirling pasta on his fork without eating it, "did you know there are rumors about students disappearing from Pinecrest?"

His mother's fork paused halfway to her mouth. "Where did you hear that?"

"Some kids at lunch. They said it happens every twelve years, and the last time was in 2013."

Dr. Rivera frowned slightly. "I did come across something in my preliminary research about incidents in 2013 and 2001, but the records indicated they were resolved runaways who returned home or were found elsewhere."

"What if they weren't runaways?" Sam pressed. "What if something else happened to them?"

His mother put down her fork, giving him her full attention. "Sam, is something bothering you about the school? Beyond these rumors?"

He shrugged, suddenly feeling foolish. "It's just... weird vibes, I guess. And the way some of the staff reacted when the topic came up."

"Schools accumulate legends and ghost stories like dust," she said gently. "It's natural, especially in buildings with as much history as Pinecrest. But I promise you, if there were actual unsolved disappearances, there would be ongoing investigations, media coverage, and concerned parents."

"Unless someone's covering it up," Sam muttered.

Dr. Rivera sighed. "Tell you what — as part of my research, I'll look into these rumors. Maybe there's a historical basis that's been distorted over time. Would that make you feel better?"

Sam nodded, though he wasn't entirely reassured. What if his mother's digging brought her too close to whatever truth lurked in Pinecrest's past?

Later that night, as he lay in bed staring at the unfamiliar ceiling, Sam's phone vibrated with another text from Leila: "FYI – The local news just reported a second missing student. Sofia Alvarez, an 8th grader from Greenbrier Middle School, was at our school sketching the east hall. She's an artist – won the regional painting competition last fall. It's happening exactly like the previous cycles."

Sam stared at the message; a mixture of dread and curiosity washed over him. Two students were missing in three days, matching the pattern Leila and her friends had described. It couldn't be a coincidence, could it? But what was the alternative? A curse? A conspiracy? Both seemed equally implausible.

Yet the facts remained: Aaron Mitchell was missing. Now Sofia Alvarez was missing, too. And if the pattern held, two more would disappear before the week was out. Sleep eluded him for hours as theories and questions tumbled through his mind. When he finally drifted off, his dreams were filled with empty classroom desks and whispered warnings from shadows in the east wing of Pinecrest Middle School.

The next morning brought rain again, drumming against the windows as Sam prepared for his second day at Pinecrest.

His mother seemed preoccupied at breakfast, scrolling through news reports on her tablet.

"Everything okay?" Sam asked, noting the crease between her eyebrows.

"Just reading about these missing students," she replied without looking up. "It's concerning. Two teenagers in three days." She finally glanced at him. "The school hasn't sent out any safety notifications yet, but I want you to be careful. Text me if you're going to be anywhere after school, and don't go off with anyone you don't know."

Sam nodded, wondering if he should tell her about his plans to meet Leila and her friends at the library. He decided against it for now – he wanted to hear more about their research first before involving his historian mother, who might dismiss it all as local folklore.

CHAPTER THREE
THE PATTERN EMERGES

The atmosphere at school was noticeably subdued. In homeroom, Ms. Bennett seemed distracted during attendance, her eyes lingering on Aaron's empty desk. During morning announcements, Principal Fletcher's voice came over the intercom, addressing the situation directly: "As some of you may have heard, two students from our district are currently missing – Aaron Mitchell from Pinecrest and Sofia Alvarez from Greenbrier Middle School. The police are investigating, and we are cooperating fully. In the meantime, we ask that students remain vigilant, travel in groups, and report any unusual activity to staff immediately. Counselors are available for anyone who needs support."

A murmur ran through the classroom as students exchanged theories and concerns. Sam noticed one boy near the front looking particularly pale, his hands clutching a pencil so tightly it seemed in danger of snapping. Throughout the morning, the disappearances were the primary topic of whispered conversations between classes.

Sam overheard fragments: "Just like what happened to my cousin's friend in 2013..."

"My mom said they're probably just runaways..."

"Always in April, that's the weird part..."

By lunchtime, Sam was eager to reconnect with Leila and her friends. He found them at the same corner table, heads bent together in intense discussion. They fell silent as he approached. "Did you see the news?"

Noah asked without preamble as Sam sat down. "Sofia Alvarez is the second one, right on schedule."

"She's an incredible artist," Mia added softly. "Her painting won first place at the regional competition last fall. It was a portrait of her grandmother that looked so real it could have been a photograph."

"So that fits your pattern," Sam acknowledged. "The scholar and the artist. Who do you think will be next? The leader or the healer?"

"Based on previous cycles, the leader," Leila answered, pulling out her grandfather's journal. "My grandfather noted the order in 1965: first the top science student, then the art club president, then the student council president, and finally a student who volunteered at the hospital after school."

"Do you have any idea who might be targeted as the 'leader' this time?" Sam asked.

The three exchanged glances before Noah spoke. "Caleb Johnson. He's the student council president. He organized that district-wide fundraiser for hurricane relief last fall."

"We tried to warn him," Mia said, frustration evident in her voice. "I messaged him on Instagram yesterday, but he probably thought I was just some random creep. Why would he believe me? I'm just a stranger to him, trying to explain a twelve-year pattern of disappearances?"

Leila turned to Sam. "That's why we need to gather more concrete evidence. Are you still coming to the library after school?"

Sam nodded. "I'll be there. But what exactly are we looking for?"

"Newspaper archives going back to when the school was first built," Noah explained. "Police reports, if we can access them. Anything that establishes the pattern beyond doubt."

"And information about the land the school was built on," Leila added. "My grandfather mentioned something about the original property being part of a plantation where something terrible happened."

"The Whitmore Plantation," Mia clarified. "There's still a historical marker near where the main house stood. It's in Northwest River Park now."

The bell signaling the end of lunch interrupted their conversation. Leila leaned in as they gathered their things and whispered to Sam, "Be careful in the east wing. Watch for anyone following you."

The warning stayed with Sam throughout his afternoon classes. When final dismissal came, he texted his mother that he was going to the public library to work on a research project with friends, promising to be home by dinner. The rain had subsided to a light drizzle as Sam walked the six blocks to the

Chesapeake Public Library, a modern building with large windows and an inviting entrance. Inside, he followed signs to the Local History section on the second floor, where he found Leila, Noah, and Mia already gathered around a large table covered with old newspapers, printouts, and notebooks.

"Finally," Noah said as Sam approached. "We've already pulled the newspaper archives from significant years." He pushed a stack of microfilm printouts toward Sam. "These are from April 1953, April 1965, April 1977, April 1989, April 2001, and April 2013. See if you notice any patterns in how the disappearances were reported."

For the next hour, the four of them combed through historical records. The earliest reports from 1953 were vague – brief mentions of 'local youths missing from school,' with follow-up articles suggesting they had 'returned to the family in North Carolina.'

By 1965, the reporting was more detailed but still contained inconsistencies. The 1977 disappearances coincided with the school's conversion to a middle school, and media attention focused more on integration challenges than the missing students. The 1989 and 2001 cases showed a pattern of initial concern followed by quietly dropped investigations. The 2013 reports were the most detailed, naming four students: Amelia Chen (robotics club president), Dominic Flores (school mural painter), Jessica Taylor (student government president), and Michael Patel (volunteer at a senior center). All were initially reported missing, then later classified as runaways despite family protests.

"Look at this," Mia said suddenly, pointing to a small article from a 1954 issue of the Chesapeake Herald. "Former Pinecrest teacher committed to a psychiatric hospital after 'unfounded accusations.'"

She read aloud:

"Dr. Walter Jenkins, formerly employed at Pinecrest High School, has been committed to Eastern State Hospital following increasingly erratic behavior. Jenkins had previously made unfounded accusations regarding the disappearance of four students in April 1953, claiming school administrators were involved in their unexplained absences. School officials expressed sympathy for Jenkins' condition and wished him a full recovery."

"They committed him for investigating the disappearances," Leila whispered. "Just like they forced my grandfather into early retirement, and that teacher who wrote the forum post."

Noah had been scanning old property records on his laptop. "I've got something on the Whitmore Plantation," he announced. "According to county historical archives, the land where Pinecrest now stands was originally part of the Whitmore Plantation, owned by the Whitmore family from 1802 until 1910, when it was sold to the county for educational purposes."

"Anything unusual about the plantation?" Sam asked.

Noah scrolled through the document. "Here's something interesting. In 1856, four enslaved people reportedly attempted escape but were captured and... executed on the property. Their names were never recorded, but local legends claim their spirits remained restless."

"That can't be a coincidence," Mia said, her voice hushed. "Four people executed on the exact same land where four students now disappear every twelve years?"

"But why twelve years?" Sam wondered. "And why those specific types of students?"

Leila had been unusually quiet, flipping through her grandfather's journal. Now she looked up, her expression grim. "My grandfather wrote about a conversation he had with the old custodian in 1965 – probably Mr. Thompson's predecessor. The man told him about a hidden room somewhere in the east wing, sealed off from regular access. He said it contained records that 'certain parties' didn't want to be found."

"A hidden room in the east wing," Sam repeated, thinking of Mr. Thompson's warning to stay away from the old storage areas.

"That's where we need to look next." Noah looked skeptical. "How exactly do we search for a hidden room without getting caught? The school's probably locked up tight by now anyway."

"Not tomorrow," Leila countered. "Tomorrow is the monthly faculty meeting after school. All teachers and administrators will be in the auditorium for at least an hour. The building will be nearly empty."

"Are you suggesting we search the east wing while the faculty meeting is happening?" Mia asked, her usual caution evident. "That's breaking about a dozen school rules."

"Four students' lives could depend on it," Leila argued. "If Caleb Johnson disappears tomorrow, we'll have one more left – the healer. We need to find out what's happening before it's too late."

They debated the plan until the library's overhead lights flickered, signaling thirty minutes until closing. Finally, they agreed: tomorrow after school, they would meet at the water fountain near the east wing entrance and begin their search for the hidden room.

As they packed up their research materials, Sam's phone buzzed with a text from his mother: "Working late on organizing the history archives. There's leftover pasta in the fridge. Don't wait up." Attached was a photo of her desk covered with file folders and boxes labeled "RECORDS" in faded marker.

Sam stared at the image, a sense of unease growing within him. What if his mother discovered something in those archives that put her in danger? The history of Pinecrest seemed increasingly sinister – teachers silenced, records altered, students vanishing without a trace. On his walk home, Sam couldn't shake the feeling of being watched. Twice, he turned around suddenly, expecting to find someone following him, but the sidewalk behind him was empty save for fallen leaves dancing in the evening breeze.

When he reached the rental house, it was dark and quiet. He reheated pasta for dinner and tried to focus on homework, but his mind kept returning to their discoveries at the library: the systematic disappearances stretching back to when the school was first built, the connection to the Whitmore Plantation, and the four archetypes—scholar, artist, leader, healer—taken every twelve years for reasons unknown.

He was still awake when his mother returned home around 10 PM, looking exhausted but oddly energized. "You wouldn't believe what I found in the old archives," she said, dropping her bag on the dining table. "Records going back to the school's founding, including some that detail the controversy surrounding its conversion to a middle school. It's fascinating material."

Sam hesitated, then decided to push a little further than he had the previous night. "Did you find anything about missing students? The ones I mentioned?"

Dr. Rivera's expression shifted subtly. "I did come across some incident reports that seemed... inconsistent. Enrollment numbers that don't quite add up, such as student transfers with incomplete documentation. Nothing concrete, but enough to raise questions."

"What kind of questions?" Sam pressed.

His mother studied him for a moment. "The kind that makes me wonder if there's more to Pinecrest's history than in the official record. But Sam, these are likely just administrative errors, especially during transitional periods like integration."

Sam wasn't convinced, but he nodded anyway. "Goodnight, Mom."

"Goodnight, Sam. And Sam?" He paused at the foot of the stairs. "Be careful with these rumors and theories. Schools like Pinecrest accumulate stories over the decades. Not all of them have substance behind them."

Something in her tone – a hint of warning or concern – stayed with Sam as he headed to his room. Later, as he lay in bed checking social media one last time, a breaking news alert appeared on his phone: "THIRD TEEN MISSING: Caleb Johnson, 14, last seen leaving Pinecrest Middle School." Sam sat bolt upright, his heart racing. The leader – the third archetype in the pattern – was missing, right on schedule.

He quickly texted the news to Leila, Noah, and Mia. Leila responded almost immediately: "It's happening exactly as predicted. Tomorrow, after school, is our only chance to find answers before the fourth disappearance."

Sleep was impossible now. Sam spent hours researching online, looking for any additional information about the previous cycles of disappearances. Around 2 AM, he found an archived blog post from 2012 titled "The Twelve-Year Cycle of Pinecrest":

"Most locals dismiss it as an urban legend, but the pattern is undeniable. Every twelve years since the school was built, four students disappear in April.

The authorities always default to 'runaway' explanations despite evidence to the contrary. What's most disturbing is the selection criteria – the missing students always represent four archetypes: the intellectual, the creative, the charismatic, and the nurturing. These archetypes mirror ancient sacrifice rituals where four aspects of humanity were offered to appease angry spirits.

Is it a coincidence that Pinecrest was built on land where four enslaved people were executed? Or is something darker at work?"

The post was deleted shortly after publication, but was preserved by someone who captured a screenshot of the post.

Sam finally drifted into uneasy sleep around 3 AM, his dreams filled with hidden rooms and desperate escapes from shadowy figures in a maze-like east wing that never ended.

Morning came too quickly. At breakfast, Dr. Rivera mentioned the faculty meeting that afternoon. "It might run late, so don't wait for dinner for me. Principal Fletcher wants to discuss safety protocols in light of these disappearances." She hesitated, coffee cup halfway to her lips. "Sam, I want you to come straight home after school today. No detours, no library visits, not until they figure out what's happening with these missing teenagers."

Sam nodded, guilt twisting in his stomach at the lie of omission. He had no intention of coming straight home – not when they had their only chance to search the east wing during the faculty meeting. The school day dragged with agonizing slowness. The news of Caleb Johnson's disappearance had spread, creating a palpable tension throughout Pinecrest.

During morning announcements, Principal Fletcher's voice was tight and strained as he acknowledged the third missing student and announced increased security measures, including police officers on campus. In the hallways between classes, Sam noticed uniformed officers patrolling, their expressions grave. At lunch, he met briefly with Leila, Noah, and Mia to confirm their plan.

"We'll meet at the water fountain at 3:15," Leila whispered. "The faculty meeting starts at 3:30 in the auditorium. We'll have at least an hour to search the east wing."

"Be careful around the officers," Noah warned. "They're watching everyone."

"What exactly are we looking for?" Sam asked. "How do we find a hidden room?"

Mia pulled out her phone. "I found blueprints of the original school building online. There's a discrepancy between the exterior dimensions and the interior layout of the east wing. There's space unaccounted for."

"A sealed-off area," Leila concluded. "Just like my grandfather described."

After lunch, Sam found it impossible to concentrate on his classes. His mind kept returning to the missing students – Aaron, Sofia, and Caleb – and wondering who would be the fourth. According to the pattern, it would be someone who fits the "healer" archetype. When the final bell rang, Sam texted his mother that he was staying after school to work on a group project, promising to be home by dinner. It wasn't entirely a lie – they were working on something together, just not a school assignment.

At 3:15, he made his way to the water fountain near the east wing entrance, where the others were already waiting. The hallways were nearly empty; most students had left for the day, and the staff was heading to the faculty meeting.

"Everyone ready?" Leila asked, her voice barely above a whisper. When they nodded, she led the way into the east wing, moving quietly along the dimly lit corridor. The east wing felt different from the rest of the school – colder, somehow, with an atmosphere of watchful silence. Display cases lined the walls, showcasing faded photographs and trophies from when Pinecrest was still a high school. At the end of the main corridor, they turned down a narrower hallway marked 'Authorized Personnel Only.'

"According to the blueprints," Mia murmured, consulting her phone, "there should be about fifteen feet of space unaccounted for at the end of this hallway."

The hallway ended at a wall that appeared solid, with a janitor's closet to the right and a storage room to the left. Noah tried both doors – the storage room was locked, but the janitor's closet opened to reveal shelves of cleaning supplies and a mop sink.

"Nothing unusual here," he reported, closing the door quietly.

Sam examined the end wall carefully. "Does it look... newer than the rest?" he asked, noticing subtle differences in the paint texture. Leila ran her hands along the baseboard.

"The molding doesn't quite match here," she noted, pointing to a section near the floor. "It's a different material."

They spent several minutes examining every inch of the wall and the surrounding area, looking for any mechanism that might reveal a hidden entrance.

CHAPTER FOUR
HIDDEN IN PLAIN SIGHT

"This is useless," Noah finally said in frustration. "Even if there is a sealed-off room, how would anyone access it?"

As if in answer, they heard the distinct sound of a key turning in a lock. They froze, expecting to be caught by a teacher or security officer. Instead, the storage room door across the hall opened to reveal Mr. Thompson, the elderly custodian. He didn't seem surprised to find them there.

"You kids are persistent, I'll give you that," he said, his expression unreadable. For a moment, no one spoke.

Then Sam stepped forward. "We know about the hidden room," he said, his voice steadier than he felt. "We know it was sealed off during the renovation, and we think it's connected to the disappearances – not just now, but every twelve years going back to when the school was built."

The custodian's expression didn't change, but something in his eyes shifted. "You don't know what you're meddling with," he said quietly. "Some doors are meant to stay closed."

"Three teenagers are already missing," Leila challenged. "A fourth will disappear today if the pattern holds. Are you going to let that happen again?"

Mr. Thompson was silent for a long moment, his gaze moving from one student to the next. Finally, he sighed deeply.

"Your grandfather was just as stubborn," he said to Leila. "Always pushing for the truth, no matter the cost."

Leila blinked in surprise. "You knew my grandfather?"

"We worked together back when this was still Pinecrest High. He was right about a lot of things, including what happened during the renovation."

Mr. Thompson leaned his mop against the wall and approached them slowly. "But knowing the truth doesn't always help. Sometimes, it just puts more people in danger."

"We're already in danger," Mia argued. "We all go to Pinecrest. Any of us could be next."

Mr. Thompson studied them for a moment longer before coming to a decision. "Step back," he ordered, moving toward what appeared to be a regular electrical outlet near the floor at the end of the hall. He withdrew a small tool from his pocket that looked like a specialized screwdriver.

"This isn't just about missing students," he warned as he worked. "It's about something older, something that's been part of this land since before the school was built."

The outlet cover came away in his hand, revealing not electrical wiring but a small keyhole. Mr. Thompson pulled a chain with an old-fashioned key from around his neck. "The school board ordered this section sealed in 1972, claiming structural issues. But that was a lie. They wanted to contain what was found here during the renovation – something that had been hidden even earlier when the original school was built in 1910."

He inserted the key and turned it with a decisive click. A section of the wall—about three feet wide—swung inward slightly, revealing darkness beyond.

"What you're looking for is in there," Mr. Thompson said, stepping back. "But I'm warning you one last time: once you know the truth, you can't unknow it. And knowledge comes with responsibility."

The four exchanged glances before Sam spoke for all of them. "We understand. But we need to know what's happening to these students."

Mr. Thompson nodded grimly. "Then may God help you." He handed the key to Sam. "I'll keep watch. If anyone comes, I'll create a distraction. But be quick – and whatever you do, don't touch the markings on the floor."

With that cryptic warning, he retreated to the janitor's closet, positioning himself where he could see anyone approaching. Sam pushed the hidden door wider, revealing a narrow passage beyond. Using their phone flashlights, they entered one by one, finding themselves in a short corridor that opened into a larger room. As their lights swept the space, they gasped in unison. The walls were covered with markings – symbols, dates, and names written in what looked disturbingly like dried blood. The floor featured an intricate design etched into the concrete: a circular pattern with four smaller circles at the cardinal points, connected by lines to a central point.

"What is this place?" Noah whispered, his voice echoing slightly in the enclosed space.

Mia's light illuminated a shelf along one wall, holding leather-bound books and what appeared to be aged scrolls. "It looks like some kind of... ritual chamber."

Leila approached a section of the wall where photographs had been pinned. "Oh my god," she breathed. "Look at these."

The photos showed students – four in each grouping – arranged in a grid. Beneath each grid was a year: 1965, 1977, 1989, 2001, 2013. The most recent photos matched the descriptions of the students who had disappeared twelve years ago.

"They documented every cycle," Leila said, her voice shaking. "Like... trophies."

"But why?" Noah asked. "What happens to these students?"

Sam's light fell on an open book on a podium in the center of the room, just beyond the circular floor marking. Carefully avoiding stepping on the etched lines, he approached it. The pages were yellowed with age, the handwriting spidery and faded.

"'April 12, 1917,'" he read aloud. "'The sacrifice is complete. Four souls to feed the hunger that dwells beneath. The barrier holds for another cycle.'" A collective shudder ran through the group.

"'April 16, 1929,'" Sam continued, turning the page. "'Again, we have paid the price. The chosen four have passed beyond, strengthening the seal that protects us all. May their sacrifice never be forgotten, though their names must be struck from the record.'"

"They're not disappearing," Mia whispered in horror. "They're being sacrificed."

Leila had moved to another shelf, where more recent documents were stored. "Look at this," she said, holding up a folder labeled "Selection Criteria."

Inside were profiles of students from Pinecrest and neighboring schools, complete with photographs, personal information, and notes about their families.

"They're selecting specific students," she realized. "But based on what?"

Sam returned to the book, flipping ahead to more recent entries. "April 8, 2013. The hunger grows stronger with each cycle. The four were chosen according to the established criteria: one with an exceptional mind, one with an artist's soul, one with a leader's heart, and one with a healer's touch. May their passage strengthen the barrier for another twelve years."

"Aaron heads the robotics club," Mia said slowly. "He's brilliant with math and science."

"And Sofia Alvarez won the regional art competition last fall," Noah added. "She's an incredible painter."

"Caleb Johnson is student council president at Hampton Roads," Leila said. "A natural leader." The implications sank in as they looked at each other. "Which means the fourth will be someone with a 'healer's touch,'"

Sam concluded. "Someone caring, nurturing."

"Lily Robertson," Noah whispered. "She volunteers at the animal shelter every weekend and wants to be a veterinarian. She sits next to me in science."

"We have to warn her," Mia insisted. "Call her, text her, something!"

Noah pulled out his phone, but the screen remained dark. "No signal in here."

A noise from the passage made them all jump.

Mr. Thompson appeared at the entrance, his expression urgent. "Someone's coming. You need to get out now!"

They rushed to gather what evidence they could – Leila stuffing the selection criteria folder into her backpack, Sam quickly photographing pages from the ritual book with his phone. As they hurried toward the exit, a voice echoed down the hallway outside.

"I know they came this way. The motion sensors picked them up." Principal Fletcher. And he wasn't alone.

"Hide," Mr. Thompson hissed, pushing them back into the chamber. "I'll try to divert them." Before they could protest, he slipped out, pulling the hidden door nearly closed behind him.

Through the crack, they could hear his conversation with the principal.

"Mr. Thompson, have you seen any students in this area?"

"No, sir. I've been checking the storage rooms for that leak you reported."

"Strange. The security system showed movement in this corridor just minutes ago."

"Probably just me, sir. These motion sensors aren't always reliable in the older parts of the building."

There was a pause, then: "Perhaps. Still, I'd like to check personally. With another student missing..."

Sam's blood ran cold. The fourth disappearance had already happened. They were too late.

The principal's voice grew closer. "And while we're here, we should ensure that certain areas remain secure. Given recent events." Mr. Thompson must have positioned himself between the principal and the hidden door.

"Sir, I've maintained this wing for decades. Everything is as it should be."

"Nevertheless, I insist." Inside the chamber, the four exchanged panicked glances. There was nowhere to hide – if the principal opened the door fully, they would be discovered.

Suddenly, another voice joined the conversation outside. "Principal Fletcher! There you are. I've been looking everywhere for you." Dr. Rivera.

Sam's heart leaped to his throat. "Dr. Rivera, I'm rather busy at the moment."

"I understand, but there's a situation in the main office that requires your immediate attention. The police are here with questions about the missing students, and they specifically asked for you."

A tense silence followed. "Very well," the principal said finally. "Mr. Thompson, we'll continue our discussion later. Please ensure all storage areas are properly secured."

Footsteps retreated down the hallway. After several agonizing minutes, the hidden door swung open again, revealing Mr. Thompson's grim face.

"You need to leave now. And take this." He handed Leila a small leather-bound book. "Your grandfather's missing journal. He documented everything about the ritual and those who maintain it. The cycle can be broken, but not by hiding in dark rooms collecting evidence."

"Who's behind this?" Sam demanded. "The principal?"

"He's just one link in a chain that stretches back generations," Mr. Thompson replied. "A society dedicated to maintaining what they call 'the barrier' – something they believe protects the entire region from a greater evil."

"By sacrificing teenagers?" Noah asked incredulously.

"By feeding an ancient hunger that grows beneath this land," the janitor corrected. "Or so they believe. Whether it's true or mass delusion doesn't change the fact that four students disappear every twelve years, all following the same pattern."

"Lily Robertson," Noah said. "Is she...?"

Mr. Thompson's expression confirmed their fears. "Reported missing an hour ago. Didn't return from lunch."

"We have to stop this," Leila insisted. "We can go to the police with what we've found."

"With what evidence?" Mr. Thompson countered. "Photographs of an old book? A hidden room that any official investigation will find empty? The society has protected itself for over a century. They have connections throughout the city – police, government, school board."

"Then what can we do?" Sam asked, desperation creeping into his voice.

Mr. Thompson looked at each of them in turn. "The ritual isn't complete until midnight on the fourth day. The students are held somewhere before their final sacrifice. Your evidence might not convince authorities, but it could help you find where they're being kept."

"And my mother?" Sam asked. "She's out there distracting the principal. Does she know about this?"

"Dr. Rivera has been asking dangerous questions since she arrived," Mr. Thompson replied. "Whether she knows everything yet, I can't say. But she's not part of their society – of that, I'm certain."

Footsteps echoed in the distance, spurring them to action. They slipped out of the hidden chamber, Mr. Thompson locking it behind them with practiced efficiency.

"Leave separately," he instructed. "Don't let anyone see you together. And whatever you do, don't return to this wing alone. They'll be watching now."

As they prepared to leave, Sam turned back to the janitor. "Why are you helping us? Why not twelve years ago or before that?"

Mr. Thompson's weathered face showed a flicker of deep sorrow. "Because I was complicit once. I believed their lies about necessity and the greater good. But no barrier, no protection is worth the price of children's lives. Your generation deserves better than to inherit our sins."

With that cryptic statement, he gestured for them to go, resuming his custodial duties as if nothing had happened. The four split up, taking different routes out of the building. As Sam hurried through the main hallway, his mind raced with what they had discovered: a hidden ritual chamber, a secret society. Four students are selected for sacrifice every twelve years to feed some ancient hunger beneath the school. It sounded impossible, insane, yet the evidence was undeniable.

Aaron, Sofia, Caleb, and now Lily had been taken, just as students before them had been taken for over a century. And somewhere, they were being held, awaiting a ritual that would complete their disappearance forever. Unless Sam and his friends could find them first, but as he slipped out of the building, another thought weighed heavily on his mind. His mother was now involved, whether she knew the full truth or not.

By distracting Principal Fletcher, Dr. Rivera had placed herself in the society's sights. And if they discovered her interference, she might become the next to vanish without a trace. Pausing at the edge of the school grounds, Sam texted Leila, Noah, and Mia: "Meet at the public library in one hour. Bring everything you gathered. We need to figure out where they're keeping Aaron, Sofia, Caleb, and Lily before midnight."

The response came simultaneously from all three: "We'll be there." Sam glanced back at Pinecrest Middle School, its east wing dark and forbidding against the afternoon sky. Beyond those brick walls, somewhere in Chesapeake, four students were being held captive by a secret society that had operated undetected for generations. A society that believed in sacrificing young lives to appease some ancient hunger beneath the earth. A society that his mother might now be investigating, putting herself in terrible danger.

The twelve-year cycle of disappearances at Pinecrest Middle School had claimed its victims once again. But this time, someone knew the truth. This time, someone was fighting back. And Sam was determined that this cycle would be the last.

CHAPTER FIVE
SHADOWS FROM RICHMOND

Sam lay on his bed, the ceiling fan spinning lazily above him as the rain pattered against the window. The events of his first few days at Pinecrest Middle School replayed in his mind like a movie he couldn't pause-the hidden room in the east wing, the ritual book, the strange symbols, and most disturbingly, the four missing students who fit the same pattern that had repeated every twelve years since the school was built.

He rolled onto his side, eyes landing on the framed photograph on his nightstand—a smiling man with Sam's same hazel eyes standing beside a younger version of Sam on a baseball field, both wearing matching Richmond Rockets uniforms. The image brought a familiar ache to his chest, one that had become his constant companion over the past eight months. His father, Dr. James Rivera, a renowned archaeologist and the best baseball coach the Richmond Rockets had ever had, according to the team, anyway. Eight months since his father had traveled to Ecuador for what was supposed to be a routine three-week excavation. Eight months since his last phone call. Eight months of unanswered questions and growing fears.

Sam reached for the photo, tracing his father's face with his finger. The scent of old books and cologne seemed to emanate from the frame, a phantom memory that transported Sam back to their home in Richmond, back to when life made sense. He closed his eyes, allowing himself to drift into the memory that visited him most often on his twelfth birthday, just two weeks before his father left for Ecuador.

Richmond Park had been vibrant with early summer colors, and their backyard had transformed into a baseball paradise. His father had surprised him by inviting Sam's entire baseball team, setting up a miniature diamond complete with bases and a makeshift pitcher's mound.

"Baseball's in our blood, Sammy," his father had said, tossing the ball high into the air and catching it with practiced ease. "Your grandfather taught me, I taught you, and someday-" he'd winked dramatically "-you'll teach your kids. It's the Rivera legacy."

The Rivera legacy. Sam returned the photo to the nightstand, the bitter irony not lost on him. What kind of legacy disappeared without a trace? What kind of father vanished into the Ecuadorian rainforest, leaving behind nothing but theories and speculation? His thoughts drifted to the cardboard box tucked beneath his bed- his father's research notes that his mother didn't know he had. He'd found them the day they'd packed up their Richmond house, hidden away in the bottom of his father's desk drawer.

Something had compelled Sam to keep them secret, to slide them into his moving box instead of showing them to his mother. Perhaps it was the way grief had hollowed her out, leaving her a shadow of the vibrant professor she'd once been. Or perhaps it was the strange notes scribbled in his father's familiar handwriting about missing children in Chesapeake, Virginia, dating back decades—notes that seemed eerily similar to what he'd learned about Pinecrest yesterday.

The sound of his mother moving around downstairs broke through his thoughts. Sam sat up, checking the time on his phone-6:30 AM. Sleep had been elusive, his mind too busy connecting dots between his father's notes and the information Leila had shared about the disappearances. He wondered what his father would make of all this.

Dr. James Rivera had built his reputation on uncovering patterns where others saw only coincidence. "History isn't random, Sam," he'd often say during their museum visits or hiking trips to historical sites. "It's a tapestry of interconnected events. Our job is to find the threads that connect them."

What threads had his father been following in Ecuador? And what threads had led him to research disappearances in Chesapeake years before Sam and his mother had any reason to move there?

Sam swung his legs over the side of the bed and reached beneath it, pulling out the battered cardboard box. He opened it carefully, the familiar scent of his father's office paper, coffee, and that peculiar mustiness that seemed to follow archaeologists washing over him. The top layer contained his father's research on the Upano Valley in eastern Ecuador, where he'd been excavating when he disappeared. Newspaper clippings, journal articles, and handwritten notes detailed the discovery of a vast network of ancient settlements hidden beneath the Amazon rainforest.

"Over 300 sq km," his father had scrawled in the margin of one article. "Dating back 2,500 years. Most significant find of the century." Sam had read these notes countless times, searching for clues about what might have happened to his father.

But the folder at the bottom of the box drew his attention, simply labeled "Chesapeake." He'd only discovered it a few weeks ago, buried beneath the Ecuador research. Inside were newspaper clippings about missing students from various Chesapeake schools, dating back to the 1950s. Red thread connected photos and dates, forming a pattern that Sam now recognized all too well: students every twelve years, always in April. His father had circled one school repeatedly: Pinecrest Middle School.

The latest article was from 2013, detailing the disappearance of four students who were later classified as runaways, though the parents insisted their children would never leave voluntarily. Besides the article, his father had written: "Same pattern. Same explanations. No one is looking at the connections. Why?"

A knock at his bedroom door startled Sam. He quickly stuffed the papers into the box and shoved it under his bed.

"Come in," he called, trying to sound like he'd just woken up. His mother opened the door, already dressed for work in a tailored blazer and pencil skirt, her dark hair pulled back in a neat bun. Despite her professional appearance, the shadows under her eyes betrayed her exhaustion. She'd been different since his father disappeared—more focused on her work, less present even when she was physically there. As if diving into her research on educational history could somehow fill the void his father had left.

"Morning, sleepyhead," she said, her smile not quite reaching her eyes. "I've got an early meeting with Principal Fletcher about those archives I found. There's cereal downstairs, and I left money on the counter in case you want to buy lunch."

She paused, studying him with the analytical gaze that had intimidated generations of university students. "Did you sleep at all? You look exhausted."

Sam shrugged, not wanting to worry her with the truth that he'd spent most of the night researching the previous disappearances at Pinecrest and trying to connect them to his father's notes. "Just adjusting to the new house. You know how it is."

Dr. Rivera's expression softened. She crossed the room and sat on the edge of his bed, the mattress dipping slightly under her weight. For a moment, she looked like the mom from before, one who'd bake cookies for his baseball team and laugh so hard at his father's terrible jokes that milk would come out of her nose.

"I know this move hasn't been easy," she said gently. "Leaving Richmond, starting at a new school in April of all times..." She trailed off, and Sam wondered if she was thinking of his father, too, of the life they'd left behind.

"But sometimes a fresh start is exactly what we need. And my research position here is a really good opportunity."

Sam nodded, not trusting himself to speak. He wanted to ask her about Pinecrest's history, the missing students, and whether she knew more than she was letting on. But the fragile smile on her face stopped him.

They'd both been walking on eggshells for months, afraid that acknowledging the void his father had left would somehow make it permanent. Instead, he said, "I met some kids yesterday. They seem cool."

His mother's smile widened, genuine relief replacing the professional mask she usually wore. "That's wonderful, Sam. I was hoping you'd make friends quickly." She stood up, smoothing her skirt. "I'd better get going. Text me if you need anything, okay?"

She hesitated at the door, turning back with an unreadable expression. "And Sam? Be careful at school today. Stay with your new friends. Don't wander off alone." Before he could ask what she meant, she was gone, her heels clicking on the hardwood floor as she headed downstairs.

Be careful. Stay with friends. Don't wander off alone. The warning echoed in Sam's mind as he got dressed, unease settling in his stomach like a cold stone. Did she know something about the disappearances? Was that why she'd taken the position at Pinecrest —not just for the research opportunity but to investigate what had happened to those students over the decades? And if so, was there a connection to his father's disappearance in Ecuador? The questions swirled in his mind as he grabbed his backpack and headed downstairs, the weight of uncertainty heavier than any school books.

Sam's breakfast consisted of a hastily eaten bowl of cereal as he scanned news articles on his phone about Aaron Mitchell, the missing student. The coverage was frustratingly vague- a fourteen-year-old honor student who hadn't returned home from robotics club. Police were investigating, but there were "no signs of foul play."

CHAPTER SIX
ECHOES FROM ECUADOR

The same phrase had been used to describe his father's disappearance in the early days before the search was scaled back and eventually abandoned. *No signs of foul play.* It is as if people just vanished into thin air without reason. Sam's throat tightened at the memory of those agonizing weeks of initial concern, the frantic calls to the American embassy in Ecuador, the search parties that found nothing, and finally, the painful transition from "missing" to "presumed dead." His mother had fought it every step of the way, insisting that James Rivera would never abandon his family. But as weeks stretched into months with no contact, ransom demands, or evidence of what had happened, she even began to accept the unimaginable.

The walk to Pinecrest gave Sam time to think and sort through the jumble of memories and new information competing for space in his mind. He remembered the day his father had announced his trip to Ecuador, bursting into their Richmond home with the energy of a hurricane.

"They've found something incredible, Olivia," he'd told Sam's mother, his eyes alight with the fervor that always accompanied a new discovery. "An entire network of ancient cities, hidden in the rainforest for over two thousand years. Settlements, roadways, agricultural systems, and this discovery rewrites everything we thought we knew about pre-Colombian civilizations in the Amazon."

He'd spread satellite images and preliminary reports across the dining table, pointing out features with childlike excitement. "The Upano Valley is going to change archaeological history, and they want me to join the team."

Sam had watched from the doorway, accustomed to his father's enthusiasm, but sensing something different this time —a deeper connection to the discovery. Later that night, he'd overheard his parents talking in hushed tones. "It's not just the archaeological significance, Liv," his father had said. "There's something about the pattern of these settlements, the way they vanished suddenly around 300 CE. It reminds me of those cases I've been tracking."

His mother's response had been skeptical. "James, you're connecting dots across continents and millennia. Sometimes disappearances are just disappearances—natural disasters, warfare, migration." His father's voice had grown more intense. "Four settlements abandoned simultaneously, at twelve-year intervals according to carbon dating. That's not a coincidence. And it matches the pattern I found in Chesapeake."

The memory stopped Sam in his tracks halfway to school. His father had been researching the pattern of disappearances at Pinecrest before his trip to Ecuador. He'd been looking for connections between ancient vanishings in South America and modern-day missing students in Virginia.

What if he'd found something, something dangerous enough to cause his own disappearance? The thought sent a chill through Sam that had nothing to do with the morning air. He quickened his pace, suddenly eager to reach the school and find Leila and the others. They needed to compare notes to see if there was a connection between his father's research and what they'd discovered in the hidden room.

Pinecrest Middle School loomed ahead, its brick facade somehow more ominous in the clear morning light than it had been in yesterday's rain. Students streamed through the main entrance, chatting and laughing, blissfully unaware of the darkness that lurked in the school's history.

Sam scanned the crowd for familiar faces, spotting Leila near the flagpole, deep in conversation with Noah and Mia. Her serious expression lifted slightly when she noticed him approaching. "You look like you haven't slept," she said by way of greeting, dark eyes assessing him with surprising perceptiveness.

"Couldn't stop thinking about yesterday," Sam admitted, glancing around to make sure no one was listening. "Plus, I found something I need to show you guys." The three exchanged looks of interest. Noah pushed his glasses up his nose, a habit Sam had noticed when he was particularly intrigued by something.

"What kind of something?" he asked, voice lowered. Sam hesitated, aware of the bustling courtyard around them. "Not here. Lunch, same table as yesterday?"

Mia nodded, her curly ponytail bouncing with the movement. "Perfect. We have more to share, too. I've been researching the 2013 disappearances and found some inconsistencies in the official reports."

The first bell rang, sending students scurrying toward the building. As they walked in together, Sam felt a curious sense of belonging- these three virtual strangers united with him in purpose, in the shared determination to uncover the truth about Pinecrest's missing students. It reminded him of his baseball team back in Richmond, that same feeling of camaraderie and common goal. For the first time since moving to Chesapeake, the hollow ache of loneliness that had been his constant companion began to recede slightly.

Sam's morning classes passed in a blur of introductions and assignments as teachers tried to help him catch up on nearly a full year's worth of material. In each class, he noted the empty desk that had belonged to Aaron Mitchell, the first of the four to disappear. The absence felt charged with meaning, as if the very air around the vacant space hummed with unspoken questions.

In English, Ms. Bennett assigned them a personal essay about a significant event in their lives. "Something that changed you," she'd said, her gaze sweeping the classroom. "Something that made you see the world differently."

Sam had stared at the blank page, pen hovering uncertainly. What could he possibly write that wouldn't expose too much? *While researching ancient civilizations, my father disappeared in the Ecuadorian rainforest, and now I'm investigating seemingly related disappearances at my new school.* Not exactly the essay that would help him blend in.

Instead, his mind drifted to Richmond, to the life he'd left behind. Before his father's disappearance, Sam had been popular at his old school—captain of the baseball team, solid student, and part of a tight-knit group of friends he'd known since kindergarten. James Rivera had coached their baseball team from T-ball through middle school, becoming a second father to many of Sam's friends. Weekend barbecues at the Rivera house had been legendary, with his father grilling burgers while telling outlandish stories about his archaeological adventures and his mother correcting the historical inaccuracies with good-natured exasperation.

All of that had changed after his father disappeared. At first, Sam's friends had rallied around him, stopping by with homework and invitations to movies or gaming sessions. But as weeks stretched into months, Sam had withdrawn, unable to bear their pity or their gradually dwindling interest in his family's tragedy. He'd quit baseball, unable to step onto the field without remembering his father's booming encouragement from the sidelines. His grades had slipped as he spent nights researching Ecuador and various theories about what might have happened. By the time his mother announced they were moving to Chesapeake for her new research position, Sam had become a ghost in his own life—present but not participating, existing but not really living.

The bell for lunch startled Sam from his memories. He packed his still-blank paper into his backpack and made his way to the cafeteria, scanning the crowded room for his new friends. They were already at the same corner table as yesterday, heads bent together in intense discussion. They fell silent as he approached, a familiar pattern that had made him feel excluded in Richmond but now signaled inclusion in something secretive and important.

"What did you find?" Noah asked without preamble as Sam sat down. Sam glanced around to ensure no one was listening before leaning in.

"My father disappeared in Ecuador eight months ago," he began, the words feeling strange on his tongue. He rarely spoke about it, especially not to people he'd just met.

"He was an archaeologist researching ancient settlements in the Amazon rainforest. But before he left, he was looking into something else—disappearances here in Chesapeake, specifically at Pinecrest." The three stared at him, varying degrees of surprise and intrigue on their faces.

"I found his research notes hidden in our old house when we were moving. He'd been tracking the twelve-year cycle of disappearances going back to when the school was first built. Four students each time, always in April."

Leila's eyes widened. "Just like my grandfather's journal," she breathed. "Did he figure out why it happens?"

Sam shook his head, frustration evident in his gesture. "Not exactly. But he thought there was a connection between the disappearances here and something he discovered about ancient settlements in Ecuador—the Upano Valley, specifically. Apparently, archaeological evidence suggested that settlements there were abandoned at regular intervals, and he thought the pattern matched what he was seeing at Pinecrest."

Mia frowned, her analytical mind visibly working through this new information. "That's a stretch, isn't it? Connecting ancient South American civilizations to a middle school in Virginia?"

Sam understood her skepticism—he'd had the same reaction when he'd first read his father's notes. "I thought so too, but then yesterday, in that hidden room, we saw those symbols on the floor and walls. I've seen similar markings in my father's research photos from Ecuador. Some kind of ritual circles or astronomical calendars, he wasn't sure."

Noah pulled out his laptop, typing rapidly. "The Upano Valley... here it is. Archaeological news from January. They've discovered a vast network of ancient cities in eastern Ecuador dating back 2,500 years. The settlements were interconnected by roads and had complex agricultural systems."

He turned the screen so they could all see a satellite image showing geometric patterns in the rainforest. "They're calling it the oldest and largest pre-Colombian urban complex found in the Amazon region."

Sam leaned forward, his heart racing. "That's where my father was when he disappeared. He was part of the research team excavating those sites."

A thought struck him, one he'd been avoiding for months. "What if... what if his disappearance is connected to what happens here? What if he found something he wasn't supposed to find?" The possibility hung in the air between them, too disturbing to be dismissed outright.

Leila broke the silence, her voice steady despite the unease visible in her expression. "My grandfather's journal mentioned something about the origins of the ritual. He wrote that when Pinecrest was first built in the 1940s, the construction workers found artifacts in the ground-strange objects that should have been in a museum but were kept quiet by the school board. Items that 'didn't belong in Virginia,' he wrote. What if they came from somewhere else? Somewhere like Ecuador?"

The implications of this connection sent a chill through the group. Sam's mind raced with possibilities, each more unsettling than the last. If his father had discovered a link between the ancient Ecuadorian settlements and the disappearances at Pinecrest, it could explain both his obsession with the research and, potentially, his disappearance. But who would want to keep such a connection secret? And what did it have to do with the four archetypes-scholar, artist, leader, healer-targeted in each cycle?

"I think we need to look at this from both ends," Mia suggested, pragmatic as ever. "Sam, you focus on your father's Ecuador research, see if there's anything specific about rituals or disappearances there. Noah, keep digging into the archaeological news to see if there are any updates about the excavation. Leila and I will concentrate on the history of Pinecrest and any evidence of those artifacts your grandfather mentioned."

The division of tasks felt natural, like a team coming together for a common purpose. It reminded Sam of the way his father would organize community digs, assigning roles based on each person's strengths.

Sam felt a curious mixture of dread and excitement as they finalized their plans. The mystery of Pinecrest's disappearances had given him something he'd been missing since his father vanished sense of purpose, a direction for the churning energy of his grief and questions. And these three new friends, bound to him by shared secrets and common goals, were filling some of the void left by the life he'd abandoned in Richmond.

For the first time in eight months, he felt like himself again—not just a shadow of the person he'd been before his father disappeared.

The bell ending lunch came too soon, forcing them to disperse to afternoon classes. As Sam headed to science, he found himself walking beside Leila, her purposeful stride matching his own. "I'm sorry about your dad," she said quietly, dark eyes studying him with an understanding that suggested personal experience with loss. "My mom died when I was eight. Cancer. It's different from a disappearance, I know, but... I understand what it's like to have this hole in your life where someone should be."

The simple acknowledgment of his pain, free from the awkward pity he'd grown accustomed to, loosened something in Sam's chest. "Thanks," he managed, the word inadequate but sincere. "The not knowing is the worst part. If he died on that expedition, why didn't they find his body? If he's alive, why hasn't he contacted us?"

He hadn't meant to reveal so much, but something about Leila invited confidence. She nodded, adjusting her glasses in a gesture that seemed both thoughtful and protective.

"That's why this investigation matters so much to you, isn't it? It's not just about saving whoever might be next on the list. It's about finding answers—maybe even about your dad."

Sam hadn't articulated this connection even to himself, but hearing Leila say it aloud, he recognized the truth in her words.

"Yeah, I guess it is. When I found his notes about Pinecrest, and then my mom coincidentally got a job here... it felt like following his footsteps somehow. Like maybe if I solve this mystery, I'll understand what happened to him, too."

They reached the science classroom, pausing outside the door. Leila's expression was solemn as she said, "We'll find the answers, Sam. For the missing students and for your dad. I promise."

The sincerity in her voice struck a chord in Sam. His friends in Richmond had made similar promises in the early days after his father's disappearance—well-meaning but ultimately empty as the case grew cold and life moved on. But Leila's promise felt different, anchored in personal determination and the shared experience of their discovery in the hidden room. He believed her, and that belief carried him through the rest of the school day with a sense of purpose he hadn't felt in months.

After the final bell, Sam headed to the library, planning to research more about the Upano Valley discoveries before meeting up with the others later. The school library was quiet, most students having rushed home or to after-school activities. Sam found a corner table partially hidden behind encyclopedias' shelves—outdated but perfect for privacy. He spread out his father's notes and opened his laptop, diving into recent archaeological news from Ecuador. The latest articles detailed laser scanning technology revealing thousands of rectangular earthen platforms, agricultural terraces, and networks of roads connecting at least fifteen distinct settlements. The complexity of these ancient cities challenged previous assumptions about pre-Colombian civilization in the Amazon.

But a smaller article, buried beneath the more sensational headlines, caught Sam's attention: *"Ritual Chambers Discovered in Upano Valley Settlements."* The piece described underground rooms found beneath several of the main plazas, their walls decorated with symbols representing the four cardinal directions and what archaeologists believed were the four elements: earth, air, fire, and water. According to the article, preliminary analysis suggested these chambers were used for ceremonial purposes, possibly including sacrifice. *"Evidence indicates that individuals representing different societal roles may have been selected for these rituals,"* the archaeologist was quoted as saying. *"We're seeing recurrent symbols associated with intellectual pursuits, artistic expression, leadership, and healing or medicine."*

CHAPTER SEVEN
THE CUSTODIAN'S BURDEN

Sam's breath caught in his throat. The four archetypes—scholar, artist, leader, healer—are the same ones targeted in the Pinecrest disappearances. His father must have made this connection, too. He scribbled notes frantically, copying the information to share with the others. As he searched for more details, a shadow fell across his table. Looking up, he was startled to find Mr. Thompson standing there, his weathered face unreadable as he studied Sam's research materials.

"Interested in South American archaeology, are you?" the custodian asked, his tone casual but his gaze sharp as it swept over the scattered papers. Sam hesitated, unsure how much to reveal. This man had helped them yesterday, showing them the hidden room, but his warnings had been cryptic, his involvement in the whole mystery unclear.

"School project," Sam lied, the words feeling hollow even to his own ears. "About ancient civilizations." Mr. Thompson's mouth twitched, almost a smile but not quite. "Your father was interested in South American archaeology, too, wasn't he? Dr. James Rivera. Quite renowned in his field, I believe."

The casual mention of his father's name sent a jolt through Sam. How did the custodian know who his father was? He'd never mentioned him by name to Mr. Thompson. "You knew my father?" he asked, unable to keep the surprise from his voice.

Mr. Thompson ran a hand along the edge of the table, his gaze now fixed on some middle distance. "Not really. But I make it my business to know about people who take an interest in Pinecrest's history. Your father visited this school once, about two years ago. Asked a lot of questions about the building and the land it was built on. Particularly interested in the east wing."

The revelation stunned Sam into momentary silence. His father had never mentioned visiting Pinecrest or investigating the school in person. Why would he keep that secret? And why hadn't his mother mentioned it when they moved here?

"What did he want to know about the east wing?" Sam finally asked, his voice barely above a whisper.

Mr. Thompson's expression darkened slightly. "Much the same as you and your friends have been asking. About the old storage rooms, about the history of the building. About students who went missing over the years."

He leaned closer, his voice dropping even lower. "I told him what I told you yesterday—some doors are meant to stay closed. Some histories are best left unexamined. He didn't listen either."

The implication hung in the air between them, unspoken but unmistakable: James Rivera's investigation into Pinecrest's secrets might be connected to his disappearance in Ecuador.

Before Sam could press for more information, Mr. Thompson straightened up, his demeanor shifting back to that of a simple school custodian. "Your mother's still in the building, working late in the history department office. Might want to pack up soon if you're expecting a ride home with her."

With that, he moved away, pushing his cart of cleaning supplies toward the next row of shelves.

Sam sat frozen, his mind racing with this new information. His father had been to Pinecrest. He'd been investigating the disappearances in person, not just through newspaper archives and secondhand accounts. And Mr. Thompson had warned him, just as he'd warned Sam and his friends. The connection to Ecuador suddenly seemed stronger, more tangible. What if his father had found something at Pinecrest that led him to the Upano Valley? What if the same people responsible for the disappearances here had somehow reached him in Ecuador?

Sam gathered his materials and stuffed them with shaking hands into his backpack. He needed to tell the others about this development, but first, he wanted to check on his mother. If she was working late in the school again, potentially near the east wing where the hidden room was located, he needed to make sure she was safe. As he made his way through the quiet corridors, the afternoon sunlight slanting through windows and creating long shadows, Sam couldn't shake the feeling of being watched. The school itself seemed to hold its breath around him, walls that had witnessed decades of disappearances observing yet another Rivera poking into secrets better left buried.

He found the history department office tucked away in a corner of the main building, not far from where the east wing began. The door was ajar, warm light spilling into the dim hallway. Sam peered in to see his mother seated at a desk covered with folders and loose papers, her reading glasses perched on her nose as she made notes on a legal pad.

She looked up at his light knock, surprise and then pleasure crossing her face. "Sam! I didn't know you were still here." She removed her glasses, rubbing the bridge of her nose where they had left slight indentations. "I got caught up in these records. The school board minutes from the 1940s and 50s are fascinating—so many details about the construction of the original building and the early years of operation."

Sam stepped into the office, glancing at the materials spread across her desk. "Find anything interesting?" he asked, trying to keep his tone casual while looking for any indication that she might be researching the disappearances specifically.

Dr. Rivera's expression brightened with scholarly enthusiasm. "Several things, actually. For one, there are discrepancies in the enrollment records for certain years, specifically 1953, 1965, 1977, and so on. Students listed at the beginning of April who aren't present by May, without transfer documentation. Could be clerical errors, of course, but it's a curious pattern."

A curious pattern. The same twelve-year cycle they'd been investigating. So his mother had noticed it too and was possibly here at Pinecrest specifically to research these disappearances. But why wouldn't she have told him that? Why maintain the fiction that this was just about her academic interest in segregated schools?

"Mom," he began, unsure how to broach the subject. "Did Dad ever talk to you about Pinecrest? About students going missing here?" The question hung in the air, heavier than he'd intended.

Dr. Rivera's hands stilled over her papers, her expression freezing momentarily before she carefully composed her features. "Why do you ask?" The deflection was an answer enough.

Sam leaned against the edge of the desk, studying his mother's face. "Mr. Thompson, the custodian, just told me that Dad visited this school two years ago and that he was asking questions about missing students and the east wing. But Dad never mentioned that to me." He paused, watching for her reaction. "And you never mentioned it either when we moved here."

His mother's shoulders sagged slightly as if the weight she'd been carrying had suddenly increased. She pushed aside the papers in front of her, creating a small, clear space on the cluttered desk. "Your father had... theories. About patterns of disappearances across different locations and time periods. Most of his colleagues considered it a side interest, not serious archaeological research."

She hesitated, choosing her words carefully. "He believed there were connections between ancient ritual practices in South America and certain events in modern times, including here in Chesapeake. I thought it was a bit far-fetched, to be honest. Until..."

"Until he disappeared in Ecuador," Sam finished for her, the pieces falling into place. "And now you're here, studying the same patterns he was."

Dr. Rivera looked up at her son, a mixture of grief and determination in her eyes. "I don't know what happened to your father in Ecuador, Sam. But I do know he was on to something about Pinecrest. The position here was a legitimate opportunity for my research on segregated education, but yes, I also wanted to look into what James had been investigating. To see if there were answers here that might lead us to him."

The confirmation of his suspicions left Sam feeling both vindicated and uneasy. His mother had been keeping secrets, just as he had been keeping his father's research notes hidden from her. They'd been working on parallel investigations, neither fully confiding in the other.

"I found Dad's notes," he admitted. "The ones about Pinecrest and the disappearances every twelve years. And yesterday, with some friends, I found something else—a hidden room in the east wing with evidence of some kind of ritual involving four students each cycle. The same kind of ritual Dad was researching in Ecuador."

Dr. Rivera's face paled, her hand reaching out to grasp Sam's arm. "You found the chamber? Sam, that's incredibly dangerous. The people involved in this—they're powerful and connected. Your father suspected they had influence throughout the city, even in the police department. That's why he kept his investigation quiet."

"Who are they?" Sam asked, the reality of the situation hitting him with full force. "What do they want with these students?"

His mother shook her head, frustration evident in the gesture. "That's what I've been trying to figure out. James had a theory about some kind of society that dates back to the founding of Chesapeake, possibly with connections to similar groups in South America. He believed they conducted rituals at regular intervals to maintain what they called 'the barrier,' though he never discovered what this barrier was supposedly protecting against."

She began gathering her papers with increased urgency. "We need to be careful, Sam. Both of us, especially now that four students are missing."

The similarity between his mother's warnings and Mr. Thompson's struck Sam forcefully. Both spoke of danger, of powerful people who wouldn't want their secrets exposed. But neither seemed to know the full story—his mother with her academic research, Mr. Thompson with his decades of observations at the school. Perhaps the answer lay in combining their knowledge with what Sam and his friends had discovered in the hidden room.

"Mom, I think we should talk to my friends—the ones who found the room with me. They've been researching this too. One of them, Leila, has her grandfather's journal from when he taught here in the 1960s. He documented the disappearances back then."

Dr. Rivera considered this, her academic mind visibly weighing the risks against the potential for new information. Finally, she nodded. "Bring them to our house tomorrow after school. We'll compare notes to see what we can piece together. But Sam—" her expression grew stern, "this stays between us and your friends. No talking about it at school, no asking obvious questions. If the people behind this realize we're investigating, we could be in danger, too."

The seriousness of her tone reminded Sam of the night before his father left for Ecuador, when he'd hugged Sam tighter than usual and said, "Take care of your mom if I'm gone longer than expected. And remember, sometimes the biggest discoveries are the ones right under our noses."

At the time, Sam had thought it was just his father's usual philosophical musings before a trip. Now, he wondered if

James Rivera had suspected he might not return—if he'd known he was getting close to something dangerous. As Sam and his mother gathered their things to head home, the weight of this realization settled over him. His father had disappeared while investigating the same mystery that now consumed Sam and his new friends. The pattern of disappearances at Pinecrest wasn't just a decades-old secret; it was personally, devastatingly connected to his family's tragedy. And solving it might be the only way to discover what had happened to his father.

The drive home was quiet; both Sam and his mother were lost in their own thoughts. The streets of Chesapeake passed by outside the car windows, ordinary houses and businesses giving no indication of the dark secrets that might lie beneath the surface of this seemingly peaceful community.

Sam thought about his life in Richmond—the baseball games, the friends he'd pushed away after his father disappeared, the normal teenage existence he'd once taken for granted. He remembered his last conversation with his best friend, Alex, the day before they moved to Chesapeake.

"You're like a zombie, man," Alex had said, frustration breaking through months of patient understanding. "It's like when your dad disappeared, you disappeared too."

The accusation had stung because it was true. Sam had withdrawn into himself, pouring all his energy into researching his father's disappearance, pushing away anyone who tried to pull him back into normal life.

But now, ironically, another mystery was bringing him back. The investigation into Pinecrest's disappearances had given him a purpose, a direction for the churning energy of his grief and questions. And Leila, Noah, and Mia—virtual strangers just days ago —had become allies in a quest that felt more significant than any baseball championship or middle school social drama. For the first time since his father vanished, Sam felt engaged with the world again, connected to people who understood the importance of seeking truth no matter how uncomfortable or dangerous it might be.

Sam noticed a small package on the front porch as they pulled into their driveway. He retrieved it while his mother unlocked the door, turning the plain brown parcel over in his hands. It was addressed simply to "S. Rivera" with no return address. Inside the house, he carefully opened it, his mother watching with curious concern from across the kitchen counter. Beneath layers of bubble wrap was an item that made both of them freeze: a small stone figurine, intricately carved to represent four human figures arranged in a circle. Sam recognized it immediately from his father's photos—an artifact from the Upano Valley excavation, similar to ones found in the ritual chambers of the ancient settlements. Wrapped around it was a note written in familiar handwriting: *"The pattern converges in April. Four become one, and one becomes none. Find me where the roads meet beneath the old trees."*

Sam's hands trembled as he held the figurine, his father's cryptic message sending a surge of conflicting emotions through him—hope that James Rivera might still be alive, fear about what his words might mean, confusion about how this package had reached their new home in Chesapeake. His mother's face had drained of color as she gently took the note, fingers tracing her husband's handwriting.

"This is recent," she whispered. "The paper, the ink—this isn't from before he disappeared." The implication hung in the air between them, too powerful to be spoken aloud immediately: James Rivera might be alive, might be trying to communicate with them about the very mystery they were investigating.

"'Where the roads meet beneath the old trees,'" Sam repeated, mind racing. "What does that mean? Is he talking about Pinecrest? About the east wing?"

His mother shook her head slowly, her analytical mind visibly working through possibilities. "Not the school itself, I think. But somewhere in Chesapeake..." She trailed off, then suddenly straightened. "The historical marker. There's an old plantation site in Northwest River Park with a historical marker about the Whitmore Plantation, the land Pinecrest was built on. It's at the intersection of two old colonial roads, with massive oak trees that date back centuries."

Sam's pulse quickened. "That has to be it. We need to go there." He was already reaching for his jacket when his mother placed a restraining hand on his arm.

"Not tonight, Sam. It's getting dark, and if this is connected to the disappearances, we need to be careful. We'll go tomorrow with your friends. More eyes, more safety."

The logic was sound, but frustration burned in Sam's chest. His father might be reaching out after eight months of silence, and they were going to wait. But the determination in his mother's eyes brooked no argument. This was Dr. Olivia Rivera, the academic, methodical, and cautious, not the impulsive woman who had once jumped into a river fully clothed because his father dared her.

"First thing tomorrow," Sam insisted, a compromise rather than a capitulation. "Before school, just you and me. Then we can bring the others after classes."

His mother considered this, then nodded reluctantly. "First light. But we stay together, and at the first sign of anything suspicious, we leave immediately."

The agreement settled, and they stood in the kitchen examining the figurine and note, both too keyed up to suggest dinner or homework or any of the normal activities that should fill a Tuesday evening.

The figurine was about four inches tall, carved from a dark green stone that felt cool and heavy in Sam's hand. The four figures were distinct, holding what appeared to be a scroll or book, another with what might be a paintbrush, a third wearing some kind of headdress or crown, and the fourth with hands outstretched as if offering healing or blessing. The scholar, the artist, the leader, the healer.

The same archetypes targeted in the Pinecrest disappearances for over seventy years. Sam couldn't shake the feeling that the figurine was both a message and a warning; his father was trying to tell them something crucial about the nature of the rituals and the danger facing the missing students.

As night fell outside their kitchen windows, Sam and his mother slowly shifted into research mode, spreading maps of Chesapeake across the table and searching for information about Northwest River Park and the Whitmore Plantation. The activity felt familiar, reminiscent of evenings in Richmond when his father would involve them both in planning his next expedition or working through an archaeological puzzle. For the first time since James Rivera disappeared, Sam felt like they were a team again- he and his mother united in purpose, following the breadcrumbs his father might have left for them.

Later, lying in bed but too wired to sleep, Sam texted Leila, Noah, and Mia about the figurine and the message, arranging to meet them before the first bell to share his discovery. As he set his phone aside and stared at the ceiling, his thoughts drifted to his father—not the missing archaeologist of the past eight months, but the dad who had taught him to throw a curve ball, who had quizzed him on historical dates during long car rides, who had always believed that the greatest discoveries came from asking questions no one else thought to ask.

"History isn't just about the past, Sammy," he'd often say. "It's about understanding patterns that repeat, cycles that keep turning until someone has the courage to break them."

Tomorrow, Sam would visit the place where his father might have left a message. Tomorrow, he would share what he'd learned with his new friends, combining their knowledge to piece together the mystery of Pinecrest's disappearances. Tomorrow, he might come one step closer to understanding what had happened to his father in the Ecuadorian rainforest.

For the first time in months, Sam fell asleep with a sense of hope alongside the ever-present worry, hope that the cycle his father had investigated could be broken, that the four missing students might be saved, that the pattern of loss that had defined his life for the past eight months might finally be coming to an end.

CHAPTER EIGHT
WHISPERS FROM THE PAST

Sam's dreams were troubled, filled with shifting images of hidden rooms and ancient stone figures. The four carved statues from his father's package seemed to move in his subconscious, their features transforming from stone to flesh and back again. In one moment, they bore the faces of Aaron, Sofia, Caleb, and Lily; in the next, they were strangers from another time, their eyes pleading for help as shadows consumed them.

"The pattern converges," his father's voice echoed through the dreamscape. "Four become one, and one becomes none." Sam tossed in his bed, the sheets tangling around his legs as his mind wrestled with connections just beyond his grasp. In the hazy logic of dreams, he found himself back in Richmond, tossing a baseball with his father in their backyard.

"You're not looking at the whole picture, Sammy," Dr. James Rivera said, his familiar voice comforting even as his words unsettled. He seemed solid and real, not like someone who had been missing for eight months. His father's hazel eyes—the same ones Sam saw in the mirror every morning-were crinkled with the familiar intensity that always accompanied his most important lessons.

"Remember what I taught you about archaeological sites? The most valuable artifacts aren't always the most obvious."

Sam tried to respond, but his dream self could only watch as his father's image began to fade, replaced by the towering oak trees of a forest he'd never seen. "Where the roads meet beneath the old trees," his father's voice whispered, now distant and echoing. "Northwest River Park. You'll understand when you see it for yourself."

In the master bedroom down the hall, Dr. Olivia Rivera sat cross-legged on the floor beside her bed, surrounded by papers she'd retrieved from the false bottom of her dresser drawer. Her dark hair was pulled back in a hasty ponytail. Her reading glasses perched on her nose as she sorted through her husband's research papers, which she'd discovered after his disappearance, and documents she'd kept hidden even from Sam. The small bedside lamp cast long shadows across the worn pages covered in James's distinctive handwriting—half-cursive, half-print, with arrows connecting seemingly unrelated facts.

Her eyes burned from fatigue, but sleep remained elusive. That afternoon, after finding the stone figurine and note, something clicked in her mind—a connection she'd missed before, hidden in plain sight among James's scattered research.

"The pattern converges in April," she murmured, repeating the words from his note. What pattern? She'd been studying the disappearances at Pinecrest, tracing the twelve-year cycle as James had, but something still eluded her. She reached for a folder labeled "Excavation Site 4B-Upano Valley" and spread the contents across the floor. Photographs of stone carvings and ritual chambers discovered in the ancient Amazon settlements stared back at her. James had circled certain symbols repeatedly-four interconnected circles arranged around a central point, eerily similar to the design on the floor of the hidden room Sam had described finding in Pinecrest's east wing. A yellow Post-it note in James's handwriting clung to one photo: "Timing critical-celestial alignment every 12 years—corresponds to school cycle?"

Olivia's hands trembled slightly as she picked up a sheet of astronomical calculations. James had mapped the positions of certain stars on dates corresponding to the Pinecrest disappearances going back decades. According to his notes, a rare alignment occurred every twelve years in April, the same month students went missing. She reached for her laptop, quietly typing a search for upcoming astronomical events. A news article about a rare alignment of planets and stars in the coming week caught her attention. If James's calculations were correct, the alignment would reach its peak three days from now, which is exactly when the ritual would be completed if the pattern were true.

Olivia rubbed her temples, trying to make sense of it all. James had been brilliant, but his work often veered into territory her more traditional academic mind struggled to follow. He saw patterns and connections across cultures and centuries that others dismissed as coincidence. She had loved that about him, wild, intuitive leaps that somehow landed on solid ground. It had also worried her, especially when he became obsessed with the Pinecrest disappearances and their possible connection to ancient Ecuadorian rituals. Even now, she wasn't sure if his theories were the product of genuine insight or if he'd fallen into a conspiracy hole. But the stone figurine had arrived at their door–tangible evidence that James might still be alive and might be trying to communicate something vital.

Olivia gathered the papers into a neat stack, her mind made up. They needed to visit Northwest River Park at first light. If James had left some clue "where the roads meet beneath the old trees," they needed to find it before the ritual. She had been truthful with Sam about her research position at Pinecrest being legitimate—her work on educational segregation and integration was respected in academic circles. But she hadn't been entirely honest about why she'd chosen this particular school, this particular time. The position suddenly opened when the previous history teacher, Dr. Eleanor Blackwood, resigned without warning in the middle of the school year. The official story was that Dr. Blackwood had left for personal reasons and a family emergency that required her immediate attention. But in academic circles, rumors swirled about a respected historian abandoning her position without proper notice, without even cleaning out her office.

During Olivia's interview, Principal Fletcher had been vague about Dr. Blackwood's departure, his usual charm faltering when Olivia pressed for details. "Sometimes people find that researching Pinecrest's history can be... overwhelming," he had said with a tight smile. "Dr. Blackwood was perhaps too dedicated to uncovering every detail of our past. I'm sure you understand that some aspects of any institution's history are best left to rest."

The words had sent a chill through Olivia then, reminding her of James's concerns about institutional cover-ups at Pinecrest. Now, in the quiet of the night, with her husband's research spread before her, those words felt like a warning she'd ignored. She had taken the position partly to continue her legitimate research but mostly to investigate what had happened to James—to follow the trail he'd been pursuing before his disappearance.

She had kept Sam in the dark, telling herself she was protecting him from painful speculation, from false hope. But now Sam was involved anyway, drawn into the mystery by his own investigation and the friends he'd made. She owed him the truth, or at least as much of it as she understood herself. A noise from Sam's room caught her attention. Sam was having a murmured conversation as if he were talking to someone. Gathering the papers quickly, she tucked them back into their hiding place and crept down the hall to check on her son. Sam's door was slightly ajar, and Olivia peered in to see him tossing restlessly, his face contorted in concentration.

"Dad?" he murmured, still deep in sleep. "I don't understand... what pattern? Where should we look?" Olivia's heart ached as she watched her son reach out in his sleep, having a conversation with the father he missed so desperately. Since James disappeared, this wasn't the first time she'd caught him sleep-talking. The psychologist had said it was normal, a way for his subconscious to process the trauma of loss and uncertainty.

"The east wing," Sam muttered, turning again in his sleep. "Hidden beneath... the marker... oaks..." Olivia stiffened, her breath catching. Sam's dreaming mind seemed to be circling the same connections she'd just been studying in James's notes. The coincidence was too strong to ignore. Making a sudden decision, she pushed the door open and crossed to Sam's bed, gently shaking his shoulder.

"Sam," she whispered, then more urgently when he didn't respond. "Sam, wake up." Sam's eyes fluttered open, confusion clouding his expression as he struggled to orient himself between dreams and reality.

"Mom? What's wrong? What time is it?"

"It's just after four," she replied, already moving to turn on his bedside lamp. "Get dressed. We need to go to Northwest River Park now, before sunrise." Sam sat up, rubbing his eyes as the remnants of his dream clung to his consciousness.

"Now? But visiting hours don't start until—"

"This can't wait," Olivia interrupted, her voice low but urgent. "I've been looking through your father's research, and there's something important at that historical marker— something connected to the disappearances and to what's happening now. You were right about the figurine being a message, but I think there's more to it than we realized."

Sam was fully awake now, swinging his legs over the side of the bed. "You found something in Dad's papers?" The question held a note of accusation that made Olivia wince inwardly. She hadn't told Sam about the additional research materials she'd discovered.

"Yes," she admitted. "I found some of his notes after he disappeared—astronomical calculations, connections between the Pinecrest disappearances, and celestial events. And something about a marker at the intersection of two colonial roads in Northwest River Park." She paused, studying her son's face. "Sam, you were just talking in your sleep about the east wing, and something was hidden beneath a marker near the oak trees. The same things your father wrote about."

Sam's eyes widened. "I was dreaming about Dad. He was trying to tell me something about the park, about looking beyond the obvious." He hesitated. "It felt real, Mom. Like he was actually talking to me." Olivia nodded, not dismissing the possibility outright as she might have months ago. Eight months of grief and unanswered questions had softened her skepticism about many things.

"Maybe he was, in some way. But right now, we need to focus on finding whatever he left at that marker. Get dressed in warm clothes and hiking boots, if you can find them. And bring your phone for photos. I'll pack some flashlights and breakfast, and we can eat in the car."

Twenty minutes later, they were in Olivia's sedan, traveling through Chesapeake's dark, empty streets. The digital clock on the dashboard read 4:47 AM as they turned onto the road leading to Northwest River Park. Sam cradled the stone figurine in his hands, studying the four carved figures in the glow of the car's interior light.

"Do you think Dad is alive?" he asked suddenly, the question hanging in the quiet car like a physical presence. Olivia gripped the steering wheel tightly, carefully considering her words.

"I don't know," she admitted, her voice steady despite the emotion behind it. "The figurine and note suggest he might be. But it's also possible someone else sent them someone who found his research or who was involved in whatever he was investigating."

She glanced briefly at her son. "I want to believe he's alive, Sam. But I also don't want to give you false hope. What matters now is finding what he wanted us to discover at the park and using it to help those missing students before it's too late."

Sam nodded, returning his attention to the figurine. "Tell me about when you and Dad met," he said after a moment. "You never really told me the whole story."

Olivia smiled despite the moment's tension, recognizing Sam's need for connection to his father through stories.

"We met in graduate school at UVA," she began, the familiar tale offering comfort as they drove through the darkness. "I was working on my PhD in educational history, and your father was completing his doctorate in archaeology. We were both teaching assistants for an interdisciplinary course on the historical impact of colonial settlements on Indigenous cultures. Professor Harrington paired us up to develop a lecture on educational practices across different cultural contexts."

She chuckled softly at the memory. "Your father was so passionate, so full of theories that connected everything from Aztec temples to colonial schoolhouses. I thought he was brilliant but undisciplined—all intuitive leaps without sufficient evidence. He thought I was too rigid, too dependent on documented facts."

Olivia's mind drifted back to that first collaborative session in the university library. Books and maps surrounded James, his dark hair falling across his forehead as he excitedly traced connections across cultures and centuries.

"Education isn't just about transmitting information, Olivia," he'd argued. "It's about preserving cultural identity, about rituals that connect one generation to the next. Look at these patterns across Indigenous communities—the selection of specific children for specialized training, the timing of initiations according to celestial events."

She'd been both exasperated and fascinated. "That's an interesting perspective, James, but we need scholarly sources, not just theories. Professor Harrington expects a well-documented presentation." He'd grinned at her, that disarming smile that would eventually break through her academic reserve.

"Then we'll give him both your meticulous research and my pattern recognition. Together, we'll change how people understand educational history." And somehow, against all odds, their presentation had been a success, her rigorous methodology providing the foundation for his innovative connections. Professor Harrington had been impressed enough to encourage them to co-author a paper, which led to long hours of research, heated debates, and, eventually, a relationship that bridged their different approaches to scholarship.

"We balanced each other," Olivia told Sam as they turned onto the road leading to Northwest River Park. "My evidence-based approach grounded his intuitive leaps. His ability to see patterns across different contexts brought life to my historical analysis."

Sam was listening intently, hungry for details about his parents' relationship before he was born. "When did you fall in love?"

Olivia felt a flush rise to her cheeks, grateful for the darkness in the car.

"About three months into working together. We were in the university archives, researching colonial-era educational practices in Virginia. Your father found a diary from a teacher at one of the first schools for freed slaves after the Civil War. The teacher described rituals the former enslaved people performed at certain times of year-ceremonies with African origins that had been preserved in secret during generations of captivity."

Her voice softened with the memory. "This evidence of cultural persistence against all odds so moved your father. He talked about how certain knowledge is preserved through rituals when written documentation is forbidden or destroyed. And I remember looking at him at that moment, eyes bright with discovery, his hands carefully turning the fragile pages of the diary, and realizing I'd never met anyone who felt history so deeply, who saw the humanity in academic subjects that others treated as merely intellectual exercises."

The memory warmed her even now, despite everything that had happened since. "We were married two years later, just after completing our doctorates. Your father got a position at VCU's Department of Anthropology and Archaeology, and I joined the History Department at the University of Richmond. We bought that little house on Maple Street, and three years after that, you came along."

Sam nodded, piecing together the timeline of his parents' lives before his memories began. "When did Dad start getting interested in the Pinecrest disappearances?" This was the question Olivia had been dreading, the point where their family history intersected with the current mystery. She slowed the car as they approached the entrance to Northwest River Park, which was still closed at this early hour. The sky was beginning to lighten imperceptibly in the east, though sunrise was still about an hour away.

"About five years ago," she answered carefully. "He was researching patterns of disappeared civilizations— communities that seemed to vanish without obvious causes like war or natural disaster. It was for a paper on cultural collapse and resilience."

She pulled the car onto a service road that curved around the park's main entrance, parking behind a stand of trees where they wouldn't be immediately visible from the road. "He came across an article about the Upano Valley in Ecuador—a network of ancient settlements that showed evidence of periodic abandonment and reoccupation at roughly twelve-year intervals. The pattern fascinated him, especially when he discovered similar cycles in other locations around the world."

Olivia turned off the engine but left the key in the ignition, turning to face her son. "While researching historical patterns in Virginia, he stumbled on news articles about missing students, Chesapeake, specifically at Pinecrest. Four students in 1989, four in 2001, and four in 2013. The twelve-year cycle caught his attention immediately."

The interior of the car felt suddenly cold despite the mild spring morning. "At first, I thought he was making connections that weren't there, seeing patterns because he was looking for them. That was always my role in our partnership, to question his intuitive leaps, to demand more evidence."

She sighed, regret heavy in her voice. "Maybe if I'd taken it more seriously from the beginning, if I'd helped him investigate instead of dismissing it as a side project..."

"It's not your fault, Mom," Sam said quietly, showing a maturity beyond his years. "You couldn't have known."

Olivia swallowed hard, the guilt she'd been carrying for months rising to the surface. "Two years ago, he visited Pinecrest for the first time. He told me he was giving a guest lecture at Old Dominion University, which was true, but he extended his trip to include research in Chesapeake. When he came back, he was different-agitated, obsessed with his notes, staying up late in his office. He told me he'd spoken with a custodian at Pinecrest who'd been there for decades, a man who confirmed his suspicions about the disappearances and mentioned something about a hidden room in the east wing."

Sam leaned forward. "Mr. Thompson. He's still there. He showed us the hidden room yesterday. He knew Dad?"

"Apparently so," Olivia confirmed. "Your father said Thompson had warned him to stop investigating, that powerful people were involved, people with connections throughout the city. But James was convinced he was onto something important that connected the Pinecrest disappearances to ancient rituals in Ecuador and other locations around the world."

She reached into her jacket pocket and pulled out a folded piece of paper, smoothing it out on the dashboard. It was a photocopy of a map with locations marked across Virginia, Ecuador, Peru, and several other countries. "He believed these were all connected sites where similar ritualistic disappearances occurred at regular intervals determined by astronomical alignments. The Upano Valley in Ecuador was the oldest and most extensively documented, which is why he was so eager to join the excavation team when the opportunity arose."

Olivia's voice faltered slightly. "I thought the trip would get it out of his system. He'd either find concrete evidence to support his theories or realize he was seeing connections that weren't there. I never imagined he wouldn't come back."

The weight of unspoken grief hung between them. After a moment, Sam broke the silence. "So when he disappeared in Ecuador, you started looking into his research more seriously."

It wasn't a question. Olivia nodded, opening her car door. "Let's continue this conversation while we walk. We need to find that historical marker before anyone else arrives at the park."

CHAPTER NINE
NORTHWEST RIVER SECRETS

They stepped out into the pre-dawn darkness, the air cool and heavy with dew. Olivia retrieved two flashlights from the trunk, handing one to Sam, along with a small backpack containing water bottles, protein bars, and a first aid kit. "The marker should be about half a mile in, where two old colonial-era roads intersected before the park was established. According to the historical society's website, it's surrounded by oak trees that are over 200 years old."

Sam activated the flashlight app on his phone as additional illumination. "Does anyone know we're here?" he asked as they started down a trail leading into the woods.

Olivia shook her head. "No, and that's probably for the best. If your father's theories are correct, and there is some kind of organization behind these disappearances, the fewer people who know what we're doing, the safer we are."

They walked silently for several minutes, the beam of their flashlights cutting through the darkness between the towering trees. The forest was alive with pre-dawn sounds, the rustle of nocturnal animals returning to their dens, and the first tentative chirps of early-rising birds. Olivia consulted a park map she'd downloaded to her phone.

"The marker should be just ahead, in a clearing where the old Portsmouth Road met the Great Bridge Turnpike." As if on cue, the trees opened up to reveal a small clearing dominated by four massive oak trees. Their gnarled branches spread across the sky like arthritic fingers, their trunks so wide that three people with outstretched arms would encircle them. In the center of the clearing stood a weathered stone marker about four feet tall, its surface discolored by decades of exposure to the elements.

Sam directed his flashlight at the inscription: "WHITMORE PLANTATION 1802-1910. Site of the main house of one of Norfolk County's largest plantations. Home to the Whitmore family for four generations. In 1856, four enslaved people attempting to escape were executed on this property. Their names were unrecorded. The land was sold to the county in 1910 for educational purposes." Below this official text, someone had carved additional words that appeared much newer: "The unnamed four still guard the barrier. Their sacrifice repeats."

Sam's breath caught as he read the unauthorized addition. "Mom, look at this." Olivia leaned closer, her flashlight illuminating the carving. "This wasn't here when the historical society documented the marker five years ago," she said, her academic mind automatically cataloging the discrepancy. "Someone added it recently."

"Dad?" Sam suggested; hope colored his voice. Olivia didn't answer immediately, circling the marker slowly, her flashlight scanning every inch of the weathered stone. "There's something else here," she said, crouching near the base of the marker. "Look at these symbols."

Sam knelt beside her, examining what appeared to be freshly carved markings near the ground, four interconnected circles arranged around a central point, identical to the pattern on the floor of the hidden room in Pinecrest's east wing and similar to symbols in his father's research photos from Ecuador. "It's the same pattern," he whispered, excitement and dread mixing in his voice.

"The four become one." Olivia ran her fingers over the carving, noting its depth and precision. "This was done with proper tools, not just a pocket knife. Someone wanted these symbols to last." She pulled out her phone and took several photos of the markings from different angles, the flash momentarily brightening the clearing.

"Your father's notes mentioned that the Whitmore Plantation originally covered over three hundred acres, including the land where Pinecrest was eventually built. The main house was here, but other structures were scattered throughout the property, including slave quarters."

Sam was examining the ground around the marker, his flashlight cutting through the early morning mist that had begun gathering in the clearing. "What do you think happened to the four slaves who tried to escape?" he asked, the historical reality suddenly more immediate and disturbing in this quiet place.

Olivia's expression darkened. "According to your father's research, they were accused of planning a rebellion—a young man who taught other slaves to read in secret, a woman known for her skills in painting and creating natural dyes, a man who had emerged as a leader among the slave community, and a woman who practiced traditional healing with herbs and plants."

"The scholar, the artist, the leader, and the healer," Sam said, the parallel to the current disappearances unmistakable. "Exactly the same archetypes as the missing students through the years."

"Yes," Olivia confirmed, her academic voice slipping into place like armor against the disturbing implications. "James believed their execution was not just a punishment but a ritual of some kind. The Whitmore family was involved in something beyond the already horrific institution of slavery. He found references in private letters and diaries to 'maintaining the barrier' and 'the necessary sacrifice to protect what lies beneath.'" She hesitated, aware of how fantastical it sounded. "He believed that whatever began here continued after the plantation was sold, with the ritual moving to Pinecrest when the school was built on part of the former plantation grounds."

Sam listened intently, connecting these revelations to what he and his friends had discovered. "The hidden room in the east wing that is where they plan the selections and perform whatever ritual is involved."

Something occurred to him suddenly. "Mom, if the missing students are meant to be sacrifices like these slaves were, does that mean they're killed?"

The question hung in the air between them, terrible in its directness. Olivia chose her words carefully. "Your father couldn't find definitive evidence of what happens to the students. The official records always list them as runaways who were later found or returned home, but he could never verify those claims. No bodies have ever been discovered, but..."

"But no one really comes back either," Sam finished for her. The implications were too horrific to dwell on. He redirected his attention to the marker, examining the ancient oaks surrounding it. "Dad's note said to find him 'where the roads meet beneath the old trees.' We found the marker, but I don't see anything that could lead us to him."

Olivia was circling the largest of the four oaks, her flashlight directed at its massive trunk. "These trees would have been witnesses to everything that happened: the plantation house, the slave community, the executions." She stopped suddenly, her beam fixed on an abnormality in the tree's bark about five feet from the ground. "Sam, look at this."

He joined her, finding a small, precise carving in the oak's trunk, the initials "JR" with an arrow pointing downward.

"Dad's initials," Sam breathed, hope surging through him. "He was here." Olivia nodded, her own emotions carefully controlled as she followed the direction of the arrow with her flashlight. The beam illuminated a section of ground at the base of the tree, where the soil appeared recently disturbed.

Sam was already kneeling, brushing away leaves and loose dirt to reveal what looked like a small metal box, the kind used for storing cash or valuable documents, with a simple combination lock securing the lid. "It's locked," he said unnecessarily, lifting the box from its shallow hiding place. It was surprisingly heavy for its size, suggesting something substantial inside.

Olivia knelt beside him, examining the lock. "Your father always used the same combination for everything—it drove me crazy from a security perspective." Her fingers spun the dials rapidly: 7-22-13. The lock clicked open.

"July 22, 2013," she explained as Sam looked at her questioningly. "It was the day we found out I was pregnant with you. He said it was the most important date in his life." The sentiment might have warmed Sam under different circumstances. Still, now he was focused entirely on the box's contents as his mother carefully lifted the lid.

Inside lay a leather-bound journal, a USB drive sealed in a waterproof bag, a small velvet pouch, and a sealed envelope with "Olivia & Sam" written on the front in James's distinctive handwriting. Olivia's hands trembled slightly as she removed the envelope, tearing it open with uncharacteristic impatience.

Inside was a single sheet of paper covered in James's handwriting. "My dearest Olivia and Sam," she read aloud, her voice steady despite the emotion evident in her eyes.

"If you're reading this, you've followed the clues I left and found this cache. I hope you're reading it together. This concerns both of you. What I've discovered about Pinecrest is that it is more dangerous and far-reaching than I initially believed. The disappearances are not isolated incidents but part of a pattern that stretches back centuries and extends beyond Chesapeake to sites around the world, including the Upano Valley excavation in Ecuador. The journal contains my complete findings, and the USB drive holds copies of all documentation and evidence I've collected. The object in the pouch is a key-not just physically but symbolically. It unlocks a door in the east wing of Pinecrest, behind the ritual chamber you've likely discovered by now."

Olivia paused, looking up at Sam in surprise. "He knew you'd find the hidden room." Sam nodded, equally startled. "Keep reading," he urged. Olivia returned to the letter.

"The organization behind these disappearances calls itself the Guardians of the Veil. They believe they're protecting humanity from something dwelling beneath Chesapeake-something that was disturbed when the first European settlers arrived and again when the plantation was established. The four archetypes—scholar, artist, leader, and healer—represent aspects of humanity that this entity feeds upon. Every twelve years, when specific celestial conditions are met, the barrier between our world and whatever lies

beneath weakens. The Guardians perform their ritual to strengthen it, using the energy life force of the four selected students."

Olivia's voice faltered slightly before continuing.

"I've traced their activities across multiple sites globally and discovered that Chesapeake is just one node in a network of similar rituals performed around the world.

My excavation work in Ecuador was a cover to investigate one of the oldest ritual sites, where I believed I might find a way to end this cycle without further sacrifices. By the time you read this, I will either have succeeded or become another disappearance myself. If I've succeeded, I'll find you. If not, everything you need to continue is in this box."

She took a deep breath before reading the final paragraph.

"The current cycle is nearly complete. Four students have already been taken. You have until the full celestial alignment to find them and break the cycle. The key opens a passage beneath Pinecrest that leads to where the students are held before the final ritual. Be careful who you trust. Guardians have members at every level of Chesapeake society, including the school board, police department, and local government. I love you both more than words can express. Find me where the veil is thinnest.

—James"

The silence that followed was profound, broken only by the increasing sounds of birds as dawn approached. Olivia carefully folded the letter and returned it to the envelope, her academic mind visibly struggling with the fantastical implications of her husband's words.

"This can't be real," she murmured, more to herself than to Sam. "Secret societies, ancient entities, ritual sacrifices... it sounds like something from one of your father's more outlandish theories." Yet even as she said it, her hands were carefully removing the journal and USB drive from the box, securing them in her jacket pockets as if they were precious artifacts.

Sam opened the velvet pouch, tipping an ornate bronze key into his palm. It was unlike any modern key, about four inches long, with an elaborate handle featuring the now-familiar symbol of four interconnected circles.

"He believed it," Sam said softly, studying the key. "And after what we found in that hidden room, after four students disappearing every twelve years following the same pattern... It's hard to dismiss."

Olivia nodded reluctantly, the historian in her giving way to the reality before them. "We need to get back to the car," she said, checking her watch. "It's almost 6:30, and the park officially opens at 7:00. We don't want to be discovered here."

CHAPTER TEN
GUARDIANS REVEALED

She helped Sam replace the now-empty metal box in its hiding place, covering it with dirt and leaves to conceal their discovery. As they stood to leave, a twig snapped somewhere beyond the clearing, the sound unnaturally loud in the otherwise quiet forest. Olivia froze, her flashlight beam sweeping toward the source of the noise. "Who's there?" she called, trying to keep her voice authoritative despite the fear clutching her chest.

No answer came, but Sam's flashlight caught a momentary glimpse of movement among the trees, a shadowy figure retreating deeper into the woods. "We're not alone," he whispered, instinctively moving closer to his mother. "We need to go. Now!"

They hurried back along the trail toward the parking lot, no longer concerned with stealth or careful observation. The eastern sky had lightened considerably, painting the forest in shades of gray and pale blue. As they approached the car, Olivia spotted a piece of paper tucked under the windshield wiper: a park citation for unauthorized entry after hours. "Someone knows we're here," she said grimly, snatching the paper and unlocking the car with trembling hands. "Get in quickly."

As Sam slid into the passenger seat, his gaze caught on something moving at the edge of the trees-another shadowy figure, too distant to make out clearly but unmistakably watching them. "Mom," he began, but Olivia was already turning the key in the ignition, the car engine roaring to life.

"I see them," she said tersely, throwing the car into reverse and backing onto the service road with more speed than caution.

"There's more than one." Sam craned his neck to look behind them as they accelerated away from the park entrance, spotting what appeared to be a dark SUV pulling onto the road some distance behind. "They're following us," he reported, fear and adrenaline sharpening his senses. "Can you lose them?"

Olivia's hands tightened on the steering wheel, her eyes flicking between the road ahead and the rearview mirror. "I'm going to try. Our best bet is to get to someplace with people." She took a sudden turn onto a side road, accelerating through the quiet residential neighborhood. "Check the journal," she instructed, her voice tight with concentration. "See if your father left any information about who these people might be, names, or specific warnings."

Sam retrieved the journal from Olivia's jacket pocket, flipping it open with shaking hands. The first pages contained field notes from Ecuador, sketches of archaeological sites, and astronomical calculations similar to those Olivia had found in James's other papers. But as he turned to later entries, dated just weeks before his father disappeared, the content became more urgent, more specific to Chesapeake.

"He mentions several names," Sam reported, scanning the pages rapidly. "Principal Fletcher is listed as a 'suspected Guardian,' along with two school board members, Davis and Hargrove. There's also a Detective Collins with the Chesapeake Police and..." he paused, swallowing hard. "And Dr. Eleanor Blackwood, the history teacher you replaced."

Olivia's sharp intake of breath was audible even over the engine's hum as she navigated another turn, momentarily losing sight of the pursuing vehicle. "Blackwood was investigating the disappearances, too," she murmured. "That's why she left so suddenly; she either discovered something that frightened her into running or..."

"Or she became another disappearance," Sam finished, the implication hanging heavy between them. "Dad writes that she'd been asking questions about the east wing, about the school's history, and specifically about the 2013 disappearances. She had accessed archived school board minutes that mentioned 'special security protocols' for the east wing dating back to the 1950s."

He turned another page, finding a hasty sketch of what appeared to be a floor plan. "There's a map here that looks like the east wing but with additional passages that don't appear on the school's official blueprints. He's marked an entrance behind the hidden room with a note saying, 'Bronze key required—leads to holding chambers.'" Sam looked up, connecting the dots.

"The students who disappear—they're kept somewhere beneath the school before the ritual. The key we found opens the way to them."

Olivia rechecked the rearview mirror, relieved to see no sign of pursuit for the moment. "If that's true, we might still have time to save them. Your father's letter said the ritual isn't completed until the full celestial alignment, that is, three days from now."

She made another turn, heading toward more populated areas as morning traffic began to increase. "We need to get to the school," she decided. "But not directly if we're being followed. We'll stop at home first, change clothes, gather some supplies, and approach Pinecrest as if it's a normal school day. I have a legitimate reason to be there as a teacher, and you have a legitimate reason to be there as a student. We'll find a way to access the east wing during lunch or after classes."

Sam nodded, returning his attention to the journal. As he turned another page, a small photograph slipped out, a faded color snapshot from what appeared to be the 1990s, showing a group of four teenagers standing in front of Pinecrest Middle School. They were smiling at the camera, ordinary students caught in an ordinary moment, unaware of what might have awaited them. On the back, in his father's handwriting: "1989 disappearances—David Chen, Maria Lopez, Tyrell Washington, Sarah Miller. No evidence they ever returned despite official reports."

Sam stared at the faces of people with real lives, families who had lost them, and futures that had been stolen. The reality of what they were dealing with hit him with renewed force. These weren't just historical patterns or academic mysteries; they were lives at stake, both those already lost and those that might still be saved. "We need to involve Leila, Noah, and Mia," he said firmly. "They've been researching this too, and they helped me find the hidden room. We'll need their help to rescue Aaron and the others."

Olivia hesitated, the protective maternal instinct warring with practical necessity. "It's dangerous, Sam. These people, Guardians, have been operating for decades, maybe centuries. They've been willing to sacrifice children to maintain whatever this 'barrier' is."

Sam met his mother's gaze steadily. "Which is exactly why we need all the help we can get. Leila's grandfather documented the 1965 disappearances. Noah's tech skills could be crucial for accessing information. And Mia knows the current missing students personally-she might notice details we'd miss."

After a moment's consideration, Olivia nodded reluctantly. "You're right. But we need to be cautious in our approach to this. No discussion at school where we might be overheard. We'll invite them to our house after school today." She checked her watch as they turned onto their street. "It's already 7:15. We have less than an hour to get ready and get to school. Go straight to the shower when we get home, and I'll pack some essentials, such as flashlights, first aid supplies, and water. We don't know what we might be facing beneath Pinecrest."

As they pulled into their driveway, both scanned the street nervously for any sign of the SUV that had followed them from the park. The neighborhood seemed calm and normal, with people leaving for work and children waiting for school buses. But Sam couldn't shake the feeling of being watched, of invisible eyes tracking their movements from behind drawn curtains or tinted windows.

Inside the house, Olivia moved with urgent efficiency, gathering supplies while Sam showered and dressed for school. The bronze key and figurine were carefully wrapped and hidden in Sam's backpack, along with his father's journal. Olivia secured the USB drive in her briefcase, along with her notebook, where she'd already begun transcribing and analyzing her husband's research.

By 7:45, they were back in the car, Olivia's hair still damp from her hasty shower. "Remember," she said as they drove toward Pinecrest, "act normal. Don't say anything about what we found to anyone except your three friends, and even then, only when you're absolutely sure you can't be overheard. Watch Principal Fletcher and any of the other names in your father's journal. Notice who they talk to, who seems to be watching you."

Sam nodded, the weight of their discovery settling onto his shoulders. "What about Mr. Thompson? Dad seemed to trust him somewhat, but he's also been at the school for decades. Could he be involved with the Guardians?"

Olivia considered this as they stopped at a red light. "Your father's notes suggested Thompson knew about the disappearances but wasn't actively participating in them. He described him as 'trapped by the knowledge he can't escape, unwilling to act but unable to fully comply.' Be cautious around him, but he might be a potential ally if approached correctly."

The conversation stalled as they pulled into the Pinecrest parking lot, which was already filling with buses and cars and dropping off students. The school looked deceptively normal in the morning sunlight, a typical middle school preparing for another day of classes. But Sam now saw it with new eyes, aware of the dark history beneath its ordinary exterior, the secrets hidden behind its institutional facade.

"Text me if you notice anything suspicious," Olivia said as they prepared to part ways at the main entrance. "I'll be in the history department office most of the morning, organizing those archives. If anyone asks about our early morning trip, say we went hiking to clear our heads after a restless night. Not entirely untrue."

Sam nodded, scanning the crowd of arriving students for his friends. "I'll try to talk to Leila, Noah, and Mia before the first bell. We usually meet by the water fountain in the main hall."

Olivia gave his shoulder a quick squeeze, an unusual public display of affection that emphasized the seriousness of their situation. "Be careful, Sam. These people have been operating unchecked for decades. They won't hesitate to act if they suspect we know too much."

With that sobering reminder, she headed toward the faculty entrance, her posture deliberately casual, just another teacher arriving for work.

CHAPTER ELEVEN
PATTERN CHANGES

Sam watched her go, then turned toward the main student entrance, steeling himself for a day of pretending everything was normal while carrying the knowledge that four students were being held somewhere beneath the school, awaiting a ritual that would claim their lives just as it had claimed others every twelve years since Pinecrest was built. And somewhere connected to all of this was his father, potentially alive, potentially nearby, potentially leaving clues to help them end this cycle once and for all.

The thought gave Sam courage as he stepped through the doors, immediately scanning the hall for Leila, Noah, and Mia. As expected, he spotted them by the water fountain, huddled in conversation that stopped abruptly when Leila noticed him approaching. Her expression shifted from concern to relief. "Sam," she said, moving to meet him halfway. "We were worried when you didn't answer our texts this morning."

He pulled out his phone, realizing he'd forgotten to check it in the rush of the early morning discovery. Five missed texts, three from Leila and one each from Noah and Mia. All expressed concern about the latest news. "What happened?" he asked, joining their huddle away from the main flow of students.

Noah pulled out his phone, showing Sam a local news notification: "SEARCH CONTINUES FOR MISSING CHESAPEAKE TEENS—Police expand the search area for four missing students, parents demand answers."

"They're publicly acknowledging all four disappearances now," Mia explained in a low voice. "It's never happened before. Usually, they try to keep it quiet and treat each one as an isolated runaway case." Leila nodded, her dark eyes intense.

"Something's different this time. The pattern is the same, but the response is changing. We think it might be because more people are connecting the dots, social media, online forums, parents organizing search parties independently of the police."

Sam glanced around to ensure they weren't being overheard before responding.

"My mom and I found something this morning," he said quietly. "We went to Northwest River Park before sunrise, to the historical marker my dad mentioned in his note. He left a hidden cache there, a journal, a USB drive, and a key. The journal confirms everything we've suspected and more."

The three leaned closer, their expressions a mixture of excitement and dread. "What did it say?" Noah asked, pushing his glasses up nervously.

Sam chose his words carefully, aware of students passing nearby. "That the disappearances are part of something bigger—a ritual performed by a group called the Guardians of the Veil. They believe they're protecting the city from something underneath it, something that requires sacrifices every twelve years when specific celestial conditions are met." He lowered his voice further. "The key opens a passage beneath the school, where the students are being held before the final ritual three days from now. We might still have time to save them."

The information had a palpable impact on the three friends. "Your dad wrote all this?" Mia asked, her usual skepticism momentarily suspended by the concrete evidence Sam had described.

He nodded. "And more, names of people involved, including Principal Fletcher and others. My mom wants us all to meet at our house after school to plan our next steps. She thinks we should try to access the passage tonight when the building is empty."

Leila glanced toward the administrative offices, where Principal Fletcher could be seen greeting students through the glass partition. "If he's involved, we need to be extremely careful today. Act normal, don't draw attention to ourselves."

The first bell rang, signaling five minutes until classes began. Noah looked nervously at his watch. "We should split up now. Meet at lunch, usual table?" The others nodded in agreement. As they prepared to part ways,

Sam caught Leila's arm. "There's something else," he said, his voice barely above a whisper. "The previous history teacher, Dr. Blackwood—my father's notes suggest she was investigating the disappearances too before she suddenly left. And..." he hesitated, not wanting to upset Leila but knowing she needed the information. "He mentioned your grandfather's journal. He believed it contained crucial information about the Guardians' origins at Pinecrest, information your grandfather was forced to hide when they pushed him into early retirement."

Leila's expression darkened. "My grandfather never trusted the school administration, even decades later. He told me to keep his journal secret and only share it with people I trusted." She hesitated, then added, "There are pages missing, torn out near the back. He always said if anything happened to him, I should look 'where knowledge is preserved but hidden from those who would misuse it.' I never understood what he meant."

The second bell rang, forcing them to separate and head to their respective homerooms. As Sam slid into his seat in Ms. Bennett's class, he couldn't help but stare at the empty desks that belonged to Aaron Mitchell and now Lily Robertson, who had also been in his homeroom. Two empty seats, two lives in danger, connected to two others in different classrooms. The normality of taking attendance and making morning announcements felt surreal against the backdrop of what he now knew.

Ms. Bennett seemed distracted during roll call, her eyes lingering on the empty desks with something more than casual concern. Could she be involved? Sam wondered. Was she a Guardian, a passive observer, or completely unaware of the dark ritual taking place beneath the school where she taught? His father's journal hadn't mentioned her name, but that didn't necessarily mean anything. The Guardians had operated in secrecy for generations; their full membership was likely known only to those at the highest levels.

Principal Fletcher's voice came over the intercom, unusually somber as he addressed the recent disappearances. "As many of you may have heard, four students from our district are currently missing. The police are conducting an intensive investigation, and we urge anyone with information to come forward immediately. Counselors are available for any students feeling distressed by these events. I want to assure all parents and students that we are taking every possible measure to ensure the safety of our school community."

The words rang hollow to Sam, given his knowledge of Fletcher's suspected involvement. Was this announcement part of the cover-up, the public face of concern masking much darker actions? Or was Fletcher merely a pawn in a larger organization, someone who followed orders without fully understanding their implications? Either way, Sam felt a chill as he listened to the man's carefully measured tones. The morning classes passed in a blur, Sam's mind preoccupied with processing everything they'd discovered and planning their next steps. In each class, he noted which teachers seemed genuinely disturbed by the disappearances and which maintained a more detached demeanor. He paid special attention to his surroundings, looking for anything unusual— students watching him too carefully, staff members appearing in hallways where they wouldn't normally be, any sign that their investigation had been noticed.

By the time lunch arrived, Sam was mentally exhausted from maintaining his facade of normalcy while conducting this covert observation. He found Leila, Noah, and Mia already at their corner table, huddled over Noah's laptop. "I've been doing some research on the Whitmore Plantation," Noah reported as Sam sat down. "County historical records confirm what your father's notes mentioned. In 1856, four slaves were executed for allegedly planning an escape.

Their names weren't recorded officially, but I found letters from the Whitmore family archived in the historical society's database that referred to them by first names only—Isaiah, described as 'too clever for his own good,' teaching others to read; Adeline, who created dyes and patterns for textiles; Marcus, who had organized harvest celebrations and was respected among the community; and Ruth, known for her knowledge of medicinal plants."

"The archetypes again," Mia murmured. "Scholar, artist, leader, healer. Just like the students who disappear." Leila had been unusually quiet, but now she pulled something from her backpack —her grandfather's leather journal, opened to a page near the back where several sheets had been cleanly torn out. "I've been thinking about my grandfather's message about knowledge being preserved but hidden. What if he hid the missing pages somewhere in the school? Somewhere, only another history teacher would think to look?"

The possibility hung in the air between them, a potential key to understanding the full scope of what they were facing. "The library," Sam suggested. "Specifically, the historical archives section. It would be the perfect place to hide information that is accessible but overlooked by most people."

Leila nodded slowly. "My grandfather was friends with the librarian before he retired. Miss Patterson. She's still there, in her seventies now, but refuses to retire. If he hid something in the library, she might know about it, might even be protecting it."

"We should check during the free period," Noah suggested. "The library's usually quiet then, and Miss Patterson tends to take her lunch break in the staff room around that time. Less chance of being observed."

Sam hesitated, wary of drawing attention from all four visiting the library together. "Maybe just Leila should go," he suggested. "She has a legitimate connection to her grandfather, and she could say she's researching family history if anyone asks. The rest of us would just make it more conspicuous."

The others reluctantly agreed to this plan. "What about tonight?" Mia asked, lowering her voice further. "Are we really going to try to find that passage beneath the school?"

Sam nodded, determination evident in his expression. "My mom thinks our best chance is after the faculty meeting this afternoon. Most teachers and administration will be occupied for at least an hour. We'll meet at my house right after school to plan, then return to Pinecrest around 4:30 when the meeting starts."

Leila looked skeptical. "Won't the building be locked?"

"My mom has keys," Sam explained. "And she knows which entrances aren't covered by security cameras. We can access the east wing through the maintenance corridor that connects to the main building."

The plan was taking shape, but Noah still looked troubled. "What exactly are we planning to do if we find the missing students? Four teenagers against an organization that's been operating for over a century? That's assuming we even find this supposed passage or that the key actually works."

It was a valid concern, one that had been nagging at Sam since their discovery that morning. "My father's journal mentioned that the ritual can only be completed during the full celestial alignment, which is still three days away. If we can find and free the students before then, we can disrupt the cycle. And suppose we can document everything, gather evidence of the Guardians, the hidden chambers, and the ritual preparations. In that case, we can expose them, making it impossible for them to continue operating in secret."

"And if we get caught?" Mia asked the practical question, hanging heavily between them.

Sam met her gaze steadily. "My father risked everything to uncover this. The missing students are risking their lives right now, not by choice. We can't walk away just because it's dangerous." The conviction in his voice settled something for the group. Even Noah nodded, his initial hesitation giving way to resolve.

The bell ending lunch came too soon, forcing them to separate for afternoon classes. As they gathered their things, Leila confirmed she would visit the library during her free period to search for her grandfather's missing journal pages.

"Text us if you find anything," Sam instructed. "And be careful who sees you looking."

The afternoon crawled by with excruciating slowness. Each class tested Sam's ability to maintain the appearance of a normal student while his mind raced with plans and possibilities. During history, he found himself studying his mother with new appreciation as she lectured on colonial education systems in Virginia. She showed no sign of the tumultuous morning they'd shared, no indication that she was planning to lead a group of teenagers into hidden passages beneath the school in search of missing students. Her academic facade was flawless, precise, engaging, and professional.

It struck Sam that this double life wasn't new to her; she'd been investigating his father's disappearance for months while maintaining her role as a grieving but functioning widow and mother. He'd underestimated her resilience, her determination. She caught his eye briefly during a discussion of educational access in post-Revolutionary Virginia, a moment of silent communication passing between them. *Be patient. Act normal. We have a plan.*

During seventh-period science, Sam's phone vibrated with a text from Leila: "Found something. Not pages but a reference. Old biology textbook, section on cellular barriers, 2 folded notes tucked inside. Meet after class by the east hallway water fountain."

The message sent a surge of adrenaline through Sam's system. Another piece of the puzzle, potentially crucial information hidden by Leila's grandfather decades ago, was preserved in the school library all this time. The final bell couldn't come soon enough. When it finally rang, Sam gathered his things with controlled urgency, making his way through the crowded hallways toward the east wing. He found Leila already waiting by the water fountain, her expression a mixture of excitement and concern.

"Look at this," she said without preamble, pulling him into a quieter alcove and unfolding two yellowed pieces of paper. The first was a hand-drawn map of what appeared to be tunnel systems beneath Pinecrest, more detailed than the sketch in James's journal.

Various chambers were labeled with cryptic notations: "Preparation Room," "Barrier Access," "Guardian Assembly," and most disturbingly, "Holding Cells." A dotted line traced a path from a point marked "East Wing Entry" to an area labeled "Central Chamber" where the tunnels converged.

The second paper contained densely written text in an elegant, old-fashioned hand:

"For those who seek to end what my silence has allowed to continue. The Guardians of the Veil established themselves in Chesapeake before the Revolutionary War, originating from a splinter group of European occultists who believed they had discovered a thin point between worlds—a place where another reality pressed against our own. According to their beliefs, this 'thinning of the veil' allowed something to begin crossing over, something ancient and hungry that feeds on human potential. The four archetypes represent the pinnacle of human achievement—knowledge, creativity, leadership, and compassion. By sacrificing individuals who embody these qualities at the moment of greatest celestial alignment, they believe they strengthen the barrier between worlds for another cycle."

Leila's eyes were wide as she looked up from the note. "This was written by Professor Edmund Clarke, a historian who taught at William & Mary in the 1950s. My grandfather corresponded with him while researching Pinecrest's history. Clarke disappeared in 1965, the same year as that cycle's student disappearances."

Sam scanned the note again, and the implications were chilling.

"So the Guardians don't just target students," he murmured. "They eliminate anyone who gets too close to exposing them." He carefully photographed both papers with his phone before returning them to Leila.

"We need to show these to my mom and the others. This map could be crucial for navigating beneath the school." As most students headed home or to after-school activities, the hallways began to thin out. Sam checked his watch. "We should go. My mom's expecting us at our house by 4:30 to plan for tonight."

CHAPTER TWELVE
HIDDEN LOCATION REVEALED

As they turned to leave, a shadow fell across them.

Mr. Thompson stood at the end of the alcove, his weathered face unreadable as he observed them huddled over the old documents. "You kids still poking around where you shouldn't," he said, his voice carrying neither surprise nor particular disapproval. "Your father had that same stubborn look, Sam. Wouldn't listen to warnings either."

Sam tensed, uncertain whether Thompson was a threat or potential ally. "We found his journal," he said carefully, watching for the man's reaction. "He trusted you to some extent. He said you weren't actively involved in the disappearances."

Thompson's expression remained impassive, but something flickered in his eyes—perhaps relief, perhaps resignation. "I've been at Pinecrest longer than most folks have been alive," he said quietly. "Seen generations of students come and go. Seen eight cycles of the ritual-thirty-two young lives taken to 'maintain the barrier.'" He spat the phrase with evident disgust. "Never participated, but never stopped it either. Too much of a coward, I suppose."

He moved closer, his voice dropping further. "Your father found what others missed—the connection between the nodes, the global network of ritual sites. That's why they came for him in Ecuador. He was too close to understanding how to break the entire system, not just the Chesapeake branch." Leila and Sam exchanged startled glances.

"You've been in contact with my father?" Sam asked, hope warring with suspicion. Thompson shook his head. "Not directly. But I hear things—the Guardians talk when they think no one's listening. Your father escaped them in Ecuador and went into hiding. Been working his way back, gathering allies, preparing to strike at multiple nodes simultaneously when the alignment peaks three days from now."

He nodded toward the papers in Leila's hands. "That map's outdated. They've changed the tunnel system since Clarke drew it, added security measures, and changed access points. If you're planning what I think you're planning, you need updated information."

He reached into his pocket and removed a folded piece of paper, offering it to Sam. "Current layout, as of last month's preparations. Security access codes for the electronic locks they've added since the 90s. And the rotation schedule for Guardian patrols in the tunnels."

Sam accepted the paper cautiously. "Why are you helping us now? You've watched this happen for decades."

Thompson's eyes clouded with what might have been a shame. "I was young when I first discovered what was happening. A maintenance assistant recently returned from Vietnam. By the time I understood the full scope, I was compromised—not a participant but a witness who'd failed to act. They made it clear what would happen to my family if I spoke up."

His gaze hardened. "But I'm an old man now. My wife passed last year, and my children are grown and moved away. And I'm tired of carrying this weight, tired of cleaning up after their rituals, tired of pretending I don't see the empty desks every twelve years." He straightened, some of his customary dignity returning. "Your father showed me there might be a way to end it, not just here but everywhere. That's worth whatever time I have left."

Leila studied him carefully. "My grandfather tried to stop it too, didn't he? That's why they forced him into retirement."

Thompson nodded, something like respect crossing his features. "Marcus Washington was a brave man. He gathered evidence for years and documented everything he could. When they discovered what he was doing, they threatened your mother, your grandmother. Said they'd be next to disappear if he didn't destroy his research and leave quietly."

He glanced at his watch. "You should go. Principal Fletcher has scheduled a walk-through of the east wing after the faculty meeting today—supposedly to assess 'maintenance needs.' Really making sure everything's ready for the final preparations."

Sam pocketed the updated map and security information. "Thank you," he said, meaning it. "For this and for helping us find the hidden room yesterday."

Thompson's expression was grim. "Don't thank me yet. You're walking into danger beyond what you can imagine. Those tunnels don't just lead to holding cells-they connect to whatever lies beneath Chesapeake, whatever the barrier is supposedly protecting us from. The Guardians believe in what they're doing—believe they're saving humanity from something worse than the sacrifice of lives."

"What do you believe?" Leila asked bluntly.

The old custodian was silent for a long moment. "I believe no god or greater good demands the sacrifice of children," he finally said. "And I believe your father is right. Sam, there's another way to maintain whatever this barrier is without feeding it young lives. Find that way, and you end centuries of suffering."

With that cryptic encouragement, he turned and pushed his cleaning cart down the hall, resuming his role as the unassuming custodian who saw everything but was seen by few. Sam and Leila watched him go, the weight of his confirmation settling over them. "We need to move fast," Sam said, checking the time again. "Mom will be waiting, and we have a lot to plan before tonight."

They hurried toward the main exit, the afternoon sun still bright as they emerged from the institutional lighting of the school into the natural world. The normality of the scene, buses lining up, students chatting and laughing, and parents waiting in cars struck Sam as surreal against the backdrop of ancient rituals and hidden chambers. Somewhere beneath this ordinary school, four students were being held prisoner, awaiting a fate that had claimed others before them, stretching back through generations. And somewhere, perhaps closer than they realized, his father was working to end the cycle once and for all. The realization filled Sam with both dread and determination as he and Leila headed toward the Rivera house, where Noah and Mia would be waiting.

The countdown to tonight's exploration of the tunnels beneath Pinecrest had begun—a race against time, against centuries of terrible tradition, against an organization with roots deeper than the nation itself. The weight of it all should have been crushing, but Sam felt a strange clarity instead. The fog of uncertainty was lifting for the first time since his father disappeared. James Rivera hadn't abandoned them; he was fighting a battle they were only beginning to understand. And now, Sam would join that fight for the missing students, for his father, and for an end to the cycle that had claimed too many lives for too many years.

CHAPTER THIRTEEN
GUARDIANS OF MEMORY

The afternoon sun cast long shadows across the empty hallways of Pinecrest Middle School as Earl Thompson pushed his cleaning cart away from Sam and Leila. His weathered hands gripped the handle with unnecessary force, knuckles whitening as the weight of his decision pressed down on him. After decades of silent complicity, he had finally chosen a side. The squeaking wheels of his cart echoed through the corridor like a metronome, counting down the minutes until everything changed.

He had given Sam the updated tunnel; there was no going back now. The memory of Sam's determined eyes, so much like his father's, stayed with him as he methodically went through the motions of cleaning the east wing. Thompson had been cleaning these same floors since before Sam's parents were born, bearing witness to the twelve-year cycle of disappearances that no one seemed to notice or question. Or rather, those who did notice tended to disappear themselves.

As he mopped the dulled terrazzo floor near the entrance to the hidden room, his mind drifted back thirty years to a different time, a different conversation in this same hallway. Marcus Washington had been standing right where Thompson now stood, his thoughtful eyes scanning the wall with suspicion behind wire-rimmed glasses that caught the fluorescent light.

"There's something off about the dimensions, Earl," Washington had said, his deep voice lowered despite the emptiness of the hallway after hours. "I've checked the original blueprints from when this was Pinecrest High. There should be at least fifteen feet of space behind this wall."

Thompson remembered the chill that had run down his spine, how he'd glanced nervously over his shoulder before responding. "Some things are better left alone, Marcus." But Washington hadn't been deterred- he never was, once he set his mind to something.

"Four students disappeared in 1965, Earl. Four more in 1977. Now it's 1989, and Tyrell, Maria, David, and Sarah have been missing for three days. The official story is that they ran away together, but that's nonsense. Tyrell was my student, planning to attend Howard University on a full scholarship. He wouldn't just disappear." Washington's voice had grown more insistent, his finger tapping on a manila folder containing newspaper clippings, old photographs, and handwritten notes. "It's always the same pattern - the brightest mind, the most talented artist, the natural leader, and the compassionate healer. Every twelve years, like clockwork."

Thompson had shifted uncomfortably, the weight of what he knew pressing down on him like a physical force. Vietnam had taught him when to fight and when to keep his head down. "Marcus, you have a wife and a daughter. Think about them."

But Washington's expression had hardened with resolve. "I am thinking about them. I'm thinking about what kind of world my Amber will grow up in if good men do nothing in the face of evil." That conversation began their clandestine investigation, a partnership formed in whispers and shared after hours in the dim light of Thompson's maintenance closet.

Washington had been the brains, the methodical researcher tracking down connections and patterns across decades. Thompson had been the access, the invisible presence that could move throughout the building unquestioned, taking measurements and photographs and, eventually, making the discovery that would haunt his dreams for decades to come.

The memory faded as Thompson finished mopping the hallway, his aged joints protesting as he wrung out the mop for the final time. He returned his equipment to the janitorial closet, checking his watch: 5:15 PM. The faculty meeting would be ending soon. He needed to leave before Principal Fletcher began his "inspection" of the east wing. As he changed out of his work uniform in the small employee restroom, Thompson's reflection caught his eyes: deep lines etched around his eyes and mouth, the silver hair that had once been black, the tired slump of shoulders that had once stood straight and proud in military uniform.

"Some things are better left alone," he had told Washington all those years ago. Perhaps he'd been trying to convince himself. After changing, Thompson slipped out through a side entrance, nodding to the security guard, who barely acknowledged him. That was the benefit of being part of the furniture: after more than fifty years at Pinecrest, people looked through him rather than at him.

His 1998 Toyota Camry, meticulously maintained but showing its age much like its owner, was parked in the far corner of the staff lot. As he settled behind the wheel, his hand reached automatically for the glove compartment, fingers finding the small leather-bound notebook he'd carried with him every day since 1970. It was his anchor, his reminder of why he had survived when others hadn't. The journal contained names- every name he could remember of those lost in the jungles of Vietnam, and later, the names of every student who had disappeared from Pinecrest during his tenure.

As his trembling fingers traced the most recent entries– Aaron Mitchell, Sofia Alvarez, Caleb Johnson, Lily Robertson, Thompson was transported back to the rice paddies outside Quang Ngai, to the moment that had defined the rest of his life.

Private Jenkins had been just nineteen, a skinny kid from Des Moines with dreams of becoming a veterinarian after the war. "The healer," Thompson thought bitterly, recognizing the archetype only in retrospect. The patrol had been ambushed, and Thompson had watched from his position of cover as

Jenkins was hit, crawling desperately toward the tree line, calling for help. Thompson could have reached him — he was certain of it — but fear had frozen him in place. By the time the firefight ended and Thompson made it to Jenkins' position, the young medic was gone, his dog tags and medical kit missing. They'd never found his body.

Thompson had returned from Vietnam with a Bronze Star for actions in a later engagement, but the memory of his failure with Jenkins hollowed out any pride he might have felt. The survivor's guilt had followed him home like a shadow, shaping his life in ways he couldn't articulate until many years later, when he recognized the same paralyzing fear as he watched Principal Henderson escort four confused students into the east wing after hours in April 1977. He'd hidden around the corner, watching as a door that shouldn't exist opened in the wall and swallowed them whole. Just as with Jenkins, Thompson had done nothing. Starting the car, Thompson pulled out of the school parking lot, his destination clear in his mind.

Eleanor Patterson lived in a small craftsman bungalow about twenty minutes from the school on a quiet street lined with mature oak trees. Like Thompson, she had devoted her entire professional life to Pinecrest, serving as the school librarian since the mid-1970s. Unlike Thompson, she had never been silent about her suspicions —at least not with him and Washington. She had been their third musketeer, providing access to records that would otherwise have been impossible to obtain, hiding their research among the library's vast archives where curious eyes wouldn't think to look.

As he drove through the early evening traffic, Thompson's mind returned to 1990, to the aftermath of the 1989 disappearances. Washington had been relentless in his investigation, gathering evidence that pointed inevitably toward a terrible conclusion involving some of Chesapeake's most prominent citizens. "It's organized, Earl," Washington had whispered urgently as they huddled over blueprints spread across a library table after hours, Patterson keeping watch at the door. "These aren't random disappearances. There's a purpose behind them, a ritual of some kind that dates back to when the school was built, maybe even earlier."

Thompson nodded, his throat dry, as he recalled what he'd seen in the hidden room: the circular pattern on the floor, the strange symbols on the walls, and the photographs of previous "selections" dating back decades.

"But why?" Patterson had asked, her voice steady despite the fear evident in her eyes. "What could possibly justify taking children?"

Washington had spent months researching occult practices, secret societies, and local history, piecing together a theory that seemed too fantastic to be true yet too consistent to dismiss. "*The Guardians of the Veil,*" he'd explained, pointing to references in old newspapers and private correspondence he'd unearthed. "I believe they're a splinter group of European occultists who settled in this area before the Revolution. They believe there's something beneath Chesapeake — some kind of doorway or thin spot between worlds. The ritual is meant to feed it, to keep whatever is on the other side from coming through."

Thompson remembered his skepticism and the desire to dismiss Washington's theory as academic overreach. Then Washington had shown them the historical record of the Whitmore Plantation, where four slaves had been executed in 1856 for attempting to escape a scholar, an artist, a leader, and a healer. The pattern had been established even then, continuing after the plantation was sold and Pinecrest was built on part of the original property. The realization that the cycles of disappearance stretched back more than a century had been chilling. Their investigation had continued for months, with Washington documenting everything in his journal, creating maps of the hidden tunnels based on Thompson's covert explorations, and compiling a list of suspected Guardians that included some of Chesapeake's most respected citizens.

Then came the day Thompson would never forget — the day Washington came to school ashen-faced, his usual confident stride replaced by a defeated shuffle. "They came to my house last night," he'd said, his voice barely audible in the empty library. "Two men in suits, very polite, very clear. They know everything we've been doing. They showed me pictures of Diane and little Amber at her daycare. Said next time, it wouldn't be just pictures."

The threat had been unmistakable. Washington had been forced into early retirement at the end of that school year, and his research was apparently abandoned. But Thompson knew better. Before he left, Washington had entrusted the most damning pages of his journal to Patterson, who had hidden them somewhere in the library where only she could find them.

CHAPTER FOURTEEN
THE LIBERATION'S TRUST

Thompson pulled into Patterson's driveway, noting the porch light was already on despite the early hour. She'd been expecting him. Perhaps she'd been expecting him for thirty years. As he approached the front door, it opened before he could knock, revealing Eleanor Patterson, still straight-backed and bright-eyed at seventy-six, her silver hair pulled into a neat bun, her gaze as penetrating as it had been when she first joined Pinecrest as a young librarian fresh from library school. "Earl Thompson," she said, her voice carrying the slight Virginia lilt that five decades in Chesapeake had never quite erased. "I've been waiting for you to find your courage."

There was no malice in her words, only a sad understanding that tightened Thompson's throat. "It's happening again, Eleanor," he said simply, following her into the house. "The Rivera boy and his friends have found the hidden room. They know about the disappearances, the pattern. And I gave them an updated map of the tunnels today."

Patterson nodded, leading him into a living room lined with bookshelves, every available surface covered with books, papers, and photographs — the home of a woman who had devoted her life to preserving knowledge.

"Marcus always said it would come full circle," she remarked, settling into a wingback chair and gesturing for

Thompson to take the seat opposite. "That's why he left those pages with me, why we've kept them safe all these years. He knew someday someone would need them, someone with the courage to finish what we started."

Thompson leaned forward, his weathered hands clasped between his knees. "Washington's granddaughter, Leila, is one of the students who found the hidden room. She has what's left of his journal, but doesn't have the missing pages. She doesn't know the full story."

Patterson studied him for a long moment as if assessing his resolve. Finally, she nodded and rose from her chair, moving to a large bookcase that dominated the far wall. "Help me with this, Earl," she said, positioning herself at one end of the bookcase. Together, they carefully pulled it away from the wall, revealing a small wall safe behind it. "Marcus designed the system," Patterson explained as she knelt before the safe, her joints protesting audibly. "Two keys, two people — neither of us could access the pages alone. That was deliberate. He didn't want either of us making a unilateral decision that might endanger the other."

From his wallet, Thompson extracted a small key he'd carried for thirty years, never quite believing he would use it. Patterson produced its twin from a chain around her neck. Together, they inserted the keys into separate locks on the safe, turning them simultaneously. The safe door swung open with a soft click.

Inside lay a sealed manila envelope, yellowed with age but intact, with "FOR LEILA" written across the front in Washington's bold handwriting.

"He knew," Thompson said softly, a lump forming in his throat. "Even then, he knew she would be involved someday."

Patterson nodded, carefully removing the envelope. "Marcus was many things, but he was, above all, a historian. He understood patterns and cycles. I knew the Rivera boy's father was onto something significant-something that connected the Pinecrest disappearances to similar events around the world. When Dr. Rivera disappeared in Ecuador, I suspected the Guardians had reached him there."

She had sealed the envelope in a larger waterproof folder and handed it to Thompson. "These pages contain everything — the complete map of the tunnel system as it existed in 1990, the names of Guardians identified up to that point, and most importantly, Marcus's theory about how the ritual could be stopped without sacrificing more children."

Thompson accepted the folder with reverence, understanding the risks Patterson had taken in preserving this information for three decades. "Why now, Eleanor? Why help them when it could still put you in danger?"

Patterson's eyes hardened, a steel beneath the grandmotherly exterior. "Because I'm seventy-six years old, Earl. I've spent fifty years watching children disappear while doing nothing but keeping secrets. What more can they take from me now? My pension?" She snorted derisively.

"Besides, those children, Aaron, Sofia, Caleb, Lily, they're still alive down there. The ritual isn't completed until the celestial alignment peaks. We still have time to save them."

Thompson nodded, feeling a weight simultaneously lifting from and settling onto his shoulders, the burden of inaction being replaced by the responsibility of action. "Dr. Rivera has invited the students to her house tonight to plan. I think we should join them and bring them this information."

Patterson was already reaching for her coat. "I'll drive," she said with a decisiveness that brooked no argument. "You navigate."

As they left the house, Thompson found himself thinking of Jenkins again and all the others whose names filled his journal. Perhaps, after all these years, he could finally do for these four students what he couldn't do for Jenkins, what he hadn't done for thirty-two other Pinecrest students over the decades. Perhaps he could finally find his courage.

The Rivera house was modestly lit as they pulled up at 6:30 PM, Thompson noting with approval the drawn curtains and the apparent normality of the scene. If the Guardians were watching, he had no doubt they would see nothing out of the ordinary. He led Patterson to the front door, knocking softly in the pattern he had arranged with Sam earlier, four quick raps followed by two slower ones.

The door opened almost immediately, revealing Dr. Olivia Rivera. Her expression shifted from wariness to surprise as she recognized Thompson. "Mr. Thompson," she said, her voice carefully controlled. "I wasn't expecting you."

"I believe your son was," Thompson replied quietly. "And I've brought someone else who can help Eleanor Patterson, Pinecrest's librarian for the past fifty years." Understanding dawned in Dr. Rivera's eyes as she glanced from Thompson to Patterson, quickly ushering them inside and securing the door behind them. The living room had been transformed into what could only be described as a war room. Maps, printouts, and photographs covered every available surface. A large whiteboard had been propped against one wall, covered with names, dates, and connecting lines tracing the pattern of disappearances back through decades.

Sam, Leila, Noah, and Mia sat around the dining table strewn with open books and laptops. All four looked up as Thompson and Patterson entered, their young faces showing a mixture of surprise, hope, and wariness. "You came," Sam said simply, his eyes moving to the folder in Thompson's hands. "And you brought the missing pages."

Leila stood slowly, her gaze fixed on Patterson, recognition dawning. "Miss Patterson," she said softly. "You worked with my grandfather."

Patterson nodded, her eyes filling with unexpected tears. "I did, child. And he was one of the finest men I've ever known —

one of the few who was willing to risk everything to uncover the truth about Pinecrest."

Dr. Rivera quickly arranged additional chairs around the dining table, and once everyone was seated, Thompson placed the waterproof folder in the center. "Before we open this," he said, his voice steadier than he'd expected, "there are things you need to understand, context that will help make sense of what your grandfather discovered."

He looked at Leila, seeing echoes of Marcus Washington in the set of her jaw, the intelligent eyes behind her glasses. "Your grandfather and I began investigating the disappearances after the 1977 cycle. I had been at Pinecrest since returning from Vietnam in 1970, working as a custodian while trying to put myself back together after the war. I'd noticed things— patterns, inconsistencies, the special attention given to the east wing. But it wasn't until I met your grandfather that I found someone else who saw what I saw."

The memory of their first real conversation came back to him vividly. Washington approached him after school hours, requesting access to the original building plans, citing a research project on educational architecture during segregation. Thompson had recognized the pretext for what it was. He'd seen Washington's interest in the east wing and had noticed him taking measurements and making notes.

"We spent years piecing together what was happening," Thompson continued. "Washington was the researcher, the theorist. I was the eyes and ears in places he couldn't access. And Eleanor," he nodded toward Patterson, "provided crucial historical records and a safe place to store our findings."

Patterson picked up the narrative, and her librarian's precision was evident in how she structured the information. "What we discovered was a pattern that stretched back to the founding of Pinecrest and, before that, to the Whitmore Plantation that originally stood on this land. Every twelve years, four students would disappear, always following the same archetypes: the scholar, the artist, the leader, and the healer. After extensive research, Marcus theorized that these disappearances were not random kidnappings or runaways but deliberate selections by a group that called themselves the Guardians of the Veil."

Noah leaned forward, adjusting his glasses. "The same group mentioned in Dr. Rivera's journal—the ones who believe they're protecting humanity from something beneath Chesapeake."

Thompson nodded grimly. "Washington discovered references to them in historical records dating back to the colonial period. They originated as a European occult group that settled in this area, believing they had discovered a 'thin point' between worlds—a place where our reality brushes against another. According to their beliefs, something began to push through from the other side, something that feeds on human potential, specifically the four aspects of humanity represented by the archetypes."

Dr. Rivera had been taking notes as they spoke, her historian's mind organizing the information into a coherent timeline. "And the ritual is performed every twelve years because...?"

"Celestial alignment," Patterson answered promptly. "Certain stars and planets align in a specific configuration every twelve years, creating what the Guardians call a 'thinning of the veil.' During this period, the barrier between worlds weakens, requiring the sacrifice to strengthen it."

Thompson watched the younger faces around the table as they absorbed this information- the mixture of horror, fascination, and determination that crossed their features reminded him painfully of Washington's expression when they'd first pieced together the full picture. "And you discovered the hidden room," he continued, "the ritual chamber where the Guardians prepare for the selections. But there's more beneath Pinecrest—a network of tunnels that lead to holding cells where the selected students are kept until the alignment reaches its peak."

Mia, who had been relatively quiet, spoke up. "The missing students—they're still alive down there? All four of them?"

Thompson nodded, understanding the personal connection Mia had mentioned at their first meeting, that she knew the missing students. "According to the Guardians' ritual requirements, all four must be alive for the sacrifice. The alignment peaks in three days. Until then, they're kept in a state of semi-consciousness in the holding cells."

Sam reached for the folder in the center of the table, looking to Thompson for permission. Sam carefully opened it at his nod, extracting the sealed manila envelope with Leila's name written across it. Wordlessly, he passed it to Leila, whose hands trembled slightly as she accepted it. "My grandfather left this for me? He knew I would be involved somehow?"

Patterson's expression softened. "Marcus understood patterns better than anyone I've ever known. He recognized that whatever was happening at Pinecrest wasn't isolated or random; it was cyclical, generational. He believed each cycle would bring new investigators and challengers to the Guardians' power. He hoped that one of these groups would eventually succeed where we had failed."

Leila carefully opened the envelope, revealing several yellowed pages covered in the same handwriting that filled the journal she'd inherited. As she began to read, her expression shifted from curiosity to shock. "These are his final conclusions," she said, her voice barely above a whisper. "Everything he pieced together about the Guardians, the ritual, and..." she looked up, eyes wide, "...how to stop it."

Dr. Rivera leaned forward. "May I?" she asked gently. Leila handed her the pages, and she began to scan them rapidly. Her academic training allowed her to process the information quickly. "This is remarkable," she murmured. "Washington didn't just document the Pinecrest disappearances connected them to similar patterns at locations around the world. Ecuador, Peru, Vietnam, China, Egypt, all places with historical accounts of cyclical disappearances following the same four archetypes."

Noah pulled his laptop closer. "That matches what we found on the USB drive from Dr. Rivera's cache. He was mapping these locations globally, identifying them as 'nodes' in what he called a 'network of thin points.'"

Thompson wasn't surprised by the connection. "Sam's dad was picking up where Washington left off, but with more resources and global connections through his archaeological work. That's why the Guardians targeted him in Ecuador. He was getting too close to understanding the global network and potentially finding a way to disrupt all the nodes simultaneously."

Dr. Rivera set the pages down carefully, her expression a mixture of professional fascination and personal anguish. "James believed the Ecuador site was one of the oldest nodes, possibly the original point where the barrier was first breached. His notes suggested he was searching for artifacts there that might offer clues to maintaining the barrier without human sacrifice." She hesitated, her voice faltering slightly. "Do you think he succeeded? Is that why he disappeared? Was it because he found something the Guardians couldn't allow to become public?"

Thompson exchanged a glance with Patterson, whose slight nod encouraged him to share what he knew. "There are rumors among the lower-ranking Guardians, the ones who don't participate directly in the ritual but support it logistically. They say Dr. Rivera escaped with something from the Ecuador site, something that could disrupt the ritual."

Sam's head snapped up, hope flaring in his eyes. "Then he might still be alive? He might be trying to find a way back to stop this?"

Thompson didn't want to offer false hope, but he could not deny the possibility. "The Guardians certainly believe he's alive. They've increased security around all local nodes, especially Pinecrest. They're afraid he might return before the ritual is complete."

Leila had continued reading her grandfather's notes, her brow furrowed in concentration. "According to my grandfather, the ritual can be disrupted if the four archetypes are united in resistance rather than sacrifice. He believed the power the Guardians harness could be redirected to permanently seal the barrier without taking lives." She looked up, meeting the gazes around the table. "But to do that, we'd need to reach the captives before the alignment peaks and somehow get them to the central chamber during the ritual itself."

Noah shook his head skeptically. "That sounds impossible. We'd be going up against an organization that's had centuries to perfect its security and methods. How could we possibly succeed where others have failed?"

Thompson answered, surprised by the conviction in his own voice. "Because for the first time, we have all the pieces: Washington's research, Rivera's global connections, and, most importantly, the two keys needed to access the deepest levels of the tunnels."

All eyes turned to Sam, who pulled out the ornate bronze key his father had left in the cache. "This is one," he confirmed. "But what's the second?"

Patterson reached beneath the collar of her blouse, extracting a chain that held an identical bronze key. "Marcus entrusted this to me thirty years ago. He discovered that the tunnel system requires two keys used simultaneously to access the central chamber—a security measure implemented by the original Guardians to ensure no single person could disrupt the ritual."

She smiled faintly at the shocked expressions around the table. "I've been wearing this key every day for three decades, waiting for the moment it would be needed."

CHAPTER FIFTEEN
A PLAN DEVELOPS

As the implications sank in, Dr. Rivera began organizing the scattered documents on the table, her academic training asserting itself in the face of overwhelming information. "We need to synthesize everything we have—Washington's research, James's global connections, the maps of the tunnel system, and the information about the current Guardians. Only then can we formulate a plan with any hope of success."

Thompson nodded appreciatively, recognizing the methodical approach that had also characterized Washington's work. Over the next hour, they spread all their materials across the dining table and the adjacent living room floor, creating a comprehensive picture of what they were facing.

Washington's missing pages included a detailed map of the tunnel system as it existed in 1990, with annotations about security measures, patrol patterns, and access points. Thompson's updated map showed changes made in recent years in electronic security systems, reinforced doors, and surveillance cameras. James Rivera's research from the USB drive provided the global context of tunnel systems that existed beneath each node, all connecting to what he called "thin points" where the barrier between worlds was weakest.

Most significantly, his notes suggested a theory that the sacrificial rituals themselves were not what maintained the barrier but rather a misinterpretation by the original Guardians of an older, non-lethal method of channeling energy at these thin points. As the pieces came together, Mia asked the question that had been hovering unspoken. "These missing students—who are they, really? I mean, I know Aaron from Math Club, and everyone knows Caleb from the student council, but why them specifically? How were they chosen?"

Thompson sighed heavily, the weight of decades of witnessed selections pressing down on him. "The Guardians have criteria for each archetype—specific qualities they believe make for the most effective sacrifice. They observe potential candidates for months, sometimes years, before making their selections."

Patterson nodded, adding, "They have members or informants throughout the school system-teachers, administrators, and counselors who identify students with the desired qualities and report back to the senior Guardians."

"Aaron Mitchell," Thompson began, putting faces to the names that had joined his journal of the lost, "was selected as the Scholar archetype. Brilliant in mathematics and robotics, constantly questioning, seeking knowledge not just for achievement but for understanding. The Guardians believe this quality of intellectual curiosity represents the pinnacle of human thought."

Noah nodded in recognition. "He won the state robotics championship last year. His design incorporated principles nobody else had considered."

Thompson continued grimly, "Sofia Alvarez, the Artist archetype. Her paintings don't just show technical skill but evoke emotion and connection. The Guardians see this creative force as representing humanity's ability to transform and transcend ordinary existence."

Mia's voice was soft as she added, "Her mural in the community center downtown—the one with the children from different backgrounds holding hands in a circle—makes you feel something just by looking at it. Like hope and sadness, all mixed together."

"Caleb Johnson," Thompson went on, "the Leader archetype. Not just charismatic or popular, but someone who genuinely inspires others to action and brings people together across divisions. The Guardians value this quality as representing humanity's capacity for unity and collective purpose."

Leila nodded. "He organized that cross-district food drive after the hurricane last fall. Got rival schools working together, raised more donations than anyone expected."

"And Lily Robertson," Thompson concluded, his voice catching slightly, "the Healer archetype. Her compassion isn't just kindness; it's an active force for helping others recover, grow, and become whole. The Guardians see this quality as representing humanity's capacity for regeneration and wholeness."

Sam, who had been listening intently, made the connection. "Like Jenkins in Vietnam. The medic who wanted to become a veterinarian."

Thompson looked up sharply, surprised by the insight. "Yes," he acknowledged, the old guilt washing over him. "How did you know about Jenkins?"

Sam gestured toward the small leather notebook visible in Thompson's shirt pocket. "I noticed you touching it when you mentioned him earlier. And my dad's journal referenced a conversation with you about Vietnam, about a young medic you couldn't save."

Thompson nodded slowly, realizing how perceptive the boy was, like his father, seeing connections others missed. "Jenkins was nineteen," he said quietly, opening the notebook to a page he knew by heart. "A farm kid from Iowa who could calm any animal with just his presence. During an ambush outside Quang Ngai, he was hit. I could have reached him-should have reached, but I froze. By the time I found my courage, he was gone."

The confession hung in the air, decades of self-recrimination distilled into a few simple sentences. "That's why you've never tried to stop the disappearances before now," Dr. Rivera said softly, not as an accusation but as understanding. "The same paralysis, the same fear."

"I told myself it wasn't my fight," Thompson admitted, shame coloring his words. "That I was just a custodian, that there was nothing I could do against powerful people. But the truth is, I was afraid. After Vietnam, I just wanted a quiet life and wanted to forget what fear felt like. So I cleaned floors, fixed leaky faucets, and pretended not to see what was happening every twelve years."

Patterson reached across the table, her hand covering his weathered one. "You weren't the only one, Earl. I kept Washington's research safe, but I never tried to use it. We all failed those children in our own ways."

Sam looked between the two elderly faces, seeing not disappointment but determination.

"But you're here now," he said simply. "You're helping us now."

Thompson straightened, drawing strength from the boy's acceptance. "Yes. And this time, we have something we didn't have before. Rivera's research on the global network, the bronze keys to access the central chamber, and most importantly, knowledge of when and how the ritual will be performed."

Dr. Rivera had been studying the combined maps, tracing the tunnel pathways with her finger. "According to these, there are three levels beneath Pinecrest. The first contains the ritual chamber you discovered in the east wing, the second houses the holding cells where the four students are kept, and the third and deepest level connects to what the Guardians call the 'Veil Chamber,' apparently where the actual barrier between worlds exists and where the final ritual is performed."

Noah frowned at the complexity of the tunnel system. "How do we even access these lower levels? The entrance we found only led to the ritual chamber."

Thompson pointed to a section of the updated map. "There's a secondary entrance behind a false wall in the ritual chamber. It leads to a stairwell down to the second level. But it requires both bronze keys to unlock—a security measure implemented after Washington and I discovered the first entrance."

Leila studied the map intently. "And once we reach the second level holding cells, how do we free the captives? Won't they be guarded?"

Patterson nodded grimly. "According to Marcus's research, the Guardians constantly watch the captives, usually two guards per eight-hour shift. The captives themselves are kept in a sedated state until just before the ritual."

Mia's expression hardened at this detail. "So they're drugging them. Keeping them helpless."

Thompson didn't dispute this, having witnessed the preparations for previous rituals. "The Guardians believe the sacrifice must be conscious but compliant during the final ritual. They gradually reduce sedation as the alignment approaches, so the captives are fully aware of the...

culmination." He couldn't bring himself to describe the ritual in greater detail, the memory of what he'd glimpsed in 1989 still too horrific to articulate.

Sam had been examining his father's journal alongside Washington's recovered pages, his brow furrowed in concentration. "Dad believed there was a way to disrupt the ritual without violence, essentially redirecting the energy the Guardians are trying to harness. But it would require getting all four captives to the Veil Chamber at the precise moment of alignment, along with some kind of artifact he discovered in Ecuador."

Dr. Rivera nodded, picking up a page of her husband's notes. "He refers to it as 'the Convergence Stone,' apparently an ancient artifact that can channel energy at thin points between worlds. If his theory is correct, the stone could be used to permanently seal the barrier without requiring sacrifice."

Noah looked skeptical. "So instead of stopping the ritual entirely, we'd be... what, hijacking it? Using their own ceremony against them? That sounds incredibly risky."

Thompson couldn't argue with the assessment. "It is risky. But Dr. Rivera wasn't a fanciful man. He believed this could work; he had evidence to support it."

Patterson had been unusually quiet, studying an old photograph that had fallen from Washington's papers. Now she spoke up, her voice soft but clear. "There's another complication we haven't addressed. The Guardians aren't just anonymous cultists; they're prominent members of the Chesapeake community. Judges, business leaders, and school board members. Principal Fletcher is just one visible member of a much larger organization."

Leila looked up sharply. "You know who they are? My grandfather identified them?"

Patterson hesitated, then carefully extracted a folded paper from among Washington's pages. "He compiled a list of confirmed and suspected Guardians as of 1990. Some have certainly passed away since then, but organizations like this recruit new members to replace those they lose."

She placed the list on the table, and Dr. Rivera scanned it quickly, her expression growing increasingly troubled. "Judge Hargrove. Commissioner Ellis. Dr. Blackwood, the previous history teacher." She looked up at Thompson. "Half the school board. The police chief." The implications were clear; they couldn't simply report their findings to authorities. The authorities themselves were compromised.

Mia voiced what they were all thinking. "So we really are on our own. We can't go to the police or trust the school administration. It's just us against them." The weight of the challenge settled over the group, the enormity of what they were contemplating becoming suddenly, starkly evident. They were planning to infiltrate a secured underground facility, rescue four captives, and disrupt a ritual that had been performed for centuries, all while opposing some of the most powerful people in Chesapeake.

Thompson looked around at the young faces, seeing the determination mixed with fear, the resolve alongside uncertainty. He was reminded painfully of the expressions he'd seen on young soldiers in Vietnam, ordinary people thrust into extraordinary circumstances, carrying burdens no one should have to bear. But he also saw something he hadn't seen in those jungle clearings: hope.

Sam broke the heavy silence. "We need a detailed plan. Entry points, timing, and contingencies if something goes wrong. And we need to consider the possibility that my father might attempt to intervene as well. If he's been tracking the cycle, he'll know the ritual is approaching its culmination."

Dr. Rivera nodded, and the mother and son demonstrated the same problem-solving method. "We should divide our preparation into four areas: infiltration, locating and freeing the captives, accessing the Veil Chamber, and disrupting the ritual itself."

Noah took out his laptop. "I can work on the security aspects, such as the electronic locks Thompson mentioned and surveillance systems. My dad's an electrical engineer; I've picked up a few things."

Leila spread out the tunnel maps. "I'll coordinate these with my grandfather's notes and identify the safest routes and potential checkpoints where Guardians might be stationed."

Mia, who had been relatively quiet, spoke up with surprising firmness. "I should be the one to make first contact with the captives if they're in a semi-conscious state. I know Aaron and Lily personally; they might respond better to a familiar voice."

Thompson was impressed by how quickly the group organized itself, assigning roles based on their strengths without ego or hesitation. It was Washington's methodical influence in Leila, James Rivera's pattern-recognition in Sam, but also something uniquely their own generation raised on dystopian novels and complex video games, conceptualizing solutions to challenges that would have overwhelmed Thompson at their age.

Dr. Rivera had moved to the whiteboard, creating a timeline based on what they knew. "The alignment peaks at midnight on Sunday, that's when the ritual would be performed. Working backward, we would need to infiltrate the tunnel system no later than 10 PM Sunday, allowing time to navigate to the holding cells, free the captives, and reach the Veil Chamber."

She tapped the marker against the board thoughtfully. "But we should consider an earlier, perhaps Saturday night, giving us more time and a backup opportunity if something goes wrong."

Thompson nodded in agreement. "The Guardians will be most vigilant on Sunday, making final preparations for the ritual. Saturday night might offer a slight advantage in terms of reduced security."

Patterson had been examining the patrol schedules Thompson had provided. "According to this, there's a shift change at 11 PM. That creates a window of approximately fifteen minutes when the tunnel system has minimal coverage."

As the planning continued, Thompson found himself studying the four students who had uncovered a secret he'd been carrying for decades. They were so young, about the same age he'd been in Vietnam, the same age as the missing students they were trying to save. Yet they attacked this impossible problem with a determination that shamed his decades of silence.

Sam, with his father's thoughtful gaze and his mother's methodical approach. Leila, carrying her grandfather's legacy with a quiet dignity beyond her years. Noah, his technical mind working through practical solutions that others might miss. With her compassion for the missing students, Mia drove past her natural caution. They reminded him of another group of four from decades past: Marcus Washington, the scholar whose research had uncovered the pattern, and Eleanor Patterson, the artist whose careful preservation of documents had created a record that survived thirty years. Thompson himself was reluctantly cast as the leader who had provided access to places others couldn't reach. Jenny Wilson, the school nurse who had noticed strange medical symptoms in the disappeared students before they vanished, was the healer whose observations had helped confirm what Thompson had witnessed.

Four archetypes working together had previously uncovered the truth about Pinecrest, and the parallels weren't lost on them. Perhaps this time, with younger energy and new information, they might actually succeed where the previous four had failed.

Dr. Rivera's voice brought him back from his reverie. "Mr. Thompson, you mentioned your Vietnam experience. Would you be comfortable advising us on the infiltration aspects of the plan? The entry points, potential patrol patterns, and what to do if confronted?" The question surprised him; he hadn't expected to be included in the actual mission. He'd seen himself as an information source, not an active participant. But looking at the earnest faces around the table, he realized he couldn't send these young people into danger alone-not again, not after decades of standing by while others disappeared. "Yes," he said, his voice more collected than he'd expected. "I can do that."

Over the next hour, they developed a preliminary plan. They would enter through the east wing after hours on Saturday night, timing their entry to coincide with the 11 PM shift change. Using both bronze keys, they would access the stairwell leading to the second level, where the holding cells were located. According to the maps, four cells were arranged around a central monitoring station, typically manned by two guards. If they could neutralize or distract the guards, they could free the captives and proceed to the third level—the Veil Chamber; according to James Rivera's theory, they would need to position the four rescued students at specific points corresponding to the cardinal directions, redirecting the energy of the alignment to seal the barrier permanently.

Noah raised the most practical concern, "Assuming we succeed in freeing them, what condition will the captives be in? Will they be able to walk and understand what's happening?"

Thompson had to acknowledge the difficulty. "They'll be disoriented at a minimum. The Guardians use a combination of drugs and some kind of ritual preparation that leaves the selected students in a highly suggestible state. They might not immediately recognize what's happening or who you are."

Mia frowned. "So we'd essentially be dragging four semi-conscious teenagers through an underground tunnel system while being pursued by a cult of powerful community leaders. No pressure."

Despite the gravity of the situation, the comment elicited a brief laugh, releasing some of the tension that had built up during the planning. Dr. Rivera smiled faintly. "When you put it that way, it does sound rather impossible. But sometimes the most impossible sounding plans are the ones that succeed precisely because no one expects them."

Patterson nodded in agreement. "The Guardians have operated without serious challenge for decades. Their security measures are designed to keep people out, not to handle an infiltration by people who know exactly what they're looking for and how to find it."

As 10 PM approached, the group outlined their basic plan, identified the equipment they would need, and assigned specific roles to each participant. Thompson would guide them through the tunnel system, using his knowledge of the patrols and security measures. Dr. Rivera and Patterson would remain at a secure location above ground, monitoring police channels and providing a backup point of contact if something went wrong. Sam, Leila, Noah, and Mia would form the primary rescue team, with specific responsibilities based on their strengths.

"Tomorrow, we gather the equipment," Dr. Rivera concluded, capping her marker. "Flashlights, communications devices, first aid supplies, and anything else we might need. We'll meet back here at 9 PM Saturday to review the final plan before heading to Pinecrest."

Thompson nodded, impressed by how thoroughly they had prepared in just a few hours. "There's one more thing," he said, his voice low but determined. "If we succeed, we rescue the four students and disrupt the ritual—the Guardians won't simply accept defeat. They've invested too much in maintaining this system. They'll come after anyone they believe was involved."

The implications hung heavily in the room. Sam was the first to respond, his young face solemn but resolute. "Then we need to gather enough evidence during the rescue to expose them completely. Make it impossible for them to retaliate without exposing themselves further."

Dr. Rivera nodded in agreement. "James's research, Washington's documentation, and what we find in the tunnels together could create a package of evidence too comprehensive to dismiss. Not just about the Pinecrest disappearances, but about the global network of similar rituals."

Thompson knew the risk they were all taking, knowing better than most what powerful, cornered people were capable of. But for the first time in decades, he felt something like hope. As the meeting concluded and preparations were made for people to leave discreetly, in different directions, and at staggered times to avoid drawing attention, Thompson found himself alone with Patterson for a moment in the kitchen. "Do you think we have a chance, Eleanor?" he asked quietly, the question he hadn't wanted to voice in front of the younger participants.

Patterson considered for a long moment before answering. "I think we have the right four people with the right information at the right time. That's more than we've ever had before." She placed her hand briefly on his arm. "And I think you've carried Jenkins long enough, Earl. Maybe it's time to set him down."

The simple statement hit Thompson with unexpected force, the understanding that his decades of inaction had been a form of penance for that single moment of paralysis in a Vietnamese jungle.

Later, as Thompson drove home through the quiet Chesapeake streets, his mind returned to that jungle clearing, to Jenkins calling for help. But the memory felt different somehow, less immediate, less accusatory. For the first time, he could see beyond that moment of failure to the possibility of redemption. He thought of Sam, Leila, Noah, and Mia, so young, so determined to right a wrong they hadn't created. He thought of the four missing students, Sofia and Caleb, and selected qualities that should have been celebrated rather than exploited. He thought of Washington, who had lost his career for daring to investigate, and James Rivera, who might have lost his life.

As he pulled into his driveway, Thompson made a silent promise to them all. This time would be different. This time, he wouldn't freeze. This time, he would reach those who needed help, whatever the cost. As he prepared for bed, Thompson placed his journal of names on the nightstand, something he'd done every night since Vietnam. But tonight, for the first time, he left it closed rather than opening it to read the names as was his custom. Instead, he found himself thinking of names not yet written, such as Aaron, Sofia, Caleb, and Lily, allowing himself to imagine a future where they remained among the living rather than joining his catalog of the lost. Thompson drifted toward sleep with a strange sense of peace, as if a burden carried for decades had begun, ever so slightly, to lighten.

CHAPTER SIXTEEN
DANGER'S REFLECTION

Across town, in the Rivera household, Sam sat on his bed, unable to sleep despite the lateness of the hour. The bronze key his father had left felt heavy in his hand as he turned it over and over, studying the intricate pattern of four interconnected circles on its handle. The events of the evening had left him simultaneously exhausted and wired, his mind racing with tunnel maps, guard rotations, and the faces of the missing students.

A soft knock at his door preceded his mother's entrance. His mom looked tired but determined, the same expression she'd worn through countless research deadlines and academic challenges. "You should be sleeping," she said, sitting beside him on the bed. "Tomorrow will be busy with preparations."

Sam nodded, still turning the key in his hands. "I keep thinking about Dad," he admitted. "If Thompson's right, if he's out there somewhere trying to stop this from happening..."

Dr. Rivera placed her arm around his shoulders, a gesture that would have embarrassed him in other circumstances but now felt necessary and grounding. "I know," she said softly. "I've been thinking the same thing. It would be so like James—to disappear not because he was running away but because he was running toward something important."

Sam leaned into his mother's embrace, allowing himself to feel young for a moment and acknowledging the fear beneath his determination. "What if we fail? What if something happens to Leila, Noah, or Mia because I convinced them to help?"

Dr. Rivera sighed, the question clearly one she'd been asking herself as well. "They chose to be involved, Sam, just as your father did. They recognized a wrong and decided to try to right it—that's courage, not coercion."

She gently took the key from his hands, examining it thoughtfully. "I've been a historian long enough to know that change rarely comes from institutions or authorities. It comes from ordinary people who refuse to accept injustice as inevitable."

She returned the key to him, closing his fingers around it. "Get some sleep. Tomorrow, we become those people." As his mother left, closing the door softly behind her, Sam placed the key beside the photo of him and his father on the nightstand. In the dim light, he could almost imagine his father's encouraging smile, the quiet confidence that had always made Sam believe anything was possible. "We're going to find you, Dad," he whispered to the photograph. "And we're going to save them."

Leila Washington sat cross-legged in her darkened bedroom on her bed, her grandfather's journal open before her, now complete with the recovered pages. Reading his accounts of the investigation he'd conducted more than three decades ago filled her with a complicated mixture of pride, sadness, and resolve. Marcus Washington had sacrificed his career and risked his family's safety, all to uncover a truth that others had worked diligently to conceal. The final entry, written the day after he'd been threatened, was particularly difficult to read: *"I am setting aside this investigation not because the truth is unimportant, but because Diane and Amber are more important. I pray that someday, someone will find what I have hidden and complete what I have begun. The children of Pinecrest deserve justice, even if I cannot be the one to deliver it."* The words brought tears to Leila's eyes, not just for the grandfather she'd adored, whose principled stand had shaped her own sense of justice, but for the burden he'd carried silently throughout her childhood.

She wondered if her parents knew the whole story and if her grandmother understood what Marcus Washington had been trying to protect when he abruptly retired from teaching. Perhaps this explained the tension she'd sometimes sensed when Pinecrest was mentioned at family gatherings and her strange reluctance to discuss her grandfather's teaching career despite his obvious love for education.

Across Chesapeake, in a modest apartment complex, Noah Chen sat surrounded by electronic components, tinkering with several small devices that looked like modified walkie-talkies. He'd promised the group he would create a secure communication system that wouldn't rely on cell networks that might be monitored or jammed. His father, an electrical engineer with a defense contractor, had unknowingly provided the base components from his home workshop. Noah felt a twinge of guilt for "borrowing" the equipment without permission, but he reasoned that saving four lives justified some creative reallocation of resources.

As he soldered a connection, his mind kept returning to Aaron Mitchell. Despite their shared interest in technology, they'd never been close friends, moving in different social circles. Aaron was brilliant in a way that made Noah slightly envious and intuitive, while Aaron was methodical and creative, and Noah was practical. If their plan succeeded, that could change. They may have a chance to become actual friends rather than distant academic competitors. The thought gave Noah's fingers new precision as he continued his work, determined that his contribution to the rescue would function flawlessly.

Mia Patel sat at her desk in a different neighborhood, carefully placing items into a small medical kit. As the daughter of two physicians, she had access to supplies most teenagers wouldn't, including sedatives that might prove helpful if they encountered guards and stimulants that could help counteract whatever the captives had been given. She'd told her parents she was assembling first aid kits for a school project, which wasn't entirely a lie. This was, in a way, the most crucial school project she'd ever undertaken.

Unlike the others, Mia had known two of the missing students personally. Aaron had tutored her in advanced mathematics last semester, patiently explaining concepts until they clicked, never making her feel inferior for asking questions. Lily had been her lab partner in biology, her gentle handling of even the most unpleasant dissections revealing her natural affinity for healing. The thought of them held captive in some underground chamber, drugged and awaiting a ritual that would claim their lives, filled Mia with a cold anger that surprised her. She was typically the cautious one, the voice of reason in any group. But in this situation, caution felt like complicity. As she closed the medical kit and slipped it into her backpack, Mia made a promise to herself: in two days, her friends would be free, or she would be captive with them. There would be no middle ground.

Earl Thompson sat at his kitchen table in his small apartment near the school, an old service pistol disassembled before him. He hadn't fired the weapon in decades and had almost forgotten its presence in the locked box beneath his bed. Now, he cleaned it methodically, muscle memory guiding his hands through the familiar process. He didn't intend to use it—violence had never solved problems in his experience, only created new ones—but its presence might prove persuasive if they encountered resistance. More importantly, the simple act of preparation helped calm his racing thoughts and focused his mind on the practical aspects of what they were planning rather than the overwhelming enormity of challenging the Guardians after decades of silence.

As he reassembled the pistol, Thompson thought about Jenkins again, about that moment of paralysis that had defined so much of his life. "Not this time," he murmured to the empty kitchen. "This time will be different." The words felt like a prayer, or perhaps a promise, not just to Jenkins, but to Washington, to Rivera, to the thirty-two students whose names filled his journal, and to the four whose names he was determined would never be added to that grim list. As midnight approached, Thompson returned the weapon to its lockbox, his decision made. He wouldn't bring it on Saturday.

This mission wasn't about fighting the Guardians but saving the captives. Violence would only escalate the situation, potentially endangering the very people they were trying to rescue. Instead, he would rely on his knowledge of the tunnel system, stealth, timing, and the strengths of the unlikely team that had come together to challenge a century of ritualized disappearances.

Eleanor Patterson sat in her living room, surrounded by books as always, but she was not reading for once. Instead, she was writing carefully, documenting everything that had transpired since Thompson had arrived at her door that afternoon. If something went wrong on Saturday night, if their attempt to save the missing students failed, she wanted there to be a record. Someone needed to know what they had discovered, what they had attempted. It wasn't just about assigning blame to the Guardians, though they certainly deserved it. It was about honoring the missing, not just the current four, but all those who had disappeared over the decades, whose lives had been cut short to maintain a ritual based on fear and misunderstanding.

As she wrote, Patterson couldn't help reflecting on her own role in this long, sad history. She had kept Washington's research safe but had never acted on it. She had watched students disappear, knowing the pattern and understanding the implications, yet had done nothing beyond maintaining her silent vigil over hidden pages. "Too little, too late," she murmured to herself as she continued writing. But perhaps it wasn't too late for Aaron, Sofia, Caleb, and Lily. This time, with this combination of knowledge, determination, and timing, they might succeed where previous attempts had failed. The thought gave her aging hands new energy as she continued her documentation, determined that the truth would finally be known regardless of the outcome.

In the tunnels beneath Pinecrest Middle School, in a dimly lit chamber deep below the east wing, four teenagers lay on narrow cots arranged at the cardinal points of a circular room. Aaron Mitchell stirred restlessly in a drug-induced haze, his brilliant mind struggling against the chemical restraints that kept him docile. Beside him, Sofia Alvarez's fingers twitched as if holding a paintbrush, creating invisible masterpieces even in her semiconscious state. Across the chamber, Caleb Johnson murmured indistinctly, his natural charisma subdued but not extinguished by whatever they had been given. And completing the quartet, Lily Robertson lay unnaturally still, her healer's intuition perhaps sensing what awaited them all if the ritual proceeded as planned.

None of them fully understood where they were or what had happened to them. Their memories were fragmented, distorted by the drugs and by the strange chanting that filled the chamber at regular intervals. But somewhere beneath the confusion, each maintained a core of self, a tiny flame of identity that the Guardians' preparations had not entirely extinguished. And in that remnant of selfhood lay their only hope that when the moment came, if rescue appeared, they might recognize it for what it was and find the strength to embrace it. Far above, in the normal world of classrooms and hallways, plans were being made, equipment gathered, and strategies developed. But here in the shadows beneath Pinecrest, time moved differently, marked not by clocks but by the gradual progression of celestial bodies toward an alignment that had dictated the rhythm of disappearances for more than two millennia.

For the captives, Saturday night would arrive not as a deadline or a target but as simply another period of twilight consciousness, punctuated by the ritualistic preparations that had grown more frequent and more intense as the alignment approached. They couldn't know that six people—an unlikely alliance of teenagers, a historian, a school custodian, and a librarian were preparing to risk everything to save them. They couldn't know that their selection, meant to maintain a barrier between worlds, might instead become the catalyst for ending cycles of sacrifice that stretched back to before Chesapeake's founding. They couldn't know that just as they had been chosen for qualities that represented the pinnacle of human potential, their would-be rescuers embodied those same qualities—scholarship, creativity, leadership, and healing, directed toward a purpose the Guardians had never anticipated: defiance.

As Thursday night deepened toward Friday morning, two parallel paths were being set, one toward ritual and sacrifice, the other toward rescue and disruption. In less than forty-eight hours, those paths would converge in the tunnels beneath Pinecrest Middle School, where the accumulated secrets of more than a century waited to be revealed and where four young lives hung in the balance between ancient fear and modern determination. The stage was set for a confrontation generations in the making, a confrontation that would determine not just the fate of four missing students but potentially the future of Pinecrest itself and perhaps even the nature of the barrier that separated one world from another.

CHAPTER SEVENTEEN
SHADOWS AND SURVEILLANCE

Friday morning arrived with the muted pastels of early dawn stretching across Chesapeake, the soft light filtering through bedroom curtains and stirring four young souls from restless sleep. Sam Rivera awoke to the gentle chime of his alarm, his hand slapping at his phone with practiced precision. For a moment, he lay perfectly still, the previous day's events washing over him like a cold tide. The missing pages from Mr. Washington's journal. The revelations from Mr. Thompson and Mrs. Patterson. The terrifying realization that four students were being held somewhere beneath Pinecrest, awaiting a ritual that had claimed countless lives over decades. He exhaled slowly, steeling himself for what lay ahead: a day of pretending everything was normal while feeling anything but.

Across town, Leila Washington sat at the edge of her bed, already dressed in jeans and a navy sweater, her grandfather's journal open beside her. She hadn't slept much, spending most of the night reading and re-reading the newly recovered pages, trying to absorb every detail of her grandfather's investigation. The weight of his legacy pressed down on her shoulders, not a burden, but a responsibility she never knew she'd been preparing for her entire life. Her fingers traced the bold, confident handwriting that was so achingly familiar. "I'll finish what you started, Grandpa," she whispered to the empty room.

Noah Chen stood under the shower, letting scalding water pound against his shoulders. He'd always been the logical one, the friend who grounded the others when their imaginations ran wild. But there was nothing logical about what they'd discovered. Hidden rooms. Secret societies. Students disappearing every twelve years. He'd seen the evidence with his own eyes, touched the weathered pages of Mr. Washington's journal, and still, part of him wanted to dismiss it all as an elaborate hoax. He leaned his forehead against the cool tile, watching water spiral down the drain. He couldn't afford doubt now. Not with four lives hanging in the balance.

Mia Patel carefully applied her usual makeup, the familiar routine offering a sliver of normalcy amidst the chaos. She winced slightly as she covered the dark circles under her eyes, evidence of the nightmare that had jolted her awake at 3 AM, dreaming of being trapped in endless tunnels while unseen figures chanted in a language she didn't understand. Mia wasn't easily frightened, but as she stared at her reflection, she couldn't shake the feeling that they were stepping into something far more dangerous than any of them realized. Still, she thought of Sofia Alvarez, how they'd partnered in art class last semester; Sofia always encouraged her when she felt her artwork wasn't good enough. She couldn't leave her down there, waiting for whatever terrible fate the Guardians had planned.

Dr. Olivia Rivera moved efficiently through her morning routine at the Rivera household, her academic mind already cataloging and analyzing everything they'd learned the previous night. After Thompson and Patterson had left, she'd stayed up for hours, cross-referencing historical accounts of the Whitmore Plantation with geological surveys of the area, searching for any scientific basis for the Guardians' beliefs. As a historian, she'd encountered many instances where ritualistic practices masked power structures designed to maintain control. However, these disappearances' methodical, cyclical nature suggested something more complex than simple power dynamics. She poured coffee into a travel mug, her eyes catching the framed photo of her husband on the counter. James had been researching similar patterns in Ecuador before his disappearance. That couldn't be a coincidence.

"Morning, Mom," Sam said, shuffling into the kitchen in jeans and a faded Pinecrest Middle School sweatshirt. His attempt at casual normality was undermined by the tension visible in his shoulders.

"Morning," she replied, handing him a plate with toast. "Did you sleep?"

"Not really." He slathered peanut butter on the toast with mechanical movements. "I kept thinking about them. Aaron, Sofia, Caleb, Lily... they're down there somewhere. Probably scared out of their minds."

Dr. Rivera's expression softened. "We're going to find them, Sam. But today, you need to focus on appearing normal. The Guardians will be watching all of you after yesterday."

"I know." He took a bite of toast, chewing thoughtfully. "Do you think they suspect we know anything?"

"Hard to say. But if they've maintained this secret for over a century, they'll be vigilant about any potential threats." She checked her watch. "We should leave in fifteen minutes. Remember..."

"Act normal, don't go anywhere alone, and stay away from the east wing unless absolutely necessary," Sam recited, having heard the instructions several times the night before. "I've got it, Mom."

She nodded, though the worry didn't leave her eyes. "I'll be meeting with Principal Fletcher and some school board members today. It might be an opportunity to gauge what they know."

"Just be careful," Sam said, an unusual role reversal that wasn't lost on either of them.

Across town, Earl Thompson carefully packed his maintenance uniform into his worn duffel bag. Leaving room for several bags of heavy-duty zip ties from the hardware store he was planning to visit before going to Pinecrest that morning. In his bathroom cabinet, behind bottles of aspirin and shaving cream, he found what he was looking for: a medium glass bottle of chloroform left over from his taxidermy hobby. He hadn't mounted an animal in years but kept the supplies, never knowing when they might prove useful. As he tucked the bottle into a secure pocket in his bag, his mind drifted back to the jungles of Vietnam, to techniques of immobilizing an enemy quickly and silently.

It had been 1969, his second tour, when Sergeant Miller had shown their unit how to approach a sentry from behind, one hand clamping over the mouth while the other pulled the head back to expose the throat. "It's not about strength," Miller had explained in hushed tones as they crouched in dense foliage, the humid air thick with the scent of vegetation and distant napalm. "It's about speed and precision. Hesitate, and you're both dead."

Thompson shook his head, dispelling the memory. He wasn't that young soldier anymore, and this wasn't war, at least, not the kind he'd fought in Southeast Asia. But some skills never left you, lying dormant until necessity awakened them again. He zipped the duffel bag closed with a sense of grim determination. Today would be reconnaissance only, gathering intelligence and finalizing their plan for tomorrow's rescue operation. But it never hurt to be prepared.

At Pinecrest Middle School, the hallways buzzed with Friday energy, students chattering about weekend plans as they navigated the institutional beige corridors. The normalcy felt surreal for Sam, Leila, Noah, and Mia, like actors who'd wandered onto the wrong set. They'd agreed to maintain their usual routines while staying hyperaware of anything unusual, meeting briefly between classes to share observations.

"Is it just me, or is everyone staring?" Noah whispered during their first conversation by the water fountain outside the gymnasium. His back was to the hall, posture casual, but his eyes darted nervously.

"It's not just you," Mia confirmed, pretending to check her phone. "Mr. Fletcher has walked past twice already, and he never comes to this part of the building on Fridays."

"Science department meeting," Leila explained, though her tone suggested she didn't entirely believe it herself. "Third Friday of every month."

"Still," Sam murmured, "keep your eyes open and stick to crowded areas."

They separated for their morning classes, each struggling to focus on lessons that seemed trivial compared to the knowledge weighing on their minds. In English, Sam stared at his copy of *"To Kill a Mockingbird,"* the words blurring together as his thoughts kept returning to the tunnels beneath their feet. Were Aaron, Sofia, Caleb, and Lily conscious? Were they being fed? He didn't know Aaron but learned that since elementary school, he had played Little League much like him, and like him, Aaron's dad was the coach. The thought of him trapped in some underground chamber made Sam's stomach clench.

In Advanced Math, Leila found herself sketching the tunnel system in the margins of her notebook instead of solving equations. Her grandfather's recovered journal pages had included detailed maps that Mr. Thompson had helped create back in 1990. Some passages might have shifted or collapsed in the decades since, but the overall layout provided crucial intelligence. The main ritual chamber was located beneath what had once been the Whitmore Plantation's main house, now part of Northwest River Park. Several tunnel branches connected it to Pinecrest, with the primary entrance hidden in the east wing's storage room, they'd discovered.

In their History class, Mia watched Dr. Rivera lecture on the Civil War with newfound respect. The teacher moved around the room with composed energy, nothing in her demeanor suggesting she was anything but a dedicated educator sharing her passion for history. Yet Mia now knew she was simultaneously gathering intelligence for their rescue mission while navigating the dangerous attention of the Guardians. Mia thought of Sofia Alvarez, whose vibrant murals brightened the school's otherwise institutional walls. Sofia had been working on a new piece for the library when she disappeared, a landscape of the Great Dismal Swamp that the art teacher had described as "showing remarkable maturity and depth." Now, that half-finished canvas sat covered in the art room, like a visual echo of her interrupted life.

By lunchtime, the strain of maintaining normalcy had left all four friends exhausted. They gathered at their usual table in the cafeteria, carefully keeping their conversation to mundane topics while communicating more meaningful information through notes passed beneath the table.

"You guys coming to Jason's party tomorrow night?" Noah asked with practiced casualness as he slid a folded paper to Sam. "I heard his parents are out of town."

"Probably not," Sam replied, glancing at the note, *East wing door locked, Thompson said, maintenance issue. Security camera installed overnight*, before passing it to Leila. "Got too much homework."

"Same," Leila agreed, scanning the message before adding her own observation and passing it to Mia. "Plus, my mom wants to do a family movie night."

"Lame," Mia commented with a believable eye roll, reading Leila's addition-*Principal Fletcher, watching us from the office doorway for the last 10 mins*, before scribbling her own note and returning it to Noah.

Noah was about to read Mia's message when a shadow fell across their table. They looked up to find Officer Daniels, the school resource officer, standing beside their table with an affable smile that didn't quite reach his eyes. Behind him stood Detective Collins and two men in suits whom Sam recognized from school board photographs in the main hallway.

"How's it going, kids?" Detective Collins asked, his tone casual but his posture rigid. "Enjoying your lunch?"

"Yes, sir," Sam answered, fighting the urge to hide the note still in Noah's hand.

"Is everything okay?"

"Everything's fine."

One of the suited men stepped forward, his silver hair and commanding presence marking him as someone accustomed to authority. "Thomas Davis, School Board President. This is my colleague, Dr. Richard Hargrove." He gestured to the other suited man, younger with carefully trimmed dark hair and wire-rimmed glasses. "We're conducting a review of the school's facilities, particularly focusing on how we might modernize some of the older sections."

"The east wing, specifically," Dr. Hargrove added, his smile revealing perfectly even teeth. "We understand you four are some of Pinecrest's most engaged students, and we'd value your input on potential improvements."

Sam felt a chill that had nothing to do with the cafeteria's aggressive air conditioning. He forced himself to maintain eye contact, remembering his mother's warning to appear normal. "That's cool of you to ask students," he said, hoping his voice sounded steadier than it felt.

"We thought perhaps you might join us for a walk-through after you finish lunch," Dr. Hargrove suggested, his tone making it clear this wasn't really a request. "Give us the student perspective on how the space could better serve your educational needs."

The four friends exchanged glances, a silent communication passing between them. Going to the east wing, surrounded by suspected members of the Guardians, was exactly what they'd been warned against. But refusing would only raise suspicions.

"Sure," Leila finally said, her voice remarkably calm. "We have about twenty minutes before our next class."

"Excellent," Collins clapped his hands together once, the sound unnaturally loud in the cafeteria. "We won't take up too much of your time."

As they gathered their belongings, Mia deliberately knocked over her water bottle, creating a distraction while Noah slipped the note into his pocket. They stood to follow the adults, each feeling as if they were walking into a trap but seeing no way to avoid it.

They had just reached the cafeteria doors when a familiar voice called out. "Oh, there you are!" Eleanor Patterson approached with surprising speed for her age, a stack of colorful construction paper in her arms. "I've been looking all over for you four. We need to finish the book fair displays for the fifth-grade orientation this afternoon." She turned to the adults, her expression pleasantly surprised. "Oh, Mr. Davis, Detective Collins, I didn't see you there. Is everything alright?"

"Just fine, Mrs. Patterson," Davis replied, his smile tightening almost imperceptibly. "We were about to show these students the east wing and get their thoughts on some planned renovations."

"Oh, but they promised to help with the book fair displays," Mrs. Patterson said, her voice taking on the slightly disappointed tone that only retired teachers can truly perfect. "The principals from both Pinecrest Middle and Pinecrest Intermediate are counting on these being ready for the orientation at three o'clock."

The adults engaged in a silent standoff, tension crackling beneath polite expressions. Finally, Dr. Hargrove broke the impasse. "School spirit and responsibility are values we certainly want to encourage," he said smoothly. "Perhaps we could reschedule our tour for after school?"

"That would be perfect," Mrs. Patterson answered before any of the students could speak. "I'm sure they'll be happy to help, once their commitment to the book fair is fulfilled."

"Four o'clock, then," Hargrove said, fixing each student with a penetrating stare. "We'll meet you by the main office."

"Yes, sir," Sam agreed, fighting to keep his relief from showing. "We'll be there."

As the men walked away, Mrs. Patterson herded the four friends in the opposite direction toward the library. She maintained her cheerful demeanor until they were safely inside with the doors closed behind them.

"That was too close," she said, her voice dropping to a whisper as she set down the construction paper. "They're accelerating their timeline. They never approach potential sacrifices directly like that."

"Sacrifices?" Noah repeated, his face paling. "You think they were going to…"

"Not today," Mrs. Patterson said quickly. "The ritual requires specific astronomical alignments. But they may have been planning to isolate you, gauge how much you know."

"Or make us disappear early if they suspected we know too much," Leila added grimly.

Mrs. Patterson nodded. "You need to be extremely careful. Thompson and I will try to run interference where we can, but we can't be everywhere."

"What about the after-school meeting?" Mia asked. "We can't exactly skip it without raising even more suspicion."

"I'll speak with Dr. Rivera. She'll figure something out," Mrs. Patterson promised. "In the meantime, stay in public spaces and stick together."

CHAPTER EIGHTEEN
GUARDIAN'S INVITATION

In Principal Fletcher's office, Dr. Olivia Rivera sat with perfect posture, her expression professionally neutral as she faced Fletcher, Detective Collins, and the two school board members who had returned from their encounter with the students. The principal's office was meticulously organized, and every item was placed with intentional precision, from the perfectly aligned pens on the desk to the symmetrically arranged photographs on the wall. Fletcher himself matched his environment: crisp white shirt, precisely knotted tie, not a hair out of place despite the late-April humidity.

"We appreciate you making time for this meeting, Dr. Rivera," Fletcher began, folding his hands on his desk. "As I mentioned, we're conducting a comprehensive review of the school's historical archives as part of our centennial preparations."

Olivia nodded, her academic mind immediately registering the inaccuracy. Pinecrest had been established in 1952, making it just over seventy years old, not anywhere near its centennial. But she kept this observation to herself, instead asking, "How can I help?"

"Your predecessor, Dr. Blackwood, was working on a special research project before his... retirement," Hargrove explained, choosing his words carefully. "Given your background in educational history, we thought you might be interested in continuing his work."

"I'd be happy to help," Olivia replied, her tone pleasant while her mind raced. Dr. Blackwood's abrupt departure mid-semester had created the opening she'd filled. The official story was a health crisis, but she'd heard whispers that he'd left town suddenly, without even clearing out his desk. "What was the nature of the project?"

Dr. Hargrove leaned forward, his expression earnest behind his glasses. "It centered on the relationship between educational institutions and the communities they serve, particularly in times of societal upheaval. Dr. Blackwood was exploring how Pinecrest's founding during the civil rights era reflected broader cultural changes."

Another historical inaccuracy, Olivia noted. Pinecrest had been founded well before the height of the civil rights movement. These men were either surprisingly ignorant of the school's history or deliberately misrepresenting it.

"Fascinating," she said, feigning enthusiasm. "That aligns perfectly with my research interests."

"We thought it might," Detective Collins remarked, studying her with an intensity that made her skin prickle. "Dr. Blackwood had access to some rather... exclusive historical resources. Private collections, family archives, not available to the general public."

"We'd like to share those resources with you," Davis added. "Perhaps starting tonight? Say, 7 PM? There's a local historical society meeting where we could introduce you to some key community members."

"And then continue through the weekend," Fletcher added. "The archives are quite extensive, and we'd value your professional assessment."

The invitation, or summons, really couldn't have been more transparent if they'd written "Guardians of the Veil recruitment session" on an official letterhead. Olivia felt a cold certainty that Dr. Blackwood had either discovered the truth about the disappearances or had been part of the conspiracy and developed a conscience. Either way, he hadn't simply retired.

"Tonight at 7 would be fine," she said, mentally calculating how this unexpected development might fit into their plans. "Where would we be meeting?"

"The Whitmore Historical Society," Fletcher replied. "It's a private facility not far from Northwest River Park. We can provide transportation if needed."

The Whitmore name sent another chill through her. According to Washington's journal, the ritual chamber was located beneath the remains of the Whitmore Plantation's main house. The "historical society" was likely a front for the Guardians themselves.

"I know where it is," she assured them, having researched the location the previous night. "I can drive myself."

"Excellent," Davis smiled, though the expression didn't soften the calculating look in his eyes. "And for Saturday and Sunday, we'd appreciate having your expertise from morning until evening. The centennial publication has a rather tight deadline."

Again, with the nonexistent centennial. Olivia nodded agreeably while internally adjusting their rescue timeline. They'd need to move quickly if she was expected to be with the Guardians all weekend.

"I'll need to make some arrangements for my son," she said, providing a plausible reason for any delay or communication she might need. "He'd planned for us to catch a movie tomorrow night."

"Of course, family first," Fletcher nodded with artificial understanding. "But we do hope you can prioritize this opportunity. It could be quite... beneficial for your career at Pinecrest."

The threat lurking beneath the suggestion wasn't subtle. Cooperate or face consequences. Olivia maintained her pleasant expression, years of academic politics having prepared her for navigating hostile territory while appearing unfazed.

"I'll make it work," she promised. "I'm very interested in learning more about Pinecrest's history." That, at least, was entirely truthful.

CHAPTER NINETEEN
HISTORICAL PROTECTION

As they filed out of afternoon classes, the four friends maintained their facade of normalcy while anxiety churned beneath the surface. Mrs. Patterson had managed to get a message to them during sixth period. The after-school meeting had been rescheduled for Monday due to a sudden "emergency school board session." The reprieve was welcome, but they all understood it was temporary at best.

Sam was gathering books from his locker when he felt a presence beside him. He turned to find Mr. Thompson methodically mopping the floor nearby while appearing to pay Sam no attention.

"Storage closet by the gym, three minutes," the janitor murmured without looking up or pausing in his work. "Come alone. Make it look casual."

Before Sam could respond, Thompson had moved further down the hallway, the squeak of his mop bucket fading into the after-school commotion. Sam finished at his locker, then made a show of checking his phone and heading in the direction of the gymnasium. He spotted Noah and gave a subtle shake of his head when his friend made a move to join him, then continued alone, projecting an air of ordinary teenage aimlessness.

The storage closet door was unlocked, as promised. Sam slipped inside to find Thompson waiting, surrounded by shelves of athletic equipment and cleaning supplies. The small space smelled of floor polish and old rubber, and the fluorescent light cast harsh shadows across Thompson's weathered face.

"Your mother's been invited to a Guardians gathering tonight," Thompson said without preamble, his voice low despite their location's privacy. "It's a historical society meeting by the park."

"I know," Sam replied. "She texted me earlier. She thinks gathering intelligence about where they're keeping Aaron and the others might be a good opportunity."

Thompson's expression darkened. "It's a recruitment session. They only invite outsiders when they're considering them for membership or assessing them as threats."

The implication hung heavily between them. Sam swallowed hard, fighting down a surge of fear for his mother. "She knows what she's doing. She won't give us away."

"It's not about giving us away," Thompson countered, his military bearing more pronounced than usual. "The Guardians have ways of... ensuring loyalty. Your mother is smart, but intelligence is no defense against certain methods of persuasion."

"What are you saying?" Sam demanded, his voice rising before he caught himself and lowered it again. "That they'll brainwash her or something?"

"Not exactly." Thompson sighed, suddenly looking every one of his seventy-plus years. "The Guardians possess knowledge-historical records, scientific data, and personal testimonials that they use to convince potential members of the necessity of their work. Your mother is a historian. They'll approach her through that lens, show her evidence that seems to validate their beliefs."

"She won't buy it," Sam insisted, though a thread of uncertainty wormed its way into his conviction. "She's too logical."

"Logic is precisely what makes her vulnerable," Thompson replied. "The Guardians don't present themselves as a cult or secret society, at least not initially. They position themselves as guardians of crucial knowledge, protectors defending humanity from threats most people can't comprehend."

Sam leaned against a shelf, processing this information. "So what do we do?"

"We proceed with the original plan," Thompson said firmly. "Your mother will join us at your house tonight after her meeting. She'll share what she's learned, and we'll finalize our approach for tomorrow's operation."

"But if they've invited her for the whole weekend-"

"Then we move tomorrow night, with or without her direct involvement," Thompson finished for him. "The alignment they need for their ritual peaks Sunday at midnight. We have to extract those students before then."

Sam nodded slowly, the reality of their timeline sinking in. Less than 72 hours to save four lives and potentially stop a cycle of disappearances that had persisted for over a century in Chesapeake.

"I should go," he said, checking the time on his phone. "The others will be wondering where I am."

"One more thing," Thompson said, reaching into his pocket and withdrawing a small object. "Take this."

He pressed a folded switchblade into Sam's hand. The handle was worn smoothly, and the mechanism was well-oiled but clearly decades old.

"Standard issue in Vietnam," Thompson explained as Sam examined it. "Not much use against firearms, but better than nothing if it comes to close quarters. Keep it hidden; use it only if absolutely necessary."

Sam stared at the knife, its weight in his palm a tangible reminder of the danger they faced. "Thanks," he managed, carefully pocketing the weapon. "I'll see you tonight."

As Sam left the storage closet, rejoining the thinning crowds in the hallway, he felt the knife's presence against his leg like a hot coal. In all his fourteen years, he'd never imagined himself in a situation where a weapon might be necessary. The reality of what they were planning—infiltrating underground tunnels to confront a powerful secret society—hit him with renewed force.

CHAPTER TWENTY
OFF THE SIDELINES

Across town, at her modest home, Miss Patterson carefully packed a small overnight bag. After decades of keeping secrets, of watching from the sidelines as students vanished, she was finally taking action. The relief of that decision mingled with anxiety about what lay ahead. She placed her medication in a side pocket—blood pressure tablets, cholesterol medication, the arsenal of pills that kept her aging body functioning, alongside a small leather-bound book that had belonged to Marcus Washington.

The journal wasn't part of the main collection they'd passed to Leila but a more personal record Washington had entrusted to her shortly before his forced retirement. "If anything happens to me," he'd said, pressing it into her hands one afternoon in the empty library, "make sure this reaches Amber when she's old enough to understand." Amber had been his daughter, just five years old at the time, now Leila's mother.

Patterson had kept that promise, delivering the journal to Amber Washington on her eighteenth birthday. But when Amber was diagnosed with cancer, she returned it to Miss Patterson and asked that she hold it for her daughter, Leila, when she was old enough. It contained not just facts about the Guardians and the disappearances but Washington's deeply personal reflections on the moral implications of their discoveries.

Now, she slipped the journal into her bag alongside a small revolver that had belonged to her late husband. George Patterson had been a security guard at the Norfolk shipyards, licensed to carry the weapon he'd insisted his wife keep after his passing. "World's not always kind to widows living alone," he'd told her during those final weeks of his illness. She'd kept the gun in her bedside drawer for fifteen years, never expecting to use it. But circumstances changed. People changed. Even seventy-six-year-old librarians could find themselves preparing for battle.

A sharp rap at her door startled her from these thoughts. Looking through the peephole, she was surprised to see Earl Thompson standing in the hallway, his expression grave. She opened the door, ushering him inside with a quick glance at the empty corridor behind him. "Earl? We weren't supposed to meet until tonight at the Rivera house."

"Change of plans," Thompson said, his voice rough with urgency. "Fletcher's called an emergency faculty meeting for 4:30. Mandatory attendance, no exceptions."

Patterson frowned, setting her bag aside. "That's unusual for a Friday afternoon."

"Exactly," Thompson agreed. "I overheard Fletcher on the phone with Hargrove as I was cleaning the main office. They're concerned about 'unauthorized access' to restricted areas of the school. I think they suspect something."

"The students?" asked Patterson.

"Maybe. Or Dr. Rivera. Or us." He ran a hand through his thinning silver hair. "They've accelerated security measures around the east wing—new cameras, electronic locks, additional patrols by Officer Daniels."

Patterson moved to her small kitchen, mechanically filling the kettle as she processed this information. "Tea?" she offered, falling back on ingrained hospitality despite the circumstances.

Thompson shook his head. "No time. I need to get back before my absence is noticed. I just wanted to warn you to be careful coming to the Rivera house tonight. Take an indirect route; watch for followers."

"I was in the French Resistance when you were still learning to tie your shoes, Earl," she reminded him with a hint of her usual spirit. At his startled expression, she allowed herself a small smile. "Well, the high school French club's reenactment of the Resistance, anyway. But I take your point. I'll be careful."

"See you at nine," Thompson said, moving toward the door before pausing, his hand on the knob. "Eleanor... are you sure about this? At our age, maybe we should leave this to younger folks. Dr. Rivera, the police..."

"The police chief is one of them," she reminded him. "And Dr. Rivera may not remain on our side after tonight's meeting." Her expression hardened with resolve. "Besides, we've been silent witnesses for too long, Earl. I can't live with that anymore. Can you?"

The question hung between them, heavy with decades of shared guilt. Finally, Thompson shook his head. "No," he admitted. "I can't."

After he left, Patterson returned to her packing with renewed determination. They might be in their seventies, their bodies betraying them in countless small ways, but they possessed something the Guardians wouldn't expect: the accumulated knowledge of decades spent watching from the shadows and the desperate courage of those who had nothing left to lose.

As the afternoon faded into evening, Dr. Olivia Rivera prepared for her meeting with the Guardians, selecting her outfit with strategic care. Professional but not intimidating, approachable but not casual—a gray blazer over a burgundy blouse, black slacks, minimal jewelry. The kind of ensemble that suggested academic competence without drawing unnecessary attention. She applied makeup with the same calculated precision, aiming for a look that conveyed polished confidence rather than trying to impress.

Sam watched from her bedroom doorway, his concern evident despite his attempts to hide it. "You sure about this, Mom? We could find another way."

"We need information," she reminded him, securing a small silver pendant around her neck inside a GPS tracking device Noah had modified from a pet tracker. "If I can learn where they're keeping Aaron and the others, it could save us hours of searching tomorrow night."

"But Thompson says they'll try to recruit you."

"I'm aware." She turned to face her son, her expression softening. "Sam, I've spent my career analyzing historical power structures and how they perpetuate themselves. The Guardians may have existed for centuries, but they're still human, still operating on recognizable patterns of indoctrination and control."

"What if they're right, though?" Sam asked, voicing the doubt that had nagged at him since his conversation with Thompson. "What if there really is something under Pinecrest, something that needs to be... I don't know, contained or whatever?"

Olivia considered her response carefully. As a historian, she'd encountered countless instances of ritualistic behaviors emerging across different cultures, often in response to natural phenomena that people lacked the scientific framework to understand. Earthquakes became angry gods.

Solar eclipses became omens. Disease became divine punishment.

"Even if there is some geological or archaeological anomaly beneath Pinecrest," she said finally, "that wouldn't justify sacrificing children to appease it. Human sacrifice has appeared in many civilizations throughout history, Sam, but it's always ultimately about power, one group asserting control over others through fear and supernatural claims."

Sam nodded, though he didn't look entirely convinced. "Just... be careful, okay? Don't let them get inside your head."

"I won't," she promised, returning to the mirror for a final appearance check. "I'll see you tonight at nine, along with everyone else. If anything changes, I'll text you." She picked up her phone, showing him the screen. "I've set up that emergency code we discussed. If I text 'running late' followed by any reference to your father, that means I'm in trouble, and you should contact Detective Chen."

Noah's mother, Detective Grace Chen, was one of the few law enforcement officers they were reasonably confident wasn't affiliated with the Guardians. She worked primarily on cold cases and had recently been asking questions about historical disappearances in Chesapeake—questions that had reportedly made Detective Collins notably uncomfortable.

"Got it," Sam confirmed, committing the code to memory. "And if you learn anything important during the meeting?"

"I'll text you about picking up milk on the way home," Olivia said. "The more mundane the message seems, the less likely they'll suspect anything if they're monitoring my communications."

At 6:30, she gathered her things—a purse, notebook, and the digital voice recorder disguised as a pen that she planned to use if possible—and headed for the door. Sam followed, hovering uncertainly in the entryway.

"Mrs. Patterson said she'll be here around 8:30 to help you prepare for the others," Olivia reminded him. "Thompson, a little after that. You've got dinner in the fridge."

"I'm not a little kid, Mom," Sam protested, though the familiar exchange provided a moment of normalcy that both of them needed.

"Could have fooled me," she teased gently, then grew serious again. "I love you, Sam. Whatever happens, remember that."

"I love you, too," he replied, the weight of unspoken fears making the simple phrase feel inadequate. "See you later."

Olivia drove carefully through the quiet Friday evening streets, taking an intentionally circuitous route to check for followers while mentally preparing herself for the encounter ahead. As a historian specializing in educational institutions during periods of social change, she'd interviewed countless individuals with extreme ideological positions. She knew how to appear receptive without actually internalizing their worldviews-a skill she hoped would serve her well tonight.

The Whitmore Historical Society occupied a stately colonial-style building set back from the road, surrounded by ancient oak trees whose sprawling branches cast long shadows in the fading daylight. A discreet sign marked the entrance to the circular driveway, the organization's name engraved in elegant script on polished brass. No hours were listed, and there was no indication that the public was welcome. This was a private club masquerading as a historical preservation society.

Olivia parked in the small lot beside the building, noting the other vehicles already present: a silver Audi, Detective Collins's department SUV, and several other expensive cars suggesting their owners' affluence. As she approached the entrance, the heavy wooden door swung open before she could knock, revealing Thomas Davis in a well-tailored gray suit.

"Dr. Rivera," he greeted her with practiced warmth. "Right on time. Please, come in."

The interior was exactly what one would expect from an exclusive historical society- gleaming hardwood floors, oil paintings in ornate frames, and glass display cases containing artifacts and documents. The lighting was soft but adequate, creating an atmosphere of refined intellectual pursuit. About a dozen people stood in small conversational clusters, most holding crystal glasses containing amber liquid.

"Allow me to introduce you to some of our members," Davis said, guiding her toward the nearest group. "Many of us have deep roots in Chesapeake, going back generations."

The next hour passed like a carefully choreographed social dance. Olivia was introduced to influential community members—the hospital administrator, a circuit court judge, the local newspaper publisher, several business owners—each interaction layered with subtle assessment. They asked about her academic background, her research interests, and her impressions of Pinecrest and Chesapeake. She answered truthfully where possible, deflected when necessary, and projected the image of a dedicated historian thrilled to access exclusive historical materials.

Eventually, the socializing gave way to a more structured presentation. The guests were ushered into an adjoining room set up with chairs facing a small stage and projection screen. Davis took center stage, his commanding presence drawing all attention.

"Friends, colleagues, guardians of our shared heritage," he began, his voice resonating with practiced authority. "We gather tonight, as we have for generations, to honor our responsibility to this community and to welcome a potential new steward of our knowledge."

Olivia felt the weight of every gaze shift toward her. She maintained a composed expression, though her pulse quickened.

"Dr. Olivia Rivera joins us from the University of Virginia, where her work on educational institutions during periods of social upheaval has earned considerable acclaim. She now brings that expertise to Pinecrest Middle School, stepping into the position recently vacated by our colleague, Dr. Blackwood."

The mention of her predecessor sent a ripple of something— tension? Concern?—through the audience. Olivia made a mental note of the reaction.

"Tonight, we begin the process of sharing with Dr. Rivera the true history of our community, knowledge that has been carefully preserved and protected since before the founding of Chesapeake." Davis gestured to Dr. Hargrove, who dimmed the lights and activated the projector. "Knowledge that carries with it both privilege and profound responsibility."

The screen illuminated with an image of an ancient stone tablet covered in unfamiliar symbols. "This artifact was discovered in 1734 by William Whitmore during the construction of his plantation home," Davis explained. "The symbols match no known language or script, yet identical markings have been found at archaeological sites across the globe, always in locations associated with geological anomalies and unexplained phenomena."

The presentation continued a methodically constructed narrative that blended verifiable historical facts with increasingly extraordinary claims. According to Davis, the Whitmore Plantation had been built atop a geological formation that indigenous peoples had considered sacred or forbidden, depending on the translation. Early settlers had experienced strange phenomena: unexplained sounds from beneath the earth, livestock behaving erratically, crop failures in otherwise fertile soil, and, most disturbingly, mental disturbances among those who spent significant time near certain locations on the property.

William Whitmore, described as a man of science rather than superstition, meticulously documented these occurrences while seeking natural explanations. His investigations led him to discover a network of caves beneath his property and evidence of previous human habitation and ritual activity within them.

"What Whitmore found," Davis continued, the images on screen changing to show old journal pages and hand-drawn maps, "was evidence of a practice spanning thousands of years across multiple civilizations. A practice born not of primitive superstition, but of hard-earned knowledge about the nature of what lay beneath the earth."

The presentation shifted to geological data-seismic readings, ground-penetrating radar images, and magnetic anomaly maps, all purporting to show something unusual beneath the Pinecrest area. Dr. Hargrove took over, his academic tone lending scientific credibility to increasingly disturbing claims. "The geological formation beneath us is what we now understand to be a thin point in the barrier between dimensional planes," he explained, displaying complex mathematical equations alongside the geological data. "Modern quantum physics is only beginning to approach the understanding that the Whitmore family and their associates gained through direct observation over two centuries ago."

Olivia maintained her expression of interested neutrality, though internally, she was analyzing every claim, noting where scientific evidence ended and speculation began. The presentation was masterfully constructed, each outlandish claim sandwiched between verifiable facts, creating a compelling narrative that would be difficult for most people to disentangle.

"The entity beneath us exists primarily in a dimensional state we cannot perceive directly," Mercer continued. "But its effects on our world are measurable and documented. When the barrier between dimensions weakens, these effects intensify, manifesting as what history has recorded as natural disasters, epidemics, and in extreme cases, mass extinction events."

The screen displayed a timeline correlating major historical catastrophes with astronomical alignments similar to the one approaching this weekend: the Black Death, the Krakatoa eruption, the Spanish Flu pandemic, and the dinosaur extinction. According to their narrative, each event coincided with a weakening of the dimensional barrier and had been preceded by geological and atmospheric anomalies similar to those currently being recorded in the Chesapeake area.

"For centuries," Davis resumed, his tone grave, "the Guardians of the Veil have maintained the integrity of this barrier through carefully timed rituals that strengthen the dimensional boundary. These rituals require significant, specifically, the life energy of individuals who possess certain unique qualities. What indigenous peoples called 'the four pillars of humanity': the mind, the heart, the spirit, and the hand. Or as we might term them today: the scholar, the leader, the artist, and the healer."

Olivia felt her blood run cold as the implications became explicit. The four missing students. Aaron Mitchell, a brilliant student with a perfect GPA. Sofia Alvarez, whose artwork had won state recognition. Caleb Johnson, who had organized a successful campaign to improve mental health resources at school. Lily Robertson, who volunteered at the local hospital and planned to become a doctor.

"The selection process is never arbitrary," Hargrove added, seeming to address the moral question before Olivia could raise it. "Those chosen possess the qualities needed for the ritual to succeed, but they also share another trait—a unique physiological marker in their cellular structure that resonates with the dimensional boundary. In a very real sense, they are born for this purpose."

"We understand how disturbing this information must seem," Davis acknowledged, his eyes fixed on Olivia. "Throughout history, many have initially reacted with horror and disbelief. Dr. Blackwood certainly did."

The mention of her predecessor hung in the air like a warning. Olivia carefully composed her response, knowing her reaction would be scrutinized. "It's certainly... unexpected," she said, choosing her words deliberately. "As a historian, I'm trained to question extraordinary claims, to seek verifiable evidence."

"Of course," Davis nodded approvingly. "Skepticism is healthy, even necessary. We wouldn't want someone who accepts such revelations without question. That's why we've prepared more concrete evidence for you to examine over the weekend: laboratory analyses, historical documents, and recorded testimonies from previous Guardians going back generations."

"And demonstrations of the entity's influence?" Olivia asked, projecting academic curiosity rather than moral outrage. "If this dimensional boundary is as tangible as you suggest, surely its effects can be observed under controlled conditions."

"Indeed, they can," Hargrove confirmed. "Tomorrow, we plan to show you precisely that. The alignment is already beginning to affect the barrier. The effects are subtle now, but measurable with the right equipment."

The meeting continued for another hour, with other Guardians sharing personal testimonies of phenomena they'd witnessed and the historical knowledge passed down through their families. Throughout, Olivia noted the careful blend of verifiable facts, pseudoscientific jargon, and emotional appeals to the protection of the community. It was a masterful indoctrination technique, one that might well have convinced her if she hadn't already known about the decades of disappearances and cover-ups.

By the time the formal presentation concluded around 8:30, returning to a more social atmosphere with refreshments, Olivia had gathered valuable intelligence. The ritual chamber was indeed beneath the old Whitmore property in what was now Northwest River Park. The ceremony would take place at midnight on Sunday when astronomical alignments supposedly reached their peak. Most importantly, the four students were still alive, being kept in a "preparation chamber" where their "energy was being purified" for the ritual.

As she accepted a glass of water from a server, Olivia found herself joined by an older woman she hadn't been introduced to earlier-elegant in a tailored navy dress, with silver hair arranged in a sophisticated updo and eyes that held the sharp intelligence of someone accustomed to assessing others.

"Dr. Rivera," the woman said, her voice cultured and measured. "I'm Margaret Whitmore. This property has been in my family for eight generations."

"It's a beautiful building," Olivia replied, genuinely impressed by the historical preservation. "You must be very proud of your family's legacy."

"The building is merely a shell," Margaret said dismissively. "It's what we've protected—what we continue to protect— that matters." She studied Olivia with uncommon intensity. "You've received a great deal of information tonight. Information that contradicts the worldview most people comfortably inhabit. I'm curious about your thoughts."

It was a test, thinly veiled. Olivia considered her response carefully. "History is full of instances where knowledge considered heretical in one era becomes accepted fact in another," she offered. "The earth revolves around the sun. Continental drift. Bacterial causes of disease. I try to maintain an open mind, especially when presented with evidence that challenges my existing understanding."

Margaret nodded slightly, seemingly satisfied with this diplomatic answer. "Your husband was researching similar phenomena in Ecuador, wasn't he? Before his unfortunate disappearance."

The casual mention of James sent a jolt through Olivia, though she maintained her composed expression through years of academic training. "Yes, he was documenting unusual geological formations and their impact on local cultural practices."

"His work was getting quite close to some sensitive areas," Margaret remarked, the statement hovering between observation and admission. "It's unfortunate he never had the opportunity to see the complete picture, as you're being shown now."

The implication was clear: the Guardians had been aware of James's research and considered it a threat. Whether they were responsible for his disappearance remained unstated but was heavily suggested. Olivia fought to keep her breathing even, her expression neutral.

"Perhaps his findings would have eventually led him to similar conclusions as your organization," she suggested, testing the waters.

"Perhaps," Margaret acknowledged with the faintest smile. "Though not everyone has the perspective necessary to understand the difficult choices required for the greater good. Some become... fixated on individual concerns at the expense of the broader view."

"Like Dr. Blackwood?" Olivia asked, seizing the opening to gather more information about her predecessor.

A flash of something—annoyance? Concern?—crossed Margaret's aristocratic features before disappearing behind her poised facade. "Edward had access to all the same evidence you're being shown, yet he chose to focus on the individuals rather than the millions who would suffer if the ritual failed. He became... unreliable."

"I see," Olivia said, though what she actually saw was confirmation that Blackwood had developed a conscience and likely paid for it. "And his current whereabouts?"

"He decided to pursue other opportunities," Margaret replied smoothly. "Far from Chesapeake."

The conversation was interrupted by Davis announcing that the evening's formal activities were concluding, with more in-depth sessions planned for the following day. Olivia expressed appropriate gratitude for the invitation and the information shared, confirming her availability for tomorrow's continuation.

As she drove home through the dark streets, her mind raced with everything she'd learned. The Guardians weren't delusional cultists in the conventional sense. They genuinely believed in the necessity of their actions, supported by what appeared to be generations of documentation and scientific data. The question was how much of that data was legitimate, how much was misinterpreted, and how much was fabricated to justify their practices.

More troublingly, they clearly had extensive influence in Chesapeake law enforcement, local government, business, and media. Their network of power would make conventional approaches to stopping them nearly impossible. If they went to the authorities, they'd simply be reporting to the Guardians themselves.

By the time she pulled into her driveway at 9:15, Olivia had formulated her assessment of the situation and potential strategies for proceeding. Inside, she found the living room transformed into a command center of sorts. Sam, Leila, Noah, and Mia clustered around the dining table with laptops and maps. Thompson and Patterson occupied the couch, deep in conversation. All looked up when she entered, conversations halting mid-sentence.

"Well?" Sam asked, unable to contain his impatience. "What happened?"

Olivia set down her purse and took a moment to gather her thoughts. "They're recruiting me," she confirmed. "And they provided quite an extensive justification for their actions. According to the Guardians, they're protecting humanity from catastrophic consequences by maintaining a dimensional barrier beneath Pinecrest. They claim previous failures of the ritual resulted in historical disasters like plagues, natural catastrophes, and even the dinosaur extinction."

"And you believe that?" Leila asked skeptically.

"I believe they believe it," Olivia clarified. "They have impressive documentation—scientific readings, historical records, and testimonials. Some of it's likely legitimate data they're misinterpreting through their particular lens. Some are probably fabricated. The question is how much of each."

"Did you learn anything about where they're keeping Aaron and the others?" Sam pressed.

Olivia nodded, moving to the dining table where a map of Northwest River Park was spread out. "They referred to a 'preparation chamber' where the students are being 'purified' for the ritual. Based on their descriptions and the historical materials they showed me, I believe it's here." She pointed to an area marked as a historical preservation site, not far from the remains of the original Whitmore Plantation house foundation. "There's apparently a network of caves beneath the property that predates colonial settlement."

"That matches what my grandfather documented," Leila confirmed, pulling out the aged journal. "He mapped tunnel access points from Pinecrest leading to a central chamber beneath the old plantation house."

"The ritual is scheduled for Sunday at midnight," Olivia continued. "That gives us roughly fifty-one hours to locate and extract the students."

"What about tomorrow?" Noah asked. "They're expecting you back for more 'education,' right?"

"Yes, beginning at 9 AM." Olivia frowned. "They're planning to show me physical evidence of this entity they believe exists beneath us, some kind of demonstration of its effects. They also mentioned extensive documentation they want me to review."

"It's a standard recruitment technique," Thompson interjected, his voice gruff with certainty. "They'll spend hours overwhelming you with evidence, wearing down your skepticism, until their worldview begins to seem not just plausible but inevitable."

"I'm aware of the methodology," Olivia assured him. "But attending tomorrow's session might provide valuable intelligence about security measures, access points, and exactly where they're holding the students."

"Or it might result in your indoctrination," Patterson countered, her academic tone matching Olivia's. "The Guardians have refined their techniques over centuries, Dr. Rivera. They're very good at what they do. Even the most rational mind can be influenced under the right circumstances."

"Which is why I'll maintain the schedule we've already established," Olivia decided. "I'll attend tomorrow's session, gather what information I can, and meet you all back here tomorrow evening to finalize our rescue plan."

"And if you start believing their dimensional monster story?" Mia asked bluntly, voicing what others seemed reluctant to.

Olivia met the girl's gaze directly. "That's a legitimate concern," she acknowledged. "To address it, I'd like Noah to modify another tracking device that can record audio and location. I'll wear it tomorrow, and you can monitor what I'm being told and how I'm responding. If you believe I'm being compromised, contact Detective Chen with the evidence we've assembled."

This solution seemed to satisfy everyone, though concern lingered in Sam's expression. As the group returned to their planning, reviewing tunnel maps, and discussing equipment needs, Olivia checked her phone and found a text message from an unknown number.

Don't trust everything or everyone you think you know. Some monsters are real. Be at Watson's Diner, booth 7, 7 AM tomorrow. Come alone.

She deleted the message after memorizing it, her mind racing with possibilities. A trap set by the Guardians? A potential ally within their ranks? Perhaps Dr. Davis himself? There was no way to know without going, and the potential intelligence was too valuable to ignore.

The planning session continued late into the evening, with Thompson providing insights from his military experience about tactical approaches and potential security measures they might encounter. Patterson contributed her encyclopedic knowledge of the school's history and the Guardians' previous patterns. The teenagers offered surprisingly practical suggestions, their digital-native perspectives identifying technological vulnerabilities that the older adults might have missed.

Around 11:45, as they were beginning to wrap up, Thompson's cell phone rang. He checked the screen, his weathered face registering surprise before he answered. "Thompson here," he said gruffly, listening for several seconds before his expression transformed into shock. He put the phone on speaker, laying it on the coffee table.

"...not much time," a man's voice was saying, the connection staticky and faint. "The pattern isn't what we thought. It's not containment, it's communication. The entity isn't trying to break through; it's trying to warn us. The sacrifices don't appease it; they empower those who..." The voice cut out momentarily, then returned even fainter. "...found similar sites in Ecuador, Peru, and Romania. All with the same markings. All with the same cycle of disappearances. The Guardians are in every..." More static. "...the door opens both ways. Find the original tablets. The translation is wrong, deliberately wrong. It's not 'through sacrifice comes protection' but 'through protection comes...'"

The call abruptly ended, leaving a stunned silence in the living room. Thompson stared at his phone, then at the others. "That was James Rivera," he said, his voice rough with disbelief. "Dr. Rivera's husband. But he's been missing for almost a year."

All eyes turned to Olivia, who had gone completely still, her face drained of color. "Play it again," she requested, her voice barely above a whisper.

Thompson replayed the message, the staticky voice filling the room once more. This time, Olivia closed her eyes, concentrating on every nuance of the familiar voice she'd thought she might never hear again.

"It's him," she confirmed when the message ended, opening her eyes with renewed determination. "That's James."

"But how?" Sam demanded, his expression a mixture of hope and confusion. "Where is he? Is he alive?"

"The call came through a satellite relay," Noah observed, examining the phone number. "It could have originated from almost anywhere with the right equipment."

"Ecuador," Olivia said with certainty. "He was in Ecuador when he disappeared, researching similar patterns of disappearances near geological anomalies. If he's alive, that's where he'd be."

"What did he mean about the translation being wrong?" Leila asked, turning to her grandfather's journal. "Is there something about tablets in here?"

"The Whitmore Tablet," Thompson supplied. "They showed it during tonight's presentation, an artifact supposedly discovered during the plantation's construction. Covered in symbols, no one could identify."

"No one except the Guardians, apparently," Patterson added dryly. "They claim to have deciphered it as instructions for the ritual that maintains the dimensional barrier."

"But if James is right, and the translation is deliberately wrong..." Olivia's voice trailed off as she processed the implications. "Everything they believe could be based on a fundamental misinterpretation or manipulation of the original text."

"Which means the ritual might not be doing what they think it's doing," Sam concluded, the pieces falling into place. "Instead of protecting people, it might be... what? Giving the Guardians power somehow?"

"Or serving some other purpose entirely," Olivia agreed. "We need to see that tablet, the original, not just their presentation of it."

"It would likely be in the Whitmore Historical Society building," Patterson reasoned. "Perhaps in a secure area, you haven't been shown yet."

"And I'm scheduled to spend all day there tomorrow," Olivia nodded, a plan taking shape in her mind. "If I can gain access to it, maybe I can document the actual symbols for independent translation."

"This changes our approach," Thompson cautioned. "If Dr. Rivera is correct, we're not just dealing with a misguided secret society, but a group that may be deliberately perpetuating false information for their own purposes."

"Which makes them even more dangerous," Leila pointed out. "People who believe they're saving the world can justify anything. People who know they're lying have even more to hide."

The group fell silent, absorbing this new dimension to their already complex situation. Finally, Sam spoke up, his young voice steady despite the fear evident in his eyes. "So what's our plan now?"

Olivia took a deep breath, centering herself. "We proceed as discussed, but with adjusted priorities. I'll attend the meeting at the Whitmore Society tomorrow, attempt to locate and document the original tablet, and gather any additional intelligence about the students' location. The rest of you will finalize preparations for tomorrow night's extraction operation." She turned to Thompson. "Can you try to trace that call? Find out exactly where it originated?"

Thompson nodded. "I have contacts from my military days who owe me favors. I'll see what they can do."

"In the meantime," Patterson added, "I'll research alternative translations of symbols similar to those described on the Whitmore Tablet. Archaeological databases might have comparable examples from other sites."

As the meeting concluded and the others began gathering their things to leave, Sam pulled his mother aside, his expression troubled. "Mom, that really was Dad, wasn't it? Not some trick?"

Olivia wrapped an arm around her son's shoulders, noticing not for the first time how he was nearly as tall as she was now. "It was him," she confirmed softly. "The connection was poor, but I'd recognize his voice anywhere."

"Then he's alive," Sam said, a complicated mix of emotions coloring his voice. "All this time, he's been alive."

"It seems that way," Olivia agreed cautiously. "But we don't know his circumstances or why he hasn't been able to contact us before now. Let's not get ahead of ourselves."

Sam nodded, though hope had kindled in his eyes, hope that Olivia was careful not to embrace completely. The timing of James's call, just as they were preparing to confront the Guardians, seemed too convenient to be coincidental. But whether it represented salvation or complication remained to be seen.

As the others filed out into the night, making plans to reconvene the following evening, Olivia found herself standing in her living room doorway, watching their departing figures with a profound sense of responsibility. Four young lives depended on their actions over the next forty-eight hours. The cycle of disappearances that had claimed dozens over the decades could potentially end with them. And somewhere in Ecuador, James might be alive, fighting the same battle from another front.

She closed the door and turned back to Sam, who was already clearing the dining table of their planning materials. "Get some rest," she told him. "Tomorrow will be a long day for all of us."

"You too," he replied, though they both knew sleep would be elusive tonight.

As Olivia prepared for bed, the text message from the unknown number weighed on her mind. *Don't trust everything or everyone you think you know. Some monsters are real.* A warning from an ally? A trap from an enemy? Or something else entirely? She will find out at Watson's Diner at 7 AM tomorrow. Until then, she had a more immediate monster to confront—the possibility that her husband had been alive for the past year, unable or unwilling to reach them until now.

Some monsters were indeed real, she reflected as she finally lay down, though not the dimensional entity the Guardians claimed to be containing. The true monsters were human: people who would sacrifice children to maintain their power, who would manipulate ancient symbols and use fear to control others. People who might have taken her husband from his family for getting too close to their secrets.

As she drifted toward uneasy sleep, Olivia Rivera made a silent promise to the four students hidden somewhere beneath Chesapeake's placid surface. Aaron Mitchell, whose brilliant mind had earned him acceptance into a prestigious Governor's STEM academy, was on track to secure a full scholarship to an Ivy League school. Sofia Alvarez, whose artwork transformed blank walls into windows to other worlds. Caleb Johnson, whose quiet leadership had created positive change throughout Pinecrest. Lily Robertson, whose compassion extended to every struggling classmate and wounded creature that crossed her path.

They would not become entries in Earl Thompson's journal of the disappeared. They would not become nameless sacrifices to feed whatever truly lay beneath the Whitmore land. They would come home to their families, to their futures, to the lives that were rightfully theirs.

Tomorrow, the true descent would begin.

CHAPTER TWENTY ONE
DINER'S REVELATION

Saturday morning arrived with the whisper of first light, a pale glow seeping through Dr. Olivia Rivera's bedroom curtains. Her alarm hadn't yet sounded, but consciousness claimed her nevertheless. Her mind immediately filled with the weight of what lay ahead: the mysterious text message, the meeting at Watson's Diner, the Guardians' orientation session that would follow, and most pressing of all, four young lives hanging in the balance beneath Pinecrest.

She glanced at the clock - 5:32 AM. Nearly thirty minutes before her alarm was set to wake her. With a soft sigh, she swung her legs over the side of the bed, abandoning any pretense of returning to sleep. In the quiet stillness of the early morning, she moved through her preparations with practiced efficiency, selecting clothing that projected professional competence without drawing attention - charcoal slacks, a deep burgundy blouse, and minimal jewelry. The small GPS device Noah had modified was tucked into a silver pendant on a delicate chain - innocent-looking enough to avoid suspicion but capable of transmitting her location to the others if trouble arose.

As she applied her makeup, Olivia's thoughts drifted to the voice on Thompson's phone - James, her husband, somehow alive after months of silence. The rational part of her mind still questioned the authenticity of the call, wondering if it might be an elaborate deception by the Guardians.

But her heart recognized the voice, the particular cadence, and the tone that belonged uniquely to James. "*The translation is wrong, deliberately wrong,*" he had said. What translation? The Whitmore Tablet, presumably - the artifact she needed to see today. She finished her preparation, pausing at Sam's door to listen for any sign that he might be awake. Hearing only the soft rhythm of his breathing, she decided to let him sleep.

The note she left on the kitchen counter was simple: "Gone to run errands. Call if you need anything. Love, Mom." No mention of Watson's Diner or the mysterious message that had summoned her there. Sam had enough to worry about without adding to his burden. The early morning air held a crisp edge as Olivia stepped outside, spring's warmth not yet having chased away the lingering chill of night. Her sedan started quietly, and she backed out of the driveway with headlights dimmed, watching for any sign of surveillance. Since learning of the Guardians' extensive influence in Chesapeake, she'd grown increasingly aware of the possibility that her movements were being monitored. The streets were largely empty at this hour, just a few delivery trucks and early-shift workers making their way through the sleeping town. Olivia took an intentionally circuitous route to Watson's Diner, doubling back twice and making several unnecessary turns to ensure she wasn't being followed. Better to be overly cautious than careless.

Watson's Diner stood on the corner of Maple and Chester, its neon sign casting a blue and red glow that seemed out of place in the gathering dawn. The establishment was a Chesapeake institution, having served the community since the 1960s with little change to its chrome-and-vinyl aesthetic. At this hour, the parking lot held just a handful of vehicles - a pickup truck, two sedans, and a motorcycle whose engine still ticked with residual heat. Olivia parked near the entrance, positioning her car for a quick exit if necessary. Inside, the diner hummed with quiet activity. A waitress moved between tables with practiced efficiency, coffee pot in hand. An elderly couple shared breakfast in companionable silence near the window. A truck driver hunched over a plate of eggs and hash browns at the counter.

And in booth seven—the booth mentioned in the mysterious text—sat a woman Olivia recognized immediately, despite having never met her in person. Dr. Eleanor Blackwood, the former history teacher at Pinecrest, whose abrupt departure had created the opening Olivia now filled. Even without an introduction, Olivia would have known her by the distinctive silver streak in her otherwise dark hair, visible in the faculty photographs still hanging in Pinecrest's main hallway. Dr. Blackwood glanced up as Olivia approached, her sharp eyes assessing the newcomer with wary intelligence.

"Dr. Rivera," she said, her voice low and measured. "Thank you for coming." Without waiting for a response, she gestured to the seat across from her. "Please, join me. We have much to discuss and limited time."

Olivia slid into the booth, noticing the two coffee cups already on the table. Dr. Blackwood had anticipated her arrival and ordered for both of them. A small gesture that underscored the seriousness of their meeting. "You're a difficult woman to contact securely," Dr. Blackwood continued, adding cream to her coffee with a steady hand that belied the tension evident in her posture. "The Guardians monitor all conventional communications in Chesapeake - phones, emails, even letters in certain cases. This was the only way I could reach you without alerting them."

Olivia wrapped her hands around the warm mug, studying the woman across from her. Dr. Blackwood appeared slightly older than her faculty photograph, her face lined with exhaustion, her shoulders carrying the weight of someone who had been looking over her shoulder for too long.

"You disappeared rather suddenly," Olivia observed, keeping her voice neutral. "The official story involves a family emergency."

A humorless smile flitted across Dr. Blackwood's face. "Yes, that's what they said. In reality, I was given a choice - leave immediately or face consequences for my 'inappropriate fixation' on historical events better left unexplored. The principal made it quite clear that my continued inquiry into the cyclical disappearances would result in consequences beyond mere termination."

She took a sip of her coffee, her gaze never leaving Olivia's face. "I chose to leave. I'm not proud of that decision, but I had my reasons." Dr. Blackwood set down her cup with deliberate care. "But I've been watching from a distance. When I learned they had hired you, a historian with expertise in educational transitions whose husband vanished while researching similar patterns in Ecuador, I knew it wasn't coincidental. They chose you specifically, Dr. Rivera. The question is: why?"

The revelation sent a chill through Olivia that had nothing to do with the diner's aggressive air conditioning. She had suspected her hiring might not have been entirely based on her qualifications, but the confirmation was unsettling. "Because of James," she said softly. "They know I'm looking for him."

Dr. Blackwood nodded. "Not just that. They believe you might have access to whatever he discovered in Ecuador - something that threatens their control over the ritual. They're watching you, evaluating whether you're an asset to be recruited or a threat to be eliminated." The waitress approached their table, coffeepot in hand. Both women fell silent as she refilled their cups, exchanging pleasantries about the early hour and the promise of good weather. When she moved away, Dr. Blackwood leaned forward, her voice dropping to barely above a whisper. "Today, they'll show you the Whitmore Tablet. It's their most sacred artifact, the foundation of their beliefs about the entity beneath Pinecrest. They'll tell you it instructs them to perform the sacrifice, that the tablet's text describes how to maintain the barrier between worlds."

She reached into her purse and withdrew a small device that looked like an ordinary pen. "This is a scanner disguised as a fountain pen. Press the clip and run it along the text if you can get close enough to the tablet. It will capture high-resolution images we can analyze later."

Olivia accepted the device, turning it over in her hands. It felt solid and expensive, the kind of technology not easily obtained by a former history teacher. "You're not working alone," she observed.

Dr. Blackwood's expression revealed nothing. "Let's just say I found allies after leaving Pinecrest. People who share my concern about what happens beneath that school every twelve years." She checked her watch, and her movements became more urgent. "We don't have much time. They already completed the fourth disappearance, yes? Lily Robertson?"

Olivia nodded, remembering the news that had reached her during her planning bell. "Then the ritual is proceeding on schedule. But there's something you need to know about this particular cycle." Dr. Blackwood withdrew a folded paper from her jacket pocket, sliding it across the table. "This is a partial translation of the tablet, not the version the Guardians use. It suggests the entity isn't what they believe it to be. It's not a threat seeking to break through - it's a consciousness trying to communicate."

Olivia unfolded the paper, scanning the handwritten notes with growing interest. "This aligns with what we heard last night," she murmured, thinking of James's broken message. "A call came through to Thompson's phone. It was James, my husband. He said something similar - that the entity is trying to warn us, not break through. That the sacrifices don't appease it but empower those who control the ritual."

Dr. Blackwood's eyes widened slightly, a flicker of hope crossing her features. "Then he's alive. We suspected as much, but to have confirmation..." She shook her head, refocusing. "This changes things. If he's managed to contact you, he must have found substantial evidence."

She glanced around the diner, her paranoia momentarily visible before she controlled it. "The Guardians don't just want to maintain the barrier, Dr. Rivera. They're harnessing energy from the ritual for their own purposes - longevity, influence, and power. Each cycle strengthens their control over Chesapeake and beyond. They've established similar nodes in other locations globally, all following the same pattern of sacrifices."

The revelation aligned with James's research, with the connections he'd been tracing between Chesapeake and similar sites in Ecuador, Peru, and beyond. Olivia felt pieces clicking into place, the scattered fragments of understanding coalescing into a clearer picture. "And the four archetypes?" she asked. "Why those specific qualities?"

Dr. Blackwood's expression darkened. "According to my research, each archetype represents an aspect of human potential - intellectual, creative, leadership, and compassion. Together, they form a complete representation of humanity's highest capabilities. The sacrifice isn't just of lives; it's of potential. Of possibility." She checked her watch again, her movements becoming increasingly urgent. "You need to go soon. The Guardians are expecting you at nine, and you can't arrive from this direction. But before you leave, there's one more thing."

She withdrew a small, flat stone from her purse, placing it on the table between them. It was dark green with veins of gold running through it, polished to a high shine, and carved with symbols similar to those Olivia had seen in James's research photos. "This is from Ecuador," Dr. Blackwood explained. "Your husband sent it to me before he disappeared, along with notes suggesting it was a key of sorts - not physical, but energetic. He believed these stones could disrupt the ritual if placed correctly within the chamber."

Olivia reached for the stone, feeling its unexpected warmth against her palm. "How did you know James?"

Dr. Blackwood's smile held genuine affection. "We corresponded for years about historical anomalies and pattern recognition in disappearance cases. I was researching Pinecrest; he was tracking similar phenomena globally. We shared data, theories, and concerns. When he found the Ecuador site, he reached out immediately - he recognized the connection to Pinecrest from my descriptions."

The connection made sense. James had always maintained an extensive network of academic contacts, especially those working in unconventional areas of research. "Keep the stone hidden," Dr. Blackwood continued, rising from the booth. "And remember - what they show you today is carefully curated to lead you toward their conclusion. Question everything, especially your own assumptions." She placed money on the table for their coffee, pausing before leaving. "One last warning, Dr. Rivera. The Guardians aren't just watching you. They've identified your son and his friends as potential candidates for the next cycle. The four of them - Sam, Leila, Noah, Mia - they match the archetypes with remarkable alignment. If they can't be used in this cycle, the Guardians will keep them under observation for the next."

The statement hit Olivia like a physical blow, momentarily robbing her of breath. She had feared for Sam's safety as the investigation progressed, but the thought that the Guardians viewed him and his friends as future sacrifices struck a primal fear in her heart. "How do you know this?"

Dr. Blackwood's expression was grim. "Because they were evaluating my students the same way when I was teaching at

Pinecrest. They maintain files on potential candidates for years in advance. Your son and his friends have already drawn attention by asking questions about the disappearances. Be careful, Dr. Rivera. And whatever happens, don't trust Fletcher or anyone connected to the school board."

With that final warning, she slipped out of the booth and headed for the door, pausing only to exchange a few words with the waitress - casual, unremarkable, the conversation of a regular customer. Through the window, Olivia watched her walk to the motorcycle in the parking lot, don a helmet that obscured her face, and drive away with the practiced ease of someone accustomed to quick departures. Olivia remained in the booth for several minutes, processing the information she'd received. The stone felt warm in her pocket, the scanner pen secure in her purse. Nine o'clock at the Whitmore Historical Society suddenly seemed both too soon and not soon enough.

CHAPTER TWENTY TWO
OMINOUS SURVEILLANCE

In the Rivera household, Sam awoke to the sound of birds outside his window and the lingering remnants of dreams about his father. He lay perfectly still for a moment, the previous day's revelations washing over him like a tide - his father's voice on the phone, the message about incorrect translations, the plans they'd made to infiltrate the tunnels beneath Pinecrest. Reality seemed increasingly fluid, the boundary between the mundane world of middle school and the shadow realm of secret societies and ancient rituals growing thinner by the day.

He reached for his phone, checking for messages from the others. Nothing from Leila or Mia yet, but a text from Noah sent at 6:23 AM: "Finished modifications to tracking devices. Added audio capability and made a camera setup, too. Coming over at 10 to test everything."

Sam texted back a quick acknowledgment, then rolled out of bed. The house was quiet; his mother apparently had already gone for her meeting with the Guardians. In the kitchen, he found her note and a covered plate of breakfast - scrambled eggs and toast, now cold but a thoughtful gesture nonetheless. Sam's mind raced with the tasks ahead as he reheated the food in the microwave. Today, they would finalize their rescue plan, gathering the equipment and information needed for tomorrow night's operation. They still lacked crucial details - exactly where the four students were being held, the specific timing of the ritual, and the security measures they would face. His mother's infiltration of the Guardians might provide those answers, but the risk she was taking made his stomach clench with anxiety.

The microwave beeped, and Sam retrieved his breakfast, eating mechanically while reviewing what they knew so far. The missing students - Aaron, Sofia, Caleb, and Lily - were being held somewhere in the tunnel system beneath Pinecrest or the old Whitmore property. The ritual would take place at midnight on Sunday when the astronomical alignment peaked. They needed both bronze keys to access the deepest levels of the tunnels - one held by Miss Patterson, the other originally belonging to his father and now in Sam's possession.

His phone buzzed with a text from Leila: "Grandpa's journal has more details about tunnel access points. Found notes from 1977 attempt to access lower levels. Coming over at 10." Followed almost immediately by one from Mia: "Put together emergency medical kits. One for each of us, plus extras for the missing students. ETA 10:30."

Their dedication continued to impress Sam. Four teenagers with no particular training or resources were preparing to challenge a secret society that had operated with impunity for over a century. The odds seemed impossible, yet here they were, collecting medical supplies and modifying tracking devices like characters in some adventure novel. The comparison might have made him smile if the stakes weren't so devastatingly real.

Four lives hung in the balance, and more would follow in future cycles if they failed to break the pattern. Sam's thoughts were interrupted by a soft knock at the front door - not the agreed-upon pattern they'd established for their group. Caution immediately heightened his senses. He approached carefully, peering through the peephole to see a man in a police uniform standing on the porch, his expression neutral but watchful.

Not just any police officer—Detective Collins, whom Sam recognized from the school, and suspected of being a member of the Guardians. Sam's heart rate accelerated, but he forced himself to remain calm. Ignoring the knock wasn't an option; the detective had undoubtedly seen movement inside. He opened the door partially, keeping the security chain engaged. "Good morning," he said, working to keep his voice steady. "Can I help you?"

Detective Collins smiled, the expression not reaching his eyes. "Good morning, Sam. I'm Detective Collins - you might remember me from school. Is your mother home?"

Sam shook his head, grateful for once that his mother had left early. "No, sir. She left a note saying she had errands to run." He gestured vaguely behind him. "She should be back around noon, I think."

The detective nodded, his gaze moving past Sam to scan what little he could see of the living room. "I see. Well, I was hoping to discuss the recent disappearances with her. As the school's history teacher, she might have insights that could help our investigation."

The statement was plainly false, and Sam almost laughed as if the Guardians needed any "insights" about disappearances they themselves had orchestrated. "I can tell her you stopped by," Sam offered, eager to end the conversation.

Collins reached into his pocket and produced a business card. "Please do. And if you happen to hear from any of your friends about the missing students—Leila, Noah, or Mia, for instance—I'd appreciate a call. We're following all possible leads."

The emphasis on his friends' names wasn't subtle. Collins was letting Sam know that they were being watched, and their connection to the investigation had been noted. "I'll let them know if I see them," Sam managed, accepting the card through the partially open door. "Thanks for stopping by."

The detective lingered a moment longer than necessary, his calculating gaze making one final sweep. "You take care now, Sam. These are concerning times for Chesapeake. Four students missing... we wouldn't want anyone else to disappear."

The thinly veiled threat sent a chill down Sam's spine despite the morning warmth. He nodded wordlessly, closing the door as Collins finally turned to leave. Through the window, Sam watched as the detective returned to his unmarked police car, parked across the street. But the car didn't pull away immediately. Instead, Collins remained inside, apparently making notes or a phone call. Surveillance. Not even attempting to be subtle about it.

Heart racing, Sam texted the group: "Detective Collins just came by looking for Mom, now sitting in the car outside watching the house. BE CAREFUL approaching. Might need to change meeting location."

The responses came quickly. Noah: "Can use back alley entry through Willow Street. My dad's friend lives at 142 - you can cut through their yard to reach your back door." Leila: "On it. Will alert Mr. Thompson and Miss Patterson to change the approach, too." Mia: "Should we cancel? Seems risky with police watching."

Sam considered Mia's valid concern. Having the group gather with a Guardian watching the house was dangerous, potentially exposing their entire plan. But postponing meant losing precious preparation time they couldn't afford with the ritual less than forty-eight hours away. "No cancellation," he decided. "But extreme caution. No one comes through the front. Use Noah's back route only. And stagger arrivals to avoid attracting attention."

With Collins watching the house, Sam's anxiety ratcheted higher. He moved through the rooms, closing blinds and curtains to limit visibility from outside while mentally cataloging what materials they needed to hide before the others arrived. Most of their planning materials from last night were still scattered across the dining table - maps of the tunnel system, printouts of historical documents, and notes about the Guardians.

He gathered everything quickly, storing it in his mother's study where they could retrieve it once everyone had safely arrived. As he worked, Sam's phone buzzed with another text - from his mother this time: "All fine. Meeting is going as expected. Will share details when I see you. Stay safe."

The deliberate vagueness suggested she suspected her communications might be monitored, reinforcing the need for caution. Sam replied with equal care: "Okay. Friends are coming over to study later. See you when you get back."

Nothing that would raise suspicions if intercepted, but enough to alert his mother that the group was gathering at the house. With Collins watching outside and the others due to arrive soon, Sam conducted a quick security review of the house, checking that all potential entry points were secured except for the back door they would be using. In his mother's study, he retrieved the bronze key from its hiding place in a hollowed-out copy of "The Once and Future King" - one of James Rivera's favorite novels and a fitting disguise for an artifact linked to ancient rituals and hidden chambers. The key felt heavier than its actual weight, the responsibility it represented adding metaphorical mass to the small object.

CHAPTER TWENTY THREE
CLEAR COMMUNICATIONS

While Earl Thompson prepared for the day ahead, his thoughts kept returning to the strange phone call from James Rivera. He'd recognized the voice immediately despite the static and distortion. Rivera had been gone for nearly a year, presumed dead by most. Yet, somehow, he'd reached out at this critical moment with a warning that upended everything Thompson thought he understood about the rituals beneath Pinecrest. The custodian moved methodically around his small apartment, packing supplies for what might prove to be the most critical operation of his life since Vietnam. The parallels weren't lost on him - once again, he was preparing to infiltrate hostile territory to extract those who couldn't save themselves. Only this time, he wouldn't freeze. This time, he would reach those who needed help.

His bronze star, awarded for actions few civilians could comprehend, sat in its case on his bedside table. The citation mentioned "exceptional courage under fire" and "saving the lives of fellow soldiers with disregard for personal safety." What it didn't mention was Captain Matthew Harrison, the man who had pulled strings to ensure Thompson received recognition rather than a court-martial for the unauthorized rescue operation that had saved six men but violated direct orders. Harrison went on to have a distinguished career in intelligence services, eventually joining the CIA's operational division before retiring. They had maintained sporadic contact over the decades—Christmas cards, occasional phone calls— but Thompson had never asked for anything—until last night.

After the planning session at the Rivera house, Thompson retreated to his apartment and placed a call to a number he had kept only in his memory. Harrison answered on the third ring, his voice raspier with age but still carrying the crisp authority that had commanded respect in the jungle clearings of Vietnam.

"Harrison." One word, neither question nor greeting. "It's Thompson, sir. Earl Thompson, from Nam. Delta Company."

A pause, and then warmth entered the voice. "Thompson. It's been, what, five years since we spoke? Everything alright?"

Thompson hesitated, the enormity of what he was about to request momentarily overwhelming him. "No, sir, it's not. I need help with something... unusual. Something involving missing children and an organization called the Guardians of the Veil."

The silence that followed lasted so long that Thompson thought the connection had dropped. Then, Harrison's voice returned, now deadly serious. "You're being monitored, Thompson. Say nothing more on this line. I'll reach out through secure channels within twelve hours."

The call had ended abruptly, leaving Thompson with nothing but the promise of contact and the hope that his former Captain's connections might provide resources beyond their small group's capabilities. Now, as he checked his prepaid phone for the fifth time that morning, Thompson wondered if Harrison had meant what he said or if the promise had been merely a way to end an uncomfortable conversation.

The phone finally buzzed at 8:27 AM. Not a call but a text message from an unknown number: "Secure package arriving by courier within the hour. Verify identity with code phrase: 'The river runs both ways.' Delete this message."

Thompson complied immediately, erasing the message after committing the code phrase to memory. While he waited, he continued his preparations, checking and rechecking the equipment he'd gathered - flashlights with extra batteries, zip ties that could serve as either restraints or fasteners, a first aid kit more comprehensive than the ones Mia was assembling, and several other items his military experience suggested might prove useful in the tunnels.

At precisely 9:15 AM, a knock sounded at his door. Thompson approached cautiously, peering through the peephole to see a young woman in a courier uniform, a small package tucked under her arm. "Delivery for Earl Thompson," she announced when he opened the door. "I was told you're expecting this?"

Thompson nodded. "The river runs both ways," he said quietly, feeling slightly foolish using such dramatic phrasing.

The courier's professionally neutral expression didn't change. "And the current never sleeps," she responded, completing the exchange. She handed him the package, had him sign an electronic pad, and departed without another word. The package was lightweight but solid, roughly the size of a hardcover book. Thompson closed and locked his door before carefully opening it to reveal a sleek satellite phone, more sophisticated than any civilian model he'd ever seen. A handwritten note accompanied it:

"Secured against all standard monitoring. Call the programmed number when ready for the retrieval of your message. Duration: two minutes max. The package includes an enhanced recording device.

−H."

Thompson activated the phone, finding a single number stored in its contacts. When he dialed, the connection was established immediately, and an automated voice instructed him to place the phone near the device containing the message he wanted enhanced. Thompson followed the instructions, playing James Rivera's fragmented call from his regular phone while the satellite device apparently recorded and processed the audio.

After sixty seconds, the automated voice returned: "Enhancement complete. Playback will begin in five seconds." The enhanced version of James's message played with remarkable clarity, and the static and breakups were significantly reduced.

"Earl, listen carefully. I don't have much time," James's voice began, the words now perfectly audible. "The pattern isn't what we thought. It's not containment, it's communication. The entity isn't trying to break through - it's trying to warn us. The sacrifices don't appease it; they empower those who control the ritual. I've found similar sites in Ecuador, Peru, and Romania. All with the same markings. All with the same cycle of disappearances. The Guardians have chapters in every major node, manipulating the energy for personal gain. The door opens both ways. Find the original tablets. The translation is wrong, deliberately wrong. It's not 'through sacrifice comes protection' but 'through protection comes understanding.' The entity is trying to communicate something vital - a warning about something approaching. The alignment creates a moment of connection, but the Guardians have corrupted it into a source of power. I've located the original stone in Ecuador - it contains the true instructions for the ritual. No sacrifice is needed, just the presence of the four archetypes in harmony rather than death. I'm trying to get back to Chesapeake, but they're watching all transportation. If you're hearing this, tell Olivia and Sam I'm alive and coming home. Tell them I—"

The message cut off there, just as it had in the original version, but the enhanced clarity transformed a fragmented, ambiguous message into a coherent explanation that aligned with Dr. Blackwood's claims at Watson's Diner. Thompson played it twice more, committing the key points to memory. The information was revelatory - not just confirmation that James Rivera was alive, but a complete reframing of the ritual's purpose.

If James was correct, the Guardians had been manipulating an ancient communication channel for their own benefit, sacrificing innocent lives to accumulate personal power rather than to protect humanity from some interdimensional threat. The implications were staggering, potentially transforming their rescue mission into something far more significant - not just saving four students but correcting a centuries-old perversion of a ritual meant for communication rather than sacrifice. Thompson checked the time, realizing he needed to leave soon to meet the others at the Rivera house.

Before departing, he placed one more call on the secure satellite phone. When Harrison himself answered, Thompson kept his message brief. "Received and processed. Thank you. The situation is as grave as I suspected, possibly worse. Any chance of additional support?"

Harrison's response was equally concise. "Assets are being positioned. Extraction capability on standby if needed. Coordinates and code word will be transmitted to this device if requested. Good luck, Thompson. Harrison out."

CHAPTER TWENTY FOUR
THE GUARDIAN'S TRUTH

At the Whitmore Historical Society, Dr. Olivia Rivera was being guided through the building's restricted areas by Margaret Whitmore herself, the elderly matriarch's aristocratic bearing at odds with the clinical nature of the facility beneath the colonial facade. What had appeared to be a simple historical society from the main entrance gave way to increasingly modern and well-equipped spaces as they descended deeper into the building. "Few visitors see these lower levels," Margaret explained as they passed through a security checkpoint where Rivera's photo was taken and an ID badge created. "Our research facilities are reserved for senior members and specially invited guests."

The research areas resembled high-end university laboratories more than historical archives - electron microscopes, spectrographic analysis equipment, and climate-controlled examination rooms where white-coated technicians studied artifacts behind glass partitions.

"Impressive facilities for a local historical society," Olivia observed, carefully maintaining her role as the interested but not yet convinced academic.

"Our work extends far beyond local history," Margaret replied with the faintest smile. "The Whitmore family has always understood that the significance of what lies beneath

Chesapeake has global implications. What you see here is merely one team in an international research network."

The statement aligned with what James had discovered about similar sites globally, each with its own version of the Guardians maintaining the ritual cycle. Olivia made appropriate noises of interest while noting security camera placements and access points, building a mental map of the facility that might prove useful later. After touring several laboratory spaces, they reached what appeared to be the heart of the complex - a circular room with a domed ceiling, its walls lined with glass cases containing artifacts from multiple historical periods and geographical locations. In the center, on a raised platform protected by what looked like bulletproof glass, sat a stone tablet approximately two feet square.

"The Whitmore Tablet," Margaret announced with reverent pride. "Discovered in 1734 by my ancestor William Whitmore during excavation for the plantation's foundation. The cornerstone of our understanding about what lies beneath Chesapeake." Olivia approached the display with genuine academic interest, studying the artifact through the protective glass. The tablet was carved from dark stone with reddish veins running through it, its surface covered in symbols that resembled no writing system she recognized from her historical studies. Concentric circles dominated the design, with smaller symbols arranged in patterns that suggested a narrative or instructions.

"The symbols defy conventional linguistic analysis," Dr. Hargrove explained, joining them from a side door. "Yet we find identical markings at archaeological sites across the globe, always in locations associated with thin points between dimensional planes." He pressed a button on a nearby console, and the protective glass panel slid noiselessly into the floor, allowing direct access to the tablet. "You may examine it closely, Dr. Rivera. Few outside our membership have such an opportunity."

Dr. Blackwood's scanner pen felt heavy in Olivia's pocket as she approached the tablet. Outwardly projecting academic curiosity, she raced her heart with the risk she was about to take. "The material isn't indigenous to this region," she observed, leaning closer to examine the stone's composition. Using the movement, she retracted the pen from her pocket.

"No," Hargrove agreed. "Spectroscopic analysis indicates the tablet originated from geological formations found in the Andes mountains, specifically regions of Ecuador and Peru. Yet it was discovered here, suggesting ancient knowledge transfer across vast distances."

Olivia nodded thoughtfully, positioning the pen over the tablet's surface. "Have you conducted a comparative analysis with similar artifacts from South American locations?"

As Hargrove launched into a detailed explanation of their research methodology, Olivia activated the scanner, running it along the tablet's surface as if gesturing to emphasize her interest in the symbols. The pen made no sound, but she felt a slight vibration, indicating it was capturing images.

"The translation required decades of research," Margaret Whitmore said, watching Olivia with sharp eyes that missed nothing. "Each symbol represents not just a word but a concept, part of a language designed to bridge the gap between dimensional realities."

Olivia completed her scan of the central portion of the tablet, mentally calculating how to reach the outer sections without appearing suspicious. "And your translation indicates instructions for a ritual to maintain this dimensional barrier?" she asked, moving to examine another section of the tablet and continuing her scanning.

"That's the essence, yes," Hargrove confirmed. "The tablet describes a thinning between worlds that occurs during specific astronomical alignments every twelve years. It prescribes a method for strengthening the barrier through the transfer of particular energy signatures - what we've identified as the four archetypes."

Olivia nodded, completing her scan of the tablet while maintaining her scholarly demeanor. "And have you considered alternative interpretations?" she asked, carefully returning the pen to her pocket. "In my experience, ancient symbolic languages often contain ambiguities that allow for multiple readings."

A flash of something - annoyance? Concern? - crossed Margaret Whitmore's aristocratic features. "We've had our best linguistic and archaeological minds working on this for generations, Dr. Rivera. While minor details might be debated, the core meaning is quite clear."

The protective glass rose back into place, once again separating the tablet from direct access. "Now, if you'll follow me, I'd like to show you evidence of the entity's influence during the previous weakening of the barrier."

The reminder of the scanning pen's presence in her pocket burned like a lump of coal on fire as Olivia followed her hosts deeper into the facility. Had they noticed her using it? Margaret's sharp eyes seemed to miss nothing, and the timing of the glass barrier's return felt potentially significant. But Margaret and Hargrove continued their tour without comment, leading her to a laboratory where monitors displayed geological readings, atmospheric measurements, and astronomical calculations.

"These are live readings from monitoring stations positioned throughout Chesapeake," Hargrove explained, indicating the data streams. "Watch what happens when I overlay historical data from previous alignment periods." He typed commands into a console, and the displays transformed to show parallel readings from 2013, 2001, 1989, and earlier cycles. The patterns were indeed similar - unusual electromagnetic fluctuations, subtle gravitational anomalies, and atmospheric composition changes that preceded each cycle of disappearances.

From a purely scientific perspective, the data was compelling. Something was occurring beneath Chesapeake during these alignment periods, something measurable and consistent. The question wasn't whether a phenomenon existed but what it represented and how the Guardians interpreted or manipulated it to serve their purposes. "Impressive data collection," Olivia acknowledged, maintaining her role as the objectively interested academic. "And your conclusion is that these readings indicate attempts by an interdimensional entity to breach the barrier between worlds?"

"That's a somewhat simplified interpretation," Hargrove replied with the faintest condescension. "The entity doesn't seek to 'breach' our world so much as it exerts influence during periods of dimensional thinning. Without the ritual to strengthen the barrier, this influence would grow exponentially, eventually resulting in catastrophic consequences."

Olivia gestured toward the historical data displays. "And you've correlated previous failures of the ritual with historical catastrophes? The evidence must be compelling."

Margaret Whitmore's thin smile didn't reach her eyes. "We have extensive documentation linking weakened barriers to everything from localized disasters to global pandemics. The

Black Death, for instance, coincided with a failed ritual at a European node. The 1918 flu pandemic followed disruption at the Romania site during World War I."

The claims were impossible to verify on the spot, but Olivia noted how carefully they were presented - correlation framed as causation, historical coincidences elevated to evidence. It was masterfully done, the kind of pseudo-scientific presentation that could convince even educated people if they weren't approaching it with healthy skepticism. "Fascinating," Olivia said, allowing genuine interest to magnify her voice. "And the students currently selected for this cycle - they're being prepared for the ritual now?" The question was direct, perhaps too direct, but she needed to confirm the location of Aaron, Sofia, Caleb, and Lily.

A cool silence followed her question, Margaret and Hargrove exchanging a glance that communicated volumes without words. "The Chosen Ones are indeed in preparation," Margaret finally said, her use of the term revealing how the Guardians viewed their victims. "Their physical forms are being maintained in a state of suspended animation while their energetic signatures are aligned for the ritual."

Not dead then, but not fully conscious either. The confirmation that the four students were still alive sent a wave of relief through Olivia, though she kept her expression neutral. "And where is this preparation taking place? I'd be interested in observing the technical aspects of the process."

This time, Hargrove answered, his tone deliberately casual. "The Preparation Chamber is located beneath the original Whitmore Plantation site, accessible only to senior members of our organization. Perhaps in time, once you've fully embraced our purpose, you might witness a preparation phase. For now, however, we should continue with aspects more aligned with your historical expertise."

The deflection confirmed another piece of information—the students were being held beneath Northwest River Park, just as they had suspected. Hargrove gestured toward another door. "We have extensive historical records, I believe would interest you—documentation of previous cycles, journals from past Guardians, and archaeological findings from before colonial settlement."

For the next several hours, Olivia was guided through the Guardians' archives, shown carefully selected historical documents that supported their narrative while omitting anything that might contradict it. The presentation was comprehensive and convincing - if she hadn't already heard James's message and met with Dr. Blackwood, she might have found herself beginning to accept their worldview. By mid-afternoon, as the tour concluded and they returned to the more conventional historical society spaces, Olivia had gathered valuable intelligence while maintaining her cover as the interested but not yet converted academic.

"You've given me much to consider," she told Margaret and Hargrove as they prepared to conclude the day's session. "I'm particularly interested in reviewing some of the original documentation regarding the early cycles. Would it be possible to access those materials tomorrow?"

Hargrove nodded, apparently pleased by her continued interest. "Of course. We'll arrange for you to have supervised access to the first-cycle journals tomorrow morning. And tomorrow evening, we'd like you to observe a demonstration of the entity's influence as the alignment begins to peak."

Margaret Whitmore stepped forward, taking Olivia's hands in her papery grip. "We understand this is a significant paradigm shift, Dr. Rivera. Few people are prepared to accept that reality extends beyond the conventional dimensions taught in universities. But I sense in you an openness to deeper truths, a quality your predecessor unfortunately lacked."

The mention of Dr. Blackwood sent a chill through Olivia, though she maintained her composed expression. "I've always believed that an academic's first duty is to follow the evidence where it leads, even when it challenges established understanding," she replied carefully. "I appreciate the trust you've shown in sharing these materials with me."

As she prepared to leave, Hargrove handed her a small device that resembled a key fob. "For tomorrow's session," he explained. "This will grant you access to the lower levels without an escort. It's programmed only for specific areas, of course, but it represents our growing trust in your discretion."

Olivia accepted the device, recognizing it for what it was - both a genuine access tool and a way to track her movements. "Until tomorrow, then," she said with a polite smile, gathering her purse and ensuring the scanner pen was securely hidden inside. As she walked to her car, Olivia maintained an unhurried pace despite her desire to get as far from the Whitmore Historical Society as possible. The weight of what she'd learned pressed down on her - confirmation that the students were alive, held somewhere beneath the old plantation site; evidence that the Guardians were misinterpreting or deliberately mistranslating the tablet; and most troublingly, the revelation that they viewed Sam and his friends as potential future sacrifices.

CHAPTER TWENTY FIVE
EXPOSED TABLET SECRETS

Once in her car, she checked her phone, finding several texts from Sam about Detective Collins watching the house and the group arriving through the back entrance. She sent a brief, careful reply indicating she would be home soon, then took an intentionally circuitous route to ensure she wasn't being followed. As she drove, her mind raced with plans for the evening ahead. They needed to review the tablet images captured by the scanner pen, compare them with the translation Dr. Blackwood had provided, and incorporate this information into their rescue plan.

The secure access device Hargrove had given her might prove useful, depending on how extensively it worked throughout the Guardians' facilities. And most urgently, they needed to address the police surveillance of their home, which threatened to complicate their entire operation. By the time Olivia arrived at the house, it was nearly 3 PM. She parked in the driveway as usual, maintaining the appearance of normal Saturday activities while noting Detective Collins' unmarked car still positioned across the street. Gathering shopping bags from a brief stop she'd made at a grocery store to maintain her cover story about running errands, she approached the front door with the casual confidence of someone with nothing to hide.

Inside, she found the group gathered in her study, the room farthest from street-facing windows and, therefore, safest from potential surveillance. Sam, Leila, Noah, and Mia sat around the desk, surrounded by equipment and notes. Mr. Thompson stood near the bookshelf while Miss Patterson occupied the desk chair. Her librarian's precision was evident in how she was organizing documents into labeled folders.

"Mom," Sam said, relief evident in his voice as she entered. "You're back."

Olivia closed the door behind her, setting down her shopping bags. "I am, and with valuable information. But first, how long has Detective Collins been watching the house?"

Thompson moved away from the bookshelf.

"Since at least 7 AM. I spotted him when I drove by earlier to check the situation. He's been relieved twice by other officers, suggesting a sustained surveillance operation." The news was concerning but not unexpected. If the Guardians suspected their involvement in investigating the disappearances, monitoring their movements would be a logical step.

"We need to assume all conventional routes are being watched," Olivia said, removing her jacket and withdrawing the scanner pen and access device from her pockets. "But I've confirmed several crucial details today that will help us refine our plan."

She quickly summarized her morning meetings with Dr. Blackwood at Watson's Diner and with the Guardians at the Whitmore Historical Society.

Noah's eyes lit up with technical interest as she described the tablet and the scanning process. "May I see the scanner?" he asked, extending his hand. Olivia passed him the device, which he examined with appreciative expertise. "This is military-grade technology, not something you'd find in a commercial product. Your Dr. Blackwood has serious connections."

He connected the pen to his laptop using a cable from his backpack. "Let's see what you captured." The group gathered around as Noah worked, his fingers flying over the keyboard as he extracted and enhanced the images. Within minutes, the Whitmore Tablet appeared on his screen in high resolution, every symbol crisp and clear.

"Impressive," Miss Patterson murmured, leaning closer to examine the symbols.

"These match descriptions in my grandfather's journal, but he never had access to the tablet." Leila nodded, opening her grandfather's journal to a page of hand-drawn symbols. "He tried to reconstruct it based on fragments he'd seen in the Guardians' documents, but this is much more complete."

Thompson had been unusually quiet, his weathered face set in thoughtful lines. Now he spoke, his voice carrying the weight of his recent discovery. "Before we go further, there's something you all need to hear."

He placed the satellite phone on the desk, drawing curious looks from everyone. "I received this device this morning from a... former military connection. It allowed me to enhance Dr. Rivera's message from last night."

He activated the device, and James Rivera's voice filled the room with remarkable clarity, delivering the complete message they had heard only in fragments before. Sam's face transformed as he listened, hope and determination replacing uncertainty. When the message ended, silence filled the room for several seconds, each person processing the implications of what they'd heard.

"So the ritual isn't about containment," Leila said finally. "It's about communication. And the Guardians have been corrupting it for their own power."

Miss Patterson nodded, her expression grim. "Which aligns with what my research suggested. The Guardians' longevity and influence have always seemed disproportionate to their numbers. If they're harnessing energy from these sacrifices for personal benefit rather than protection..."

Olivia retrieved the stone Dr. Blackwood had given her, placing it beside the laptop displaying the tablet images. "This is apparently from the Ecuador site. James sent it to Dr. Blackwood before he disappeared, believing it was key to disrupting the ritual-or rather, correcting it."

Noah studied the stone with interest. "It matches the material description of the tablets, according to your account. And these markings..." He pointed to symbols etched into the stone's surface. "They correspond to sections of the tablet."

Leila had been comparing the tablet images to notes in her grandfather's journal, her brow furrowed in concentration. "The central section here," she said, pointing to the screen. "My grandfather believed it was mistranslated deliberately. The Guardians' version reads 'Through sacrifice comes protection,' but he suspected it actually meant something closer to 'Through union comes understanding.'"

Thompson nodded, tapping the satellite phone. "This matches what Dr. Rivera said about the true translation: 'Through protection comes understanding,' not 'Through sacrifice comes protection.' The essence is the same - the ritual was never meant to involve killing."

Mia, who had been relatively quiet, spoke up. "So instead of sacrificing the four archetypes, the ritual was supposed to unite them? To have them work together somehow?"

Olivia considered this, thinking back to Dr. Blackwood's partial translation. "That aligns with what I learned today. The four archetypes represent aspects of human potential - intellectual, creative, leadership, and compassion. Together, they form a complete representation of humanity."

Sam's eyes widened with realization. "That's why the Guardians are watching us, too. We match the archetypes—

like Aaron, Sofia, Caleb, and Lily. I'm the son of a historian, following clues and solving puzzles." He gestured to his friends in turn. "Leila, with her connection to her grandfather's research, and her habit of documenting everything. Noah, with his technical skills, creating devices to help us. And Mia, with her medical knowledge, always thinking about how to care for others."

Once articulated, the parallel was striking. Their group mirrored the captured students in composition, if not in specific talents. "Which means," Thompson said slowly, "we might be able to use the correct ritual to counter what the Guardians are attempting. If we can reach the chamber before midnight tomorrow with the captured students and your group, we might be able to disrupt their corrupted ritual and establish the proper connection."

Miss Patterson's academic mind was already analyzing possibilities. "But the logistics would be challenging. We'd need to free Aaron, Sofia, Caleb, and Lily first, then somehow get all eight of you to the central chamber during the ritual itself."

Noah had been working on his laptop while they discussed, enhanced, and analyzed the tablet images. "I think I've found something," he announced, turning the screen so everyone could see. "There's a section here that appears to be instructions, not for sacrifice but for positioning. Look at these four symbols arranged around the central circle."

The symbols were distinct - one resembling a stylized brain, another like an artist's paintbrush, a third suggesting a crown or leadership emblem, and the fourth reminiscent of outstretched hands or a healing touch.

"The four archetypes," Olivia confirmed. "And they're arranged at cardinal points around a central symbol."

Noah nodded excitedly. "Exactly! And if I'm interpreting this correctly, the pattern suggests they're meant to be connected, not separated. The lines between them form a complete circuit."

Leila's eyes lit with understanding. "Not destruction but connection. The ritual was designed to create a unified energy circuit, allowing communication across the dimensional barrier."

The revelation felt right, aligning with everything they had discovered. If the original purpose of the ritual had been communication rather than sacrifice, it transformed their rescue mission into something even more significant - not just saving four lives but potentially correcting centuries of misused power and establishing the proper connection the ritual was designed for.

"We need to revise our plan," Olivia said decisively. "Not just extraction, but substitution. We need to free the captured students, yes, but we also need to position ourselves to complete the proper ritual if possible."

CHAPTER TWENTY SIX
GET OUT NOW!

The conversation was interrupted by a soft chime from Thompson's satellite phone, indicating an incoming message. He checked it, his expression growing serious. "From my contact: Police activity has increased around your house within the last hour. Multiple unmarked vehicles are now positioned within the vicinity. Aerial surveillance drone deployed. Recommendation: immediate relocation via secondary exit routes."

The news sent a jolt of alarm through the group. "They're preparing to move against us," Thompson continued. "Likely planning to take us into custody to prevent interference with tomorrow night's ritual."

Miss Patterson's eyes narrowed with determination. "Then we need to leave now before they can establish a complete perimeter." Noah was already packing his equipment with practiced efficiency. "I've been monitoring police frequencies on my laptop," he explained. "There was a spike in encrypted communications about thirty minutes ago. I assumed it was routine, but this explains it."

Mia looked frightened but resolute. "Where do we go? If they're watching this house, they might be watching all our homes."

Thompson considered for a moment. "My church, on Maple Street. The van is parked behind the building, and the keys are hidden in the usual place. No one would connect it to us. Pastor Williams never asks questions when the van occasionally disappears for community service projects."

Olivia nodded, quickly calculating their best options. "We need to split up. Different exit routes and different timings are needed to reconvene at the church. Thompson, you take Sam and Leila through the back route. Miss Patterson, can you guide Mia and Noah through the side neighbor's yard?"

The elderly librarian nodded, her demeanor shifting from academic to surprisingly tactical. "The Henderson property has a path through their garden that connects to the alley running parallel to Willow Street. We can use that."

As they prepared to leave, gathering only essential equipment and materials, Olivia added, "I'll create a diversion to draw attention from your departures. Give me five minutes, then move out in sequence, not all at once."

Sam looked alarmed. "Mom, no. They could arrest you."

Olivia squeezed his shoulder reassuringly. "They won't. The Guardians still believe I'm a potential recruit. And even if they detain me briefly, I have a legitimate reason to leave my own house. You don't. Besides, I have the access device Hargrove gave me - my movements won't seem suspicious to them."

Though clearly uncomfortable with the plan, Sam nodded reluctantly. "Okay. But how will you find us if you get away?"

Olivia touched the pendant containing Noah's tracking device. "I'll find you. Now, prepare to move out. Five minutes."

With the efficiency of a military operation, the group gathered their essential materials - Thompson securing the satellite phone and enhanced audio recording, Noah backing up the tablet images to a cloud server before packing his equipment, Leila carefully storing her grandfather's journal in a waterproof bag, and Mia distributing the medical kits she'd prepared.

Miss Patterson removed her reading glasses, tucking them into a sturdy case before pulling a black knit cap from her purse and placing it over her distinctive silver hair. The subtle but effective transformation made her appear like a different person entirely. "Old habits," she explained with a thin smile when she noticed Olivia watching. "The French Resistance taught me a few things about quick disguises, even if it was just a high school reenactment."

Thompson checked his watch. "Three minutes," he announced quietly. "Final equipment check."

Sam approached his mother before they separated, his young face set with a determination that squeezed Olivia's heart. He looked so much like James in that moment - the same resolute expression, the same quiet courage. "Be careful," he said simply. "We need you."

Olivia hugged him quickly, allowing herself this moment of maternal connection before they resumed their roles in the operation. "I will. Trust the plan, follow Thompson's lead, and I'll see you soon."

When the five minutes elapsed, Olivia moved to the front door, car keys in hand, shopping bags retrieved from where she'd left them earlier. She opened the door casually, locking it behind her with the unhurried movements of someone running routine Saturday errands. As she approached her car, she noticed Detective Collins straightening in his seat, watching her movements. She waved pleasantly, the gesture of a neighbor acknowledging another's presence, then called out, "Forgot milk! Be back in twenty."

She backed out of the driveway and drove away at precisely the speed limit, noting in her rearview mirror that Collins had started his engine, preparing to follow. Perfect. With Collins focused on her movements, the others would have a better chance of slipping away unnoticed. She drove toward the nearest grocery store, maintaining a normal pace while keeping an eye out for additional surveillance. As expected, Collins followed at a discreet distance, making no attempt to hide his presence.

What he didn't know was that Olivia had no intention of reaching the store. Since moving there, she had extensively studied Chesapeake's street layout, identifying potential routes for quick direction changes and surveillance evasion.

Three blocks from home, she made a sudden right turn onto Cedar Lane, then immediately left into the parking lot of an apartment complex with multiple exits.

Weaving through the parking lot at a brisk pace, she emerged on the opposite side onto Elmwood Drive, quickly turning right, then left again to reach Parkway Avenue. The maneuver would force Collins to either reveal himself by accelerating to catch up or lose visual contact altogether. From her mirror, she saw his unmarked car hesitate at the apartment complex entrance, giving her crucial seconds to extend her lead.

Meanwhile, back at the house, Thompson led Sam and Leila through the rear exit, moving with the quiet efficiency that had served him well in Vietnam. "Stay low, move quickly, but don't run," he instructed, guiding them across the backyard to the fence line. They slipped through a gap in the wooden fence that Sam had identified earlier, emerging into the neighbor's yard at 142 Willow Street. The property belonged to Mr. Abernathy, Noah's father's friend, who worked night shifts at the hospital and would be sleeping at this hour.

They crossed his yard in silence, passing beneath a clothesline laden with sheets that provided additional visual cover from any aerial surveillance. Reaching the alley behind the properties, Thompson paused, checking both directions before motioning them forward. "Three blocks to Maple

Street," he whispered. "Standard file formation, five-yard spacing."

The instruction initially made no sense to Sam until he saw Thompson and Leila spread out, maintaining distance between them as they moved down the alley. The formation would make it harder for anyone watching to connect them as a group, just three separate individuals happening to walk in the same direction. Following their lead, Sam maintained his position in the formation, keeping his pace casual despite the anxiety churning in his stomach.

Behind them, Miss Patterson demonstrated surprising agility for her age as she led Noah and Mia through the Henderson property. Mrs. Henderson, a retired English teacher with a passion for gardening, had created an elaborate landscape of shrubs, trellises, and winding stone paths that provided excellent concealment for their movement. "Mrs. Henderson was in the same book club as your grandmother," Miss Patterson explained to Leila as they navigated the garden. "They used to joke that her garden was designed for clandestine meetings because of all the gothic romances they read together." The random personal detail, shared in a moment of high tension, somehow humanized their situation, reminding them that even in extraordinary circumstances, they remained connected to the ordinary world of book clubs and neighborhood friendships.

By the time they reached Maple Street, the three separate groups had managed to avoid detection, converging near the back entrance of Faith Community Church, where Thompson served as a deacon. The church was a modest brick building with a small parking lot in the back, currently empty on a Saturday afternoon.

"The van is in the maintenance bay," Thompson explained, leading them to a small outbuilding at the edge of the property. Inside, a white passenger van with the church's name and logo on the side stood waiting.

"Not the most inconspicuous vehicle," Leila observed, eyeing the prominent 'Faith Community Church - Serving God's People' painted on the side panels.

Thompson shrugged. "Actually, it's perfect. Church vans are everywhere, and no one pays attention to them. Plus, it seats twelve, so we'll all fit comfortably." He retrieved the keys from a magnetic holder hidden beneath the rear bumper, unlocking the vehicle with practiced familiarity. "Now we wait for Dr. Rivera."

Olivia's evasion tactics had successfully shaken Detective Collins, at least temporarily. After a series of quick turns and doubling back through a shopping center parking lot, she'd confirmed no tail before making her way toward the church via a deliberately roundabout route. She parked three blocks away in a public lot, walking the remaining distance with the casual air of a Saturday shopper.

When she arrived at the church's rear entrance, relief visibly washed over the group. "They'll notice our absence soon," she warned as she joined them in the van. "We need to move quickly."

Thompson nodded, starting the engine. "I know a place we can go, a fishing cabin owned by Pastor Williams on the edge of Northwest River Park. Remote enough to avoid attention but close to where we need to be for tomorrow night's operation."

The van pulled away from the church, Thompson driving with careful adherence to speed limits and traffic rules. No behavior that might attract attention. Noah had already set up his laptop in the back, working to establish a secure connection. "I've got the tablet images uploaded to a protected server," he announced. "We can analyze them at the cabin. I've also prepared the recording equipment we discussed - modified GoPro cameras with encrypted transmission capabilities. Whatever we discover in those tunnels, we'll have documented evidence."

Mia was checking her medical supplies, mentally preparing for potential injuries they might need to treat. "I included flumazenil that could help with waking up the captives," she explained. "If they've been drugged as Thompson suggested, they might need help adjusting when we free them."

Leila had spread her grandfather's journal across her lap, comparing his notes with printouts of the tablet images Noah had provided. "There's something here about access points," she said, pointing to a hand-drawn map. "Alternative entrances to the tunnel system that might not be as heavily guarded."

The collaborative focus of the group, each person contributing their specific expertise to the shared mission, created a sense of purpose that transcended the fear they all undoubtedly felt. They weren't just teenagers and adults thrown together by circumstance; they had become a team, united by the urgent need to save four lives and possibly correct a centuries-old perversion of an ancient ritual.

As Thompson guided the church van toward the outskirts of Chesapeake, Olivia shared additional details from her meeting with the Guardians. "The students are definitely being held beneath the original Whitmore Plantation site, in what they call the 'Preparation Chamber.' They're in some form of suspended animation - alive but not fully conscious." The confirmation brought both relief and renewed urgency to their mission.

"And the ritual chamber?" Thompson asked as he kept his eyes on the road. "Location confirmed?"

Olivia nodded. "Deepest level of the tunnel system, directly beneath what was the main house foundation. The alignment peaks at midnight tomorrow, just as we suspected."

Noah looked up from his laptop. "Speaking of alignment, I've been cross-referencing astronomical data. This particular alignment is more significant than the usual twelve-year cycle. It's a conjunction of four celestial bodies that only occurs every 144 years - essentially, every twelfth cycle is especially powerful."

The information sent a chill through the group. "Which would explain the Guardians' heightened security and urgency this time," Miss Patterson observed. "If this alignment creates a stronger connection than usual, they'd be particularly determined to ensure the ritual proceeds as they've designed it."

Sam had been unusually quiet, processing everything they'd learned. Now he spoke up, his voice steady despite the tension evident in his posture. "So our plan needs to change. We're not just rescuing the four students anymore; we're potentially conducting the correct version of the ritual ourselves. How does that work exactly?"

All eyes turned to Olivia, who had captured the most complete information about the tablet. "According to what I gathered today, combined with James's message, the ritual requires the four archetypes positioned at cardinal points around a central focus. Not sacrificed, but united in purpose." She glanced at the stone Dr. Blackwood had given her. "And this stone somehow facilitates the proper connection - perhaps it needs to be placed at the center of the formation."

Leila was nodding, excitement building as she matched this description to her grandfather's notes. "That's consistent with what my grandfather theorized. He believed the ritual was meant to create a circuit of energy, connecting the four archetypes into a unified representation of humanity's potential."

The conversation continued as Thompson turned onto a narrow gravel road that wound through increasingly dense forest, eventually arriving at a small clearing where a rustic cabin stood beside a calm stretch of the Northwest River. "Pastor Williams' fishing retreat," he explained as they parked behind the cabin, concealing the van from the road. "He only uses it during fishing season, which doesn't start for another month."

CHAPTER TWENTY SEVEN
HIDDEN CABIN

The cabin was simple but adequate - two bedrooms, a main living area with a fireplace, and a basic kitchen. Solar panels on the roof provided limited electricity, enough to power lights and essential equipment. As they settled in, establishing a temporary command center on the cabin's wooden dining table, the full weight of their situation became increasingly clear. They were now fugitives of sorts, having fled police surveillance, preparing to infiltrate a secret facility controlled by some of Chesapeake's most powerful citizens. The danger was real and immediate, with lives hanging in the balance.

Yet despite the risks, a sense of rightness permeated their planning. This wasn't just about saving four students but correcting a fundamental wrong that had persisted for generations. Noah had his equipment spread across one end of the table, working to extract and enhance every detail from the tablet images. "I think I've found something important," he announced after nearly an hour of focused analysis. "The tablet doesn't just describe the positioning for the ritual; it includes warnings about misuse."

He turned his laptop so the others could see, pointing to a section of symbols arranged in a pattern resembling a cautionary border around the main text. "These symbols recur in sections that Dr. Blackwood's partial translation identified as warnings. And they're identical to markings found in the Ecuador site, according to Dr. Rivera's research."

Olivia leaned closer, recognizing similarities to photographs in James's files. "You're right. These appear to be warning indicators, possibly describing consequences of ritual misuse."

Miss Patterson, who had been cross-referencing historical texts she'd brought, looked up with concern. "If the ritual has been misused for centuries, corrupting its original purpose, what happens when it's suddenly corrected? After all this time, could there be... side effects to restoring the proper connection?" The question hung in the air, unanswerable with their current knowledge yet impossible to ignore.

Every action had consequences, and they were preparing to fundamentally alter a system that had operated, however perversely, for centuries. "We'll have to be prepared for anything," Thompson said finally, his practical military mindset asserting itself. "But the alternative is allowing four more young lives to be sacrificed, with more to follow every twelve years. Whatever the risks, they're worth taking."

As evening approached, they refined their plan, incorporating the new information about the ritual's true purpose. "We should limit the infiltration team," Thompson suggested, drawing on his tactical experience. "Smaller groups move faster and attract less attention. I propose that three of us enter the tunnel system to locate and extract the captives."

After the discussion, they settled on Thompson, Sam, and Leila as the primary infiltration team. Thompson's knowledge of the tunnels made him essential. Sam's connection to the bronze key inherited from his father gave him a practical role. Leila's familiarity with her grandfather's research and the tablet made their team well-rounded.

"The rest of us will establish a support position at the secondary tunnel entrance near the park boundary," Olivia continued, indicating a location on the map spread before them. "We'll be ready to receive the freed students and provide medical assistance if needed."

Noah, who had been working on his equipment throughout the discussion, presented small wireless earpieces to the infiltration team. "Communications devices," he explained. Secure frequency, minimal chance of interception. And these are the modified GoPro cameras." He handed each of them a small camera in a head-mount configuration. "They'll transmit back to my laptop in real time, recording everything you see and hear. If something happens to you, we'll still have the evidence."

The implications of that statement - that they might not all return from this mission - sobered the group momentarily. But the alternative was unthinkable, and they pushed forward with their preparations. Dinner was a simple affair of sandwiches and snacks from supplies Thompson had brought and eaten while continuing to analyze the tablet images and refine their approach. As night fell, they established a watch rotation, recognizing that the Guardians would be actively searching for them now that their absence from the Rivera house had certainly been discovered.

Thompson took the first watch, his military training making him the logical choice for the initial security assessment of their location. While the others continued working inside, he circled the cabin's perimeter, checking sight lines and potential approach routes, establishing mental markers to distinguish between normal forest sounds and possible intrusions. This routine, so familiar from his time in Vietnam, triggered memories he'd spent decades trying to suppress—the hyper-vigilance of jungle patrols, the weight of responsibility for others' lives, and the constant calculation of risk versus necessity. Yet strangely, the revival of these old habits brought a clarity, an almost welcome sense of purpose that had been missing from his decades of quiet custodial work.

Inside the cabin, Noah made a breakthrough with tablet translation, combining Dr. Blackwood's notes with symbols in Marcus Washington's journal and reference points from James Rivera's research. "I think I understand the core instruction now," he announced, drawing the others around his laptop. "The tablet describes a 'convergence of essences' - the four archetypes - creating a 'bridge of understanding' across the 'veil between realms.' The positioning is critical - each archetype at a cardinal point, with the facilitating stone at the center."

He pointed to a diagram he'd created based on the tablet's instructions. "When properly aligned, they create what translates roughly as 'the voice of humanity' - a unified representation that can communicate across the dimensional barrier."

Leila nodded excitedly, finding confirmation in her grandfather's notes. "That matches what my grandfather theorized. He believed the entity wasn't malevolent but simply different, operating according to perceptions and physics beyond our understanding. The ritual was designed by ancient cultures as a communication method, not a containment strategy."

Olivia considered this information, correlating it with what James had discovered in Ecuador. "And the Guardians corrupted this purpose, transforming communication into sacrifice to harness power for themselves."

The pieces were fitting together, creating a coherent alternative to the Guardians' narrative. But questions remained, particularly about the entity itself and what it might be trying to communicate.

"If my dad is right," Sam said, voicing what they were all thinking, "the entity is trying to warn us about something. What could be so important that communication attempts have persisted for centuries despite being corrupted?"

Miss Patterson looked up from the historical texts she'd been consulting. "Throughout history, major civilizational collapses have often been preceded by environmental changes or natural disasters. Perhaps the entity perceives such threats from a perspective we can't access - seeing patterns or approaching dangers beyond our current scientific understanding."

The hypothesis was plausible, aligning with the cross-cultural nature of the ritual sites James had identified globally. Different human civilizations, separated by vast distances, all establishing communication protocols with the same entity or type of entity, all focused on the same astronomical alignments. It suggested a coordinated effort to share information vital to human survival, which over time became corrupted by those who saw opportunities for personal gain.

Around midnight, Thompson returned from his final perimeter check to report all clear, and Olivia took over the watch. Under the canopy of stars visible through breaks in the forest cover, she patrolled the cabin's surroundings, her mind processing everything they'd learned while remaining alert for any sign of pursuit.

Inside, the atmosphere had shifted from active planning to quiet preparation for rest. They would need to be at full strength for tomorrow night's operation. Sleeping bags and blankets were distributed, creating makeshift beds in the cabin's limited space. Despite the physical discomfort and the tension of their situation, exhaustion eventually claimed most of them. Sam, however, found sleep elusive. He sat on the cabin's small porch, keeping his mother company during her watch, the bronze key turning over and over in his fingers as he contemplated what lay ahead. "Do you think Dad will make it back in time?" he asked softly, the question emerging from the quiet weight of uncertainty that had accompanied him since his father's disappearance.

Olivia considered her answer carefully, balancing hope against realism. "I don't know, Sam. If he's in Ecuador as the call suggested and the Guardians are monitoring transportation as he claimed, it would be difficult for him to reach Chesapeake by tomorrow night."

She saw the disappointment in her son's expression and added, "But your dad has always been resourceful. If anyone could find a way, it would be him." The conversation lapsed into a comfortable silence, mother and son united in their concern while also focused on the immediate challenges before them. After a while, Sam posed another question that had been troubling him. "The Guardians think we match the archetypes, just like Aaron, Sofia, Caleb, and Lily. Does that mean they've been watching us specifically? Evaluating us as potential... sacrifices?"

The question cut to the heart of Olivia's deepest fear - that Sam had been drawn into this dangerous situation not by random chance but by deliberate targeting. "From what Dr.

Blackwood told me, the Guardians maintain files on potential candidates well in advance. They would have identified promising students within days of our arrival." She hesitated, then decided Sam deserved the full truth. "And given your father's research, they may have been aware of you even before we moved here. Part of why they offered me the position could have been to bring you within their reach."

The revelation didn't shock Sam as much as she'd expected, suggesting he'd already considered this possibility. "That's messed up," he said finally, his understated teenage phrasing somehow perfect for the twisted situation they found themselves in. "So if we fail tomorrow, if we can't stop the ritual this time..."

"Then you guys might become their targets for the next cycle," Olivia confirmed, the reality of that threat stealing her resolve further. "Which is why failure isn't an option."

As the night deepened around them, the sounds of the forest created a natural symphony of rustling leaves and distant animal calls. Mother and son maintained their vigil together, each drawing strength from the other's presence.

When morning arrived, it brought renewed purpose and accelerated preparations. Thompson, who had taken the pre-dawn watch, reported that the area remained quiet around their location. But they all understood that the Guardians would be intensifying their search, particularly as the ritual's timing grew closer. Breakfast was a hurried affair of instant oatmeal and coffee prepared on the cabin's small propane stove. As they ate, they conducted a final review of their plans, equipment, and contingencies.

"The first phase begins at 9 PM," Thompson reminded them, indicating the timing on a hand-drawn schedule. "We'll approach through the Northwest River Park, using the service road access to reduce visibility. The infiltration team enters the secondary tunnel entrance at 9:30, proceeding to the holding area where the captives are located."

Leila had been studying her grandfather's maps of the tunnel system, committing the layout to memory in case they became separated. "According to this, the Preparation Chamber is approximately fifteen minutes from the entrance, assuming no resistance," she noted. "Then another ten minutes to reach the exit point where the support team will be waiting."

Mia, ever focused on the medical aspects, raised a concern. "What condition will the captives be in? If they've been sedated or drugged, they might not be able to walk unassisted."

The question triggered a cascade of practical considerations. How would they transport four potentially incapacitated teenagers through narrow tunnels while potentially evading pursuit? What if one or more required medical interventions before they could be moved? The infiltration team would need to be prepared for multiple scenarios, adding complexity to an already challenging operation.

"I've modified the medical kits to include stimulants that might help counteract sedation," Mia continued, demonstrating her thoughtfulness. "But we should be prepared for the possibility that they'll need to be carried."

Thompson nodded, making adjustments to their equipment list. "We'll find or maybe make a collapsible stretcher. It's lightweight and can be assembled quickly if needed." Practical problem-solving continued throughout the morning, each person contributing their expertise to anticipate challenges and develop solutions.

Noah finalized his communications setup, ensuring the cameras and earpieces were functioning perfectly. "The signal should penetrate up to fifty feet of earth and concrete," he explained. "Beyond that, we might experience interruptions. If that happens, the cameras will still record locally, so we won't lose the documentation."

Miss Patterson, drawing on her extensive knowledge of the Guardians' patterns, provided insights about potential security measures. "They typically use a combination of technology and human surveillance," she explained. "This includes electronic locks, motion sensors, and guards positioned at key junctions. But their overconfidence is a weakness—they've rarely been challenged directly, so they may not be prepared for a coordinated infiltration."

By mid-afternoon, their preparations were as complete as possible, given the limitations of their resources and information. Thompson suggested a few hours of rest before the operation, recognizing that physical and mental fatigue could be as dangerous as any external threat.

While the others attempted to nap or at least relax, Olivia found herself drawn to the small dock extending into the river behind the cabin. The water flowed calmly, indifferent to the human drama unfolding along its banks. She sat at the edge, feet dangling above the surface, trying to quiet her mind enough to focus clearly on what lay ahead. The weight of responsibility pressed heavily, not just for the four captured students or for Sam and his friends, but potentially for correcting a fundamental corruption that had claimed countless lives over centuries.

The scope of it seemed almost too vast to comprehend, yet the immediate actions required were concrete and specific. Find the captives. Free them. Reach the ritual chamber. Establish the proper configuration. Simple objectives masking incredibly complex challenges. A soft footstep on the dock alerted her to Thompson's approach. He sat beside her without speaking, his weathered face revealing the same mixture of determination and concern she felt within herself. "In Vietnam," he said after a while, his voice low and steady, "before an operation, I'd always try to find a quiet place like this. Somewhere to center myself, to remember why we were fighting, beyond the immediate mission objectives."

Olivia appreciated the parallel he was drawing, acknowledging the quasi-military nature of what they were preparing to undertake. "Did it help?" she asked.

Thompson considered the question, his gaze fixed on the distant shore. "Sometimes. Other times, nothing could quiet the fear. But I learned that fear isn't the enemy of courage—it's part of it. The ones who claimed they felt no fear were usually the first to break under pressure."

He glanced at her, his expression softening slightly. "Your husband understood that. When we spoke about his research and what he'd discovered in Ecuador, he was terrified of the implications. But he kept pushing forward because the truth mattered more than his comfort."

The mention of James brought a fresh wave of emotion that Olivia carefully contained. "Do you think he's really alive? That it was actually him on that call?"

Thompson nodded without hesitation. "It was him. I served with men for years in Vietnam; you learn to recognize a voice like you recognize a face. That was James Rivera, and he was trying to warn us about what's really happening beneath Pinecrest." The confirmation from someone who had no reason to offer false hope strengthened Olivia's resolve. If James had survived and was still fighting this battle from another front, she would ensure his efforts weren't in vain.

"Thank you," she said simply. "For everything you're doing. For not remaining silent this time."

Thompson's eyes reflected decades of regret but also newfound purpose. "Some debts can never be fully repaid," he said quietly. "But perhaps they can be honored through different actions."

As evening approached, they gathered for a final briefing, reviewing each phase of the operation one last time. The infiltration team—Thompson, Sam, and Leila—would enter the tunnel system and locate the captives. The support team— Olivia, Noah, Miss Patterson, and Mia—would establish a position at the secondary exit point, ready to receive the freed students and provide immediate assistance. "If everything goes according to plan, we'll have all four students extracted by 11 PM," Thompson summarized. "That gives us one hour to reach the ritual chamber and implement the correct configuration before the alignment peaks at midnight."

Noah distributed the final pieces of equipment—extra batteries for the cameras, backup communication devices, and small LED flashlights that could be attached to clothing for hands-free illumination. "The GoPros are fully charged and transmitting," he confirmed. "We'll be seeing everything you see, recording all of it as evidence."

Mia handed out the medical kits, providing last-minute instructions on using the stimulants and sedatives if necessary. "The blue capsules might help counteract whatever they've been given," she explained. "But be careful with dosing, start with half if they seem particularly weak."

Miss Patterson's contribution was knowledge—detailed briefings on the tunnel layout based on Marcus Washington's maps and her own research over decades. "The security patterns suggest rotation changes at the top of the hour," she noted. "That creates a potential window of reduced vigilance at 10 PM, which might be your best opportunity to access the Preparation Chamber."

Leila had been unusually quiet during the final preparations, and the weight of her role in the mission was evident in her focused expression. When the others finished their briefings, she spoke up, her voice steady despite the tension in her posture. "My grandfather spent years investigating the disappearances, documenting everything he could find about the Guardians and their rituals. He was forced into retirement before he could act on what he'd discovered." She looked around at each of them, her gaze settling finally on Thompson. "He would be grateful to know his work is finally being used to save lives."

The personal statement added emotional weight to their mission, reminding them that they were part of a lineage of resistance against the Guardians' corruption, a struggle that had claimed careers, reputations, and possibly lives over generations. As darkness fell, they loaded the essential equipment into the church van, leaving behind anything that wasn't absolutely necessary for the operation. The cabin had served its purpose as a temporary haven, but now they needed to position themselves for the critical phase of their mission.

With Thompson at the wheel, they drove carefully along back roads toward Northwest River Park, avoiding main thoroughfares where police might be watching for them. The park would normally be closed at this hour, but Thompson knew of a service entrance used by maintenance personnel that would provide access with minimal visibility. They parked the van in a secluded area near this entrance, concealing it beneath low-hanging branches and undergrowth. From there, they would proceed on foot to their respective positions. Before separating, they gathered in a tight circle for a final confirmation of the plan. No rousing speeches or dramatic declarations—just the quiet determination of people unified in purpose, aware of the dangers but committed to the necessity of their actions.

Thompson checked his watch; it was 8:45 PM. "Infiltration team moves out in fifteen minutes," he said, his voice low but clear. "Support team establishes position at the secondary exit and maintains communication. If anything goes wrong, if we lose contact for more than thirty minutes, implement the contingency plan."

The contingency plan was straightforward but difficult: if the infiltration team was captured or communication was lost, the support team would contact Detective Grace Chen, Noah's mother, providing her with all their evidence about the Guardians and the ritual. It wasn't ideal, potentially exposing their activities without guaranteeing intervention, but it was the best fallback they could establish with their limited resources.

Sam approached his mother before they separated, the bronze key secure in his pocket, Thompson's switchblade tucked into his boot. No words seemed adequate for the moment, so he simply hugged her tightly, trying to communicate everything he couldn't articulate—his love, his fear, his determination. Olivia returned the embrace with equal intensity, then pulled back to look him in the eyes. "You can do this," she said with quiet confidence. "You're braver than you know."

Then, with a professional shift that impressed Sam with its discipline, she turned to address the infiltration team. "Cameras on, communications check before you enter the tunnel. We'll be watching and listening. Good luck."

With that, they separated—the infiltration team heading toward the concealed tunnel entrance Thompson had identified from Marcus Washington's maps, the support team moving toward the secondary exit point where they would eventually receive the freed captives. As Sam followed Thompson and Leila through the darkened forest, navigating by the dim glow of their covered flashlights, he felt a strange calmness descend. The uncertainty and fear remained, but beneath them ran a current of rightness, of necessary action that transcended personal safety. Four lives hung in the balance tonight, with potentially countless more to follow in future cycles if they failed. The responsibility was enormous, but they carried it together, steps aligned in the darkness, moving toward whatever awaited them beneath Pinecrest.

CHAPTER TWENTY EIGHT
PREPPED AND READY

Sunday night descended upon Chesapeake with an unnatural stillness, as if the very air sensed the impending confrontation between ancient darkness and determined light. Pastor Williams's fishing cabin stood on the edge of Northwest River Park, its weathered exterior blending with the darkening shadows cast by towering pines. Inside, lamplight illuminated tense faces gathered around a rough-hewn table covered with maps, diagrams, and equipment. The scent of brewing coffee mingled with the cabin's permanent aroma of old wood and fish tales, creating an oddly comforting backdrop for the dangerous mission ahead. Sam Rivera checked his watch for the fifth time in as many minutes-8:57 PM.

In just three minutes, they would begin the operation that would determine the fate of four missing students and potentially end a cycle of disappearances that had haunted Pinecrest for over a century. "Final equipment check," Thompson announced, his weathered hands distributing earpieces to each team member. The former janitor moved with unexpected precision, his military training evident in every efficient gesture.

"Testing communications," Noah responded, adjusting settings on his laptop where multiple screens displayed security camera feeds, building schematics, and a tracking map with seven blinking dots representing each team member. "Everyone, tap your earpiece twice when you hear me." A series of gentle taps followed as each person confirmed their communication link was functioning.

"Medical supplies ready," Mia reported, kneeling beside a duffel bag containing sedatives, stimulants, and basic trauma equipment she'd assembled with guidance from her father's medical texts. Her hands moved confidently through the inventory, belying the anxiety visible in her tight expression.

Dr. Olivia Rivera stood slightly apart from the group, studying the strange artifact Dr. Blackwood had given her during their clandestine meeting at Watson's Diner yesterday morning. The stone disk, no larger than her palm, was etched with symbols matching those shown on the Whitmore Tablet during her orientation with the Guardians. "The true translation," Dr. Blackwood had whispered across the diner table, "reveals that the ritual was never meant to require sacrifice. It was about connection—forming a circle to channel energy back into the earth, not taking life to appease some dimensional monster. The Guardians corrupted the meaning to gain power for themselves." Turning the disk over in her hands now, Olivia struggled to reconcile its ancient significance with the very modern rescue operation unfolding around her.

Eleanor Patterson approached Olivia quietly, her seventy-six years carried with the dignity of someone making peace with their final mission. "It will work," she said, nodding toward the disk. "Marcus Washington believed the original ritual was about harmony, not sacrifice. The Guardians perverted it to maintain their control."

Leila finished checking her backpack, her grandfather's journal securely tucked inside alongside a digital camera, and the folded pages of Thompson's updated tunnel maps. At fourteen, she appeared impossibly young for such a dangerous undertaking, yet her eyes held a determination that transcended her years. "We should get moving," she said, glancing toward Thompson. "The shift change happens at 11:00 PM, which gives us less than two hours to get into position."

Thompson nodded gravely, the weight of decades of inaction visible in the set of his shoulders. For the first time since Vietnam, he was moving toward danger rather than away from it. "Remember the plan," he said, his voice steady despite the emotion beneath it. "Infiltration team—myself, Sam, and Leila—enters through the maintenance tunnel access point in Section C of Northwest River Park. We proceed to the holding cells, neutralize any guards, and extract the captives."

Noah swiveled in his chair, the blue glow from his laptop screen illuminating his focused expression. "Support team monitors from here. I'll guide you through the tunnels using thermal imaging from the satellite feed Captain Harrison provided. Dr. Rivera, Miss Patterson, and Mia will prepare the medical station and be ready to receive the students when you bring them out."

Sam caught his mother's eye across the room, a silent conversation passing between them. They had argued intensely about who would be on the infiltration team, with Olivia initially insisting she should go instead of her son. However, Sam's knowledge of the tunnels, combined with Thompson's assessment that a smaller team had better chances of moving undetected, had eventually won out. "Be careful," she mouthed to him now, fighting to maintain her professional composure while maternal fear tightened around her heart.

Miss Patterson stood by the window, peering out at the darkness that seemed to press against the glass. "It's time," she announced, her voice carrying the quiet authority of someone who had waited decades for this moment. The atmosphere in the cabin shifted instantly, conversation ceasing as everyone moved into final preparations with practiced coordination.

Thompson shouldered a backpack containing tools for bypassing electronic locks, rope, and basic defensive equipment. At the same time, Sam and Leila double-checked the small packs they would carry. As they prepared to depart, Thompson paused at the doorway, turning back to face those who would remain behind. "If we're not back by 1:00 AM, contact Detective Chen with the evidence package. Don't attempt to follow us."

The unspoken implication hung heavily in the air: if the infiltration team wasn't back by then, they likely wouldn't be coming back at all. Outside, the night air carried the earthy scent of the river and the distant chorus of spring peepers, an incongruously peaceful backdrop for their clandestine mission. Thompson led Sam and Leila along a narrow path that wound through dense underbrush toward the park's maintenance area. They moved silently, three shadows barely distinguishable from the darkness surrounding them. As the cabin disappeared from view, Sam felt the weight of their mission settle fully upon his shoulders. Somewhere beneath their feet, four students waited in drugged captivity for a ritual that would claim their lives before dawn.

The knowledge propelled him forward, each step a defiance against the century of silence that had allowed the Guardians to continue their horrific tradition. Noah established final connections inside the cabin with the satellite uplink Captain Harrison had arranged. The retired CIA director had been skeptical when Thompson first contacted him, but the evidence they'd assembled—historical records of disappearances, photographic documentation from Washington's journal, and thermal imaging showing human forms beneath Northwest River Park—had been compelling enough to secure limited support.

"Infiltration team moving into position," Noah reported, tracking the three blinking dots representing Thompson, Sam, and Leila as they approached the park's maintenance shed. "All systems online."

CHAPTER TWENTY NINE
INFILTRATION

Mia arranged the makeshift medical area, transforming the cabin's small bedroom into a recovery station with four cots and monitoring equipment borrowed from her dad's home clinic. Her hands moved with practiced efficiency, but her mind raced with anxiety. *Would the students be conscious enough to move under their own power? Would the drugs the Guardians used have lasting effects?* She had prepared counter-agents based on Thompson's descriptions, but without knowing the exact compounds used, she could only hope they would be effective.

Dr. Rivera watched the tracking screen over Noah's shoulder, her historian's mind trying to process the reality that she was witnessing the culmination of a pattern that stretched back over a century.

"They've reached the access point," Noah announced, his fingers flying across the keyboard to enhance the satellite imagery. "Thompson is disabling the electronic lock now."

Outside the maintenance shed, Thompson worked methodically on the keypad that secured the entrance. Despite his age, his fingers moved with the precision of someone well-versed in covert operations. "Military intelligence trained us for this kind of thing in '69," he murmured to Sam and Leila as the lock disengaged with a soft click. "Never thought I'd be using it again, especially not back home."

The door swung open silently, revealing a small room filled with park maintenance equipment—leaf blowers, grass trimmers, and bags of fertilizer stacked against the walls. Thompson moved directly to the back corner, shifting aside a metal storage cabinet to expose a trapdoor set into the concrete floor.

"This wasn't on any of the official blueprints," he explained softly as he knelt to examine the lock. "Found it by accident in '83 while helping the park service install new drainage systems. Connects directly to the tunnel network beneath the old Whitmore property." Working carefully, he bypassed the sizeable padlock with tools from his pack, lifting the heavy door to reveal a dark shaft with metal rungs embedded in the concrete wall. The smell that rose from the opening was ancient and damp, earth and stone and something else— something that raised the fine hairs on Sam's arms and neck.

"I'll go first," Thompson whispered, already lowering himself onto the ladder. "Sam follows, then Leila. Move quietly and watch for motion sensors at the bottom." One by one, they descended into darkness, the beam of Thompson's flashlight illuminating the rough stone walls of a tunnel that predated Pinecrest, the Whitmore Plantation, and perhaps even colonial settlement. Sam felt the weight of history pressing down as they reached the bottom, standing in a passageway barely tall enough for Thompson to stand upright. "Tunnel access confirmed," Thompson murmured into his earpiece. "Moving to checkpoint Alpha."

Noah's voice came through clearly: "Copy that. Thermal imaging shows two heat signatures approximately fifty meters ahead—likely guards at the first intersection. The holding cells appear to be on the level below your current position, accessed through the central chamber."

Back at the cabin, Dr. Rivera studied the thermal images with growing concern. "Those signatures in the holding cells are too still," she noted, pointing to four prone forms visible as orange-yellow shapes against the blue-purple background. "Their core temperatures are lower than normal, consistent with sedation."

Noah adjusted the satellite feed, zooming in for a clearer image. "There's a fifth signature I didn't notice before," he said suddenly, pointing to a slightly separated form in an adjacent chamber. "Someone else is being held there."

Olivia's heart clenched painfully in her chest. "James," she whispered, hardly daring to hope. "It might be James." In the tunnels, Thompson led Sam and Leila through the narrow passage with the confidence of someone following a map etched in memory. Each step was carefully placed to avoid loose stones or puddles that might betray their presence. The walls around them were hewn from the earth itself in some sections, while others showed the deliberate stone masonry of colonial construction. Decades of moisture had encouraged the growth of pale fungi that cast an eerie phosphorescent glow, providing just enough natural light to discern the tunnel's dimensions.

"Stop," Thompson whispered suddenly, raising his hand. Ahead, a faint glow indicated artificial lighting. "Checkpoint Alpha. Guards ahead." He motioned for Sam and Leila to press themselves against the wall, then removed something from his pack—a small canister with a modified cap. "Smoke grenade," he explained softly. "Non-toxic, but it'll create enough confusion for us to move past. Keep your bandanas ready."

Sam and Leila pulled bandanas over their noses and mouths as Thompson prepared the grenade. With practiced movements, he released the pin, counted silently to three, and then tossed the canister around the corner toward the intersection. A soft hiss followed, then surprised shouts as thick white smoke billowed through the passage.

"Now," Thompson urged, already moving forward. They rushed through the choking white cloud, Sam's eyes watering despite the protection of the bandana. Through the haze, he glimpsed two figures in dark clothing, hands raised to shield their faces as they coughed and stumbled. Before the guards could recover, Thompson was upon them, applying pressure to specific points on their necks that rendered them unconscious within seconds. "Checkpoint Alpha secured," he reported into his earpiece, already zip-tying the guards' hands and feet. "Two hostiles neutralized, non-lethal."

Noah's voice crackled with static: "Copy that. Proceed to checkpoint Bravo. The central chamber should be twenty meters ahead of your current path."

Leila consulted the tunnel map, confirming their position against her grandfather's notes. "The holding cells are accessed through the floor of the central chamber," she whispered. "There should be a spiral staircase leading down to the second level."

The tunnel widened as they approached the central chamber, ancient stone giving way to more recent construction. The space they entered was circular, its domed ceiling supported by columns inscribed with the same symbols Sam had seen in the hidden room at Pinecrest. In the center of the floor, a large circular pattern matched the design from Dr. Rivera's artifact, with four smaller circles positioned at the cardinal points, all connected by lines to a central point.

"The ritual chamber," Thompson confirmed grimly. "This is where they will bring the students for the final ceremony." Leila pointed to a metal hatch on the floor near the far wall. "There, that must lead to the holding cells." As they approached the hatch, a low humming became audible, machinery of some kind operating beneath them. Thompson examined the lock mechanism, his expression troubled.

"Electronic," he muttered. "More sophisticated than I expected."

Noah's voice came through their earpieces, tense but controlled: "I'm picking up increased activity on the thermal scan. Multiple heat signatures are moving toward your position from the north tunnel. ETA three minutes."

Thompson worked frantically on the lock, connecting a small device from his pack to the keypad. "Bypass sequence initiated," he reported. "Thirty seconds to access."

The humming below grew louder, and Sam felt a growing sense of urgency that transcended their immediate danger. Something was happening in the holding cells—something related to the approaching ritual.

"Twenty seconds," Thompson counted down, watching the device cycle through possible combinations. "Fifteen... ten..." A sudden shout echoed from the north tunnel—they had been discovered. "Five seconds," Thompson continued, his voice steady despite the approaching threat. "Three, two, one— " The lock disengaged with a heavy clunk, and Thompson heaved the hatch open to reveal a spiral metal staircase descending into pulsing, blue-tinted darkness. "Go," he ordered, already turning to face the north tunnel, something in his hands that Sam recognized with shock as a handgun. "I'll hold them off. Get the captives."

Leila was already descending the stairs, but Sam hesitated. "We stick together," he insisted. "That was the plan."

Thompson's weathered face softened briefly. "Plans change, son. Those kids need you more than I do. Now go, I'll be right behind you." The confidence in his voice didn't reach his eyes, and Sam knew with sudden clarity that Thompson was preparing to make a stand— perhaps his final one.

"Thompson— " Sam began, but the older man cut him off.

"Go," he repeated, positioning himself with a clear line of sight to the north tunnel. "Don't make the same mistake I did with Jenkins. Don't freeze when others need you." The reference to the young medic Thompson had failed to save in Vietnam, struck Sam like a physical blow. With a final nod of understanding, he turned and followed Leila down the spiral staircase, leaving Thompson alone to face whatever came from the darkness.

CHAPTER THIRTY
HOLDING CELL DISCOVERY

The holding cells were arranged in a circular pattern around a central monitoring station, just as Washington's journal had described. Blue light pulsed from equipment that hummed with increasing intensity, casting eerie shadows across the unconscious forms visible behind glass walls.

"There," Leila whispered, pointing to the first cell. Inside, a teenage boy lay on a narrow cot, an IV line running from his arm to a bag of clear fluid hanging above. "Aaron Mitchell." They moved quickly to the locking mechanism—a simpler design than the hatch above, requiring only a key card that Thompson had taken from one of the unconscious guards. The door slid open with a pneumatic hiss, allowing them access to the brilliant mind the Guardians had selected as their "scholar."

Mia's voice came through their earpieces, professional despite her youth: "Check his pulse and pupil response. We need to know how deeply he's sedated."

Sam placed two fingers against Aaron's neck, finding a slow but steady pulse. When he lifted one eyelid, the pupil contracted sluggishly in response to his flashlight. "He's alive but heavily sedated," he reported. "Mia, how do we disconnect this IV safely?"

Her calm instructions guided him through clamping and removing the line, while Leila moved to the next cell containing Sofia Alvarez, the artist. The same procedure was repeated, Sofia's breathing more rapid than Aaron's but still within concerning ranges.

As they worked to free Caleb Johnson from the third cell, a distant sound of scuffling reached them through the open hatch above. The unmistakable sound of a gunshot echoed through the chamber, followed by Thompson's strained voice over the earpiece: "Multiple hostiles engaged. Holding position, but won't be able to maintain it for long. Hurry."

Sam worked faster, adrenaline sharpening his focus as he and Leila moved to the fourth cell containing Lily Robertson. The healer's slight form seemed especially vulnerable beneath the harsh blue lighting, her face pale but peaceful in unconsciousness. "All four captives secured," Sam reported into his earpiece. "But they're completely non-responsive. We can't move them without help."

Noah's voice came back immediately: "There's a fifth heat signature in a separate chamber to your east. Slightly higher temperature than the others–possibly less sedated."

Leila was already moving toward the indicated direction, finding a heavy door marked "SPECIAL CONTAINMENT." The key card granted them access, revealing a smaller room with a single occupant strapped to a metal examination table. Sam instantly recognized him even in the blue-tinted darkness, even with days of beard growth and hollowed cheeks. "Dad," he gasped, rushing forward. Dr. James Rivera's eyelids fluttered at the sound of his son's voice, a low groan escaping his lips as consciousness began to return.

"Sam?" he whispered, voice rough from disuse. "How... where...?"

"Dad, it's me," Sam confirmed, quickly working to release the restraints that held his father to the table. "We found you. We're getting everyone out."

Dr. Rivera struggled to focus, fighting against whatever drugs remained in his system. "The ritual," he managed, grasping Sam's arm with surprising strength. "They can't complete it. The translation... wrong..."

Leila appeared in the doorway, her expression urgent. "Sam, we need to move. I can hear more people coming." The sounds of conflict above had intensified, Thompson's periodic updates becoming shorter and more strained. With Leila's help, Sam supported his father as they returned to the main holding area, where the four students remained unconscious on their cots.

"Dad, we can't carry all five of you," Sam said desperately. "Can you walk?" James Rivera forced himself to stand straighter, shaking his head as if to clear it. "Yes," he said, his voice growing stronger with each passing second.

"The drugs they used on me were designed to keep me aware but unable to move. They... they wanted me to witness the ritual, to see what would happen to those who interfered with their plans." He stumbled toward the nearest captive, Aaron Mitchell, and checked the boy's vital signs with practiced movements. "We need to counteract the sedatives," he concluded. "They've been preparing them for days, gradually deepening the trance state."

Mia's voice came through the earpieces: "Dr. Rivera, I have flumazenil and epinephrine along with other counter-agents in the medical kit. Would any of those work?" James looked around in confusion until Sam tapped his own earpiece in explanation. "Yes," he answered, speaking toward Sam's device. "Flumazenil would help, but we need to be careful with the dosage. Too much could send them into shock."

Another gunshot echoed from above, followed by Thompson's voice, now clearly strained: "Can't hold position much longer. Multiple hostiles, armed. You need an exit strategy now."

CHAPTER THIRTY ONE
REVIVAL AND ESCAPE

Noah's urgent response followed: "Thermal shows at least six hostiles converging on Thompson's position. There's another exit, a southeast tunnel that should connect to the old storm drain system. It can lead you to the river about half a kilometer from the cabin."

Leila was already consulting her map, tracing the potential escape route with her finger. "He's right," she confirmed. "But we still can't move four unconscious teenagers and Dr. Rivera quickly enough to escape."

James looked around the chamber, his gaze settling on a cabinet marked "MEDICAL" near the monitoring station. "There," he said, moving toward it with increasing steadiness. They keep emergency supplies here, including stimulants for the final phase of the ritual. The Guardians need the sacrifices to be conscious for the ceremony to work."

The cabinet yielded exactly what they needed: pre-filled syringes labeled "REVIVAL COMPOUND" with each student's name written in neat handwriting. "This will counteract the sedatives temporarily," James explained, already administering a dose to Aaron. "It won't last more than an hour, but it should give them enough awareness to move with assistance."

Sam relayed the information to Mia, confused about how he could help, not realizing that he was his dad's voice.

"I don't know what is in those syringes," said Mia. "But I think you should be able to add the flumazenil to their IV." Mia frantically looked up dosage amounts on her computer. "According to what you described, I believe you can give each of them 1 milligram over 30 seconds, and it should help wake them up. I don't think it's too much and should work pretty quickly."

"Dad, Mia says that you can use 1 milligram of the flumazenil by putting it in the IV for 30 seconds," Sam said. "She did some calculations and thinks it won't hurt them."

"Got it," James said, breathing heavy, still groggy from his ordeal. He pulled out the bottle of flumazenil, found four packaged syringes, and extracted 1 milligram in each. He started to slowly put the medication into the injection port for each IV, counting to 30 as he slowly injected.

CHAPTER THIRTY TWO
ESCAPING A FAILED RESCUE

Sam contacted Noah while his father worked: "My dad's trying to revive the students, but we still need to extract Thompson before we can escape." Above them, the sounds of conflict had ceased, replaced by an ominous silence that suggested either Thompson had prevailed or, more likely, had been overwhelmed. "I'll go check on him," Sam decided, drawing the pocketknife Thompson had given him from his pocket. "Dad, you and Leila get the students ready to move. I'll be right back."

Before anyone could object, Sam was already climbing the spiral staircase, moving as silently as his racing heart would allow. He emerged into the central chamber to find Thompson kneeling on the floor, hands bound behind his back, surrounded by four figures in dark clothing. Detective Collins stood before him, pistol aimed at the janitor's head. "You've proven remarkably resilient for a man your age," Collins was saying, his tone conversational despite the violence it promised. "But your interference ends here. Where are the others?"

Thompson's bloodied face remained impassive, his silence a continuation of the defiance he'd shown in holding the tunnel entrance. Collins sighed theatrically, adjusting his grip on the weapon. "You know what happens to those who interfere with the Guardians' work. Surely, you understand that some sacrifices are necessary for the greater good."

From his position at the top of the staircase, partially concealed by shadow, Sam assessed the situation with growing despair. Four armed men against his small switchblade presented impossible odds, yet he couldn't leave Thompson to his fate. As Collins continued his monologue, Sam noticed something his father had pressed into his hand before he ascended, one of the syringes from the medical cabinet.

A desperate plan formed in his mind. Moving with deliberate slowness, he unscrewed the cap from the syringe and then waited for his moment. It came when one of the guards shifted position, temporarily blocking Collins's line of sight to the staircase entrance. In that instant, Sam darted forward, driven by the same instinct that had propelled Thompson to act after decades of passivity. Before the guards could react, Sam had plunged the syringe into the nearest one's neck, depressing the plunger fully before diving toward Thompson.

The effect was instantaneous and terrifying. The guard convulsed violently, then began screaming, his body arching as the revival compound, designed to counteract days of specialized sedation, flooded his system with overwhelming stimulation. In the chaos that followed, Sam managed to reach Thompson, slicing through his restraints with the pocketknife while the other guards struggled to control their thrashing colleague.

"Run!" Sam urged, helping Thompson to his feet. But the older man stumbled, his leg clearly injured from the earlier confrontation. "Go," Thompson insisted, pushing Sam toward a different tunnel than the one they had entered through.

"Southeast passage, like Noah said. I'll create a diversion." Before Sam could protest, Thompson had lunged toward the disoriented guards, tackling one to the ground with surprising strength for his age. "Go!" he shouted again, grappling with the guard as Collins raised his weapon. Sam hesitated only a fraction of a second longer, torn between loyalty and necessity, before racing back to the staircase. The sound of another gunshot followed him down into the holding cells, where he found his father and Leila had managed to rouse all four captives to varying states of consciousness. Aaron Mitchell sat upright on his cot, blinking rapidly as his brilliant mind struggled to process his surroundings. Sofia Alvarez stood shakily, supported by Leila, while Caleb Johnson and Lily Robertson remained seated but aware, their confused expressions giving way to fear as the gunshot echoed from above.

"Thompson's been captured," Sam reported breathlessly. "Collins and at least three guards. They're right above us. We need to move now, southeast tunnel." James nodded grimly, already helping Aaron to his feet. "Lily, can you walk?" he asked the girl, who nodded hesitantly, her healer's instinct prompting her to check on Caleb beside her immediately.

"Southeast tunnel leads to the river," Leila confirmed, consulting her map. "But it's a narrow passage, we'll have to move single file, and it hasn't been used in decades."

They had no choice. With James supporting Aaron, Leila helping Sofia, and Sam assisting both Caleb and Lily, they moved toward a narrow archway on the eastern side of the holding area.

Behind them, heavy footsteps and voices could be heard descending the spiral staircase. "Hurry," Sam urged, ushering the others ahead of him as he prepared to defend their retreat if necessary. The southeast tunnel was even narrower than the main passage they had entered through, its ceiling so low that James had to stoop to avoid hitting his head.

They moved as quickly as the recovering students could manage, guided by flashlights and the increasingly urgent instructions from Noah through their earpieces. "You're headed in the right direction," he confirmed. "But thermal is showing pursuit–four signatures about fifty meters behind you and closing."

The ancient tunnel twisted and turned, occasionally branching into smaller offshoots that would have been easy to get lost in without Leila's map. Water seeped through cracks in the stone walls, forming slippery patches that further slowed their progress. Despite the revival compound, the four students struggled to maintain awareness, occasionally stumbling or stopping in confusion. "Keep moving," James encouraged them. "Just a little further." He seemed to be regaining his strength with every passing minute, his protective instinct toward the disoriented teenagers overriding his own physical limitations. After what felt like hours but was only five minutes, they reached a junction where the tunnel widened slightly.

CHAPTER THIRTY THREE
LOCKED IN

Ahead, a rusted metal grate blocked their path, the entrance to the storm drain system Noah had mentioned. "It's locked," Leila reported, examining the heavy padlock securing the grate. Behind them, flashlight beams and voices grew closer. They were trapped between their pursuers and the locked exit. "Stand back," James said suddenly, removing something from the heel of his shoe, a small package wrapped in oilcloth. Inside was a compact object that Sam recognized immediately as an explosive device, similar to what his dad showed him during one Fourth of July in Richmond. "Standard excavation equipment," James explained, already working to position it around the padlock. "Focused charge, minimal blast radius. Everyone, back around the corner."

They retreated as instructed, the four students huddling together in confusion while James set the device. A muted thump followed, then the sound of metal hitting stone as the destroyed lock fell away. "Now!" James called, already helping Aaron through the newly opened passage.

One by one, they squeezed through the grate into the storm drain beyond-a large concrete tunnel with a shallow stream of water flowing through its center. They had barely cleared the opening when flashlights illuminated the junction behind them. "Stop right there!" Collins's voice echoed through the stone passageway. "There's nowhere to go!"

Rather than responding, James urged them forward, deeper into the drainage system. "The river is less than one hundred meters ahead," he encouraged. "Once we reach it, they won't be able to track us easily." A shot rang out, the bullet ricocheting off concrete well above their heads, a warning, not meant to hit them, but the message was clear. The next one wouldn't miss. Sofia stumbled, nearly falling into the shallow water before Leila caught her arm. "I can't," the young artist gasped, her enhanced consciousness already beginning to fade as the revival compounds wore off. "So tired..."

Caleb Johnson, the natural leader even in his compromised state, moved to help support Sofia from the other side. "Together," he insisted, his voice gaining strength. "All of us together." The gesture inspired the others. Aaron and Lily drew closer as they continued their desperate flight through the dark tunnel. Behind them, splashing footsteps indicated their pursuers had made it through the grate and were closing the distance. The drain tunnel gradually widened as it approached its outlet, the sound of the Northwest River growing louder ahead. Fresh air carried the scent of mud and vegetation, a promise of freedom that energized their final push. They emerged onto a concrete apron where the storm drain emptied into the river, moonlight reflecting off the dark water before them.

CHAPTER THIRTY FOUR
SACRIFICED DIVERSION

"Which way?" Leila asked urgently, consulting her map. James pointed downstream, where the river curved around a wooded peninsula. "The cabin is about half a mile that way, but we can't risk leading them directly to it. We need to create a false trail."

From their earpieces came Noah's voice, less clear now that they were outside but still audible: "Backup is on the way. Captain Harrison contacted local FBI assets when Thompson missed his check-in. ETA twelve minutes to your current position."

Twelve minutes might as well be twelve hours, given how quickly their pursuers were gaining on them and how rapidly the four students were fading back toward unconsciousness as the revival compound wore off.

"There," James said suddenly, pointing to a small dock about fifty meters downstream where a rowboat was tied. "If we can reach that boat, we can cross to the other side and double back to the cabin." They moved along the riverbank as quickly as their bedraggled group could manage. Sam and Leila practically carried Lily and Aaron, while James and Caleb supported Sofia between them. Behind them, Collins and his men emerged from the storm drain, immediately spotting their quarry in the moonlight.

"Stop, or we'll shoot!" Collins called, his weapon raised. The threat spurred them to greater speed, James positioning himself between the Guardians and the teenagers as they stumbled toward the boat. They had almost reached the dock when a shot rang out, the bullet striking the water just inches from where they stood.

"Next one won't miss," Collins warned, advancing steadily along the bank. James motioned for the others to continue to the boat while he turned to face their pursuers, empty hands raised. "This ends tonight, Collins," he called, his voice carrying clearly across the water. "You've maintained this perversion for too long."

Collins laughed, the sound stripped of humor. "You still don't understand, Rivera. The ritual doesn't serve us; we serve it. Without the sacrifice, the barrier weakens. You've seen the evidence yourself in Ecuador."

James shook his head, backing slowly toward the dock where Sam and the others were struggling to untie the boat. "I saw evidence of your organization's global reach, manipulating similar geological formations for your own benefit. The original tablet never mentioned sacrifice, which was your translation, designed to maintain your power through fear."

Collins's expression hardened, his weapon still trained on James. "You're too late anyway. The alignment peaks at midnight–less than two hours from now. Even if you escape with these four, we can get replacements. The ritual will be completed." Behind Collins, his men had spread out along the bank, effectively cutting off any retreat back toward the storm drain. Sam had managed to untie the boat and was helping the increasingly disoriented students aboard, but it was clear they wouldn't all fit. The small craft could hold four comfortably, perhaps five at most, but not all seven of them.

"Dad," Sam called urgently, "we have to go now!" James continued his slow retreat, keeping Collins's attention focused on him rather than the boat. "You know your justification is based on a deliberate mistranslation," he called to Collins. "How many children have been sacrificed because of that lie?"

The distraction worked, Collins advancing angrily toward James while Sam helped Lily, the last of the four students, into the boat. "You weren't there when the barrier nearly broke in '37," Collins snarled. "My grandfather was. He saw what came through the cracks, saw what happens when the hunger isn't appeased." While Collins focused on James, Sam had managed to position the boat for rapid departure, with Leila already aboard, steadying the weakening students.

They had room for one more, either Sam or his father, but not both. The realization hit them simultaneously, father and son exchanging a look of understanding across the short distance that separated them.

"Go," James mouthed, giving an almost imperceptible nod. Sam shook his head desperately, unwilling to leave his father behind after just finding him.

James made the decision for him, suddenly lunging toward Collins with arms outstretched. The unexpected move caught the detective off guard, causing him to stumble backward as James crashed into him. "Now, Sam!" James shouted, grappling with Collins while his men raced toward the commotion. "Get them to safety!" In that moment, Sam faced the same choice Thompson had confronted so many years ago in the same paralysis, threatening to take him to the spot as someone he cared about called for help. But unlike Thompson with Jenkins, Sam moved, pushing the boat away from the dock with a powerful shove before leaping into it. The current immediately caught them, carrying them toward the center of the river as shots rang out from the bank.

Leila had taken control of the oars, rowing with all her might, seemingly possessed by five grown men, despite her size, steering them toward the opposite shore while Sam crouched low, shielding the semi-conscious students with his body. On the bank behind them, James had managed to disarm Collins in their struggle, the detective's weapon splashing into the shallow water at the shore's edge. But the other Guardians were closing in, their flashlights illuminating the scene as James broke free and sprinted along the bank, drawing their hunt away from the boat's trajectory.

"Dad!" Sam called desperately as his father disappeared into the underbrush, followed closely by Collins and his men. "Heading your way," Leila reported into her earpiece, her voice strained with the effort of rowing. "Four students secure but fading fast. Dr. Rivera is creating a diversion on the east bank."

Noah's response came back immediately: "Copy that. Support team moving to extraction point Charlie. FBI assets vectoring to your last GPS signal now." Sam trained his flashlight on the four students huddled at the bottom of the boat, their conditions deteriorating rapidly as the compounds wore off. Aaron's eyes were already closed again, his brilliant mind succumbing to the sedatives still in his system. Sofia murmured incoherently, artistic hands twitching as if painting in her semi-conscious state. Caleb maintained awareness the longest, his natural leadership extending to this most desperate situation, but even he was fighting a losing battle against the drugs.

"Stay with us," Sam urged them, patting Lily's cheek gently when her eyes began to close. "We're almost there." The reality was more complex; they were still minutes away from the extraction point, and their passengers might be fully unconscious by then.

CHAPTER THIRTY FIVE
ILLUMINATED RESCUE

Something odd was happening in the dark water around them. A faint luminescence seemed to be spreading beneath the surface, tendrils of pale blue light following their boat like curious fingers reaching up from the depths. "Leila," Sam whispered, gesturing toward the water.

She followed his gaze, her rowing faltering momentarily as she observed the phenomenon. "It's the same as the marking on the floor," she realized. "The same pattern, forming in the water around us." The glowing pattern expanded, its circular shape now unmistakable as it surrounded their small craft. Within the main circle, four smaller circles of light pulsed at positions corresponding to where each student sat.

"It's responding to them," Sam said with growing alarm. "To the four archetypes—scholar, artist, leader, healer." As if in confirmation, the light intensified beneath each student, tendrils rising from the water to wrap around the boat in a spectral embrace. Rather than feeling threatening, however, the phenomenon carried a sense of protection; the boat moved more swiftly through the water despite Leila's slowing strokes.

Back at the cabin, Noah tracked their progress on his laptop, and the strange energy pattern was visible even on the thermal imaging as an anomalous cold spot in the river.

"Something's happening," he reported to Dr. Rivera and Miss Patterson, who had been preparing to move to the extraction point. "The boat is accelerating, but there's an unusual energy signature surrounding it."

Dr. Rivera studied the screen, the stone disk from Dr. Blackwood warm in her hand as if responding to what they were seeing. "The original ritual is asserting itself," she whispered, a historian witnessing ancient forces awakening in real-time. "The true purpose was never sacrifice, it was protection."

Miss Patterson nodded slowly, her eyes reflecting a lifetime of accumulated knowledge. "Marcus Washington believed the four archetypes were meant to channel energy back into the earth, creating harmony rather than taking life. Perhaps the river itself is recognizing them."

Mia, who had been monitoring the medical equipment, looked up with concern. "Their vital signs are fading on the trackers," she reported. "We must reach them with the counter-agents as soon as possible."

Dr. Rivera made a quick decision. "Noah, stay here and coordinate with the FBI assets tracking James. Mia, Miss Patterson, and I will move to the extraction point, Charlie, now."

On the river, the luminescent pattern had completely encircled the boat, accelerating their movement toward the western shore where a small inlet offered a natural landing place. The four students were now fully unconscious again, the temporary effects of the revival compound completely dissipated. As they approached the bank, Sam could see flashlights moving through the trees—the support team arriving to help.

Leila guided the boat into the shallow water of the inlet, jumping out to pull it firmly onto the muddy shore. "We made it," she breathed, exhaustion evident in her voice.

Dr. Rivera emerged from the trees, rushing toward them with Mia close behind, a medical kit already open. "Sam!" she called, relief breaking through her professional demeanor as she embraced her son briefly before turning her attention to the unconscious teenagers. "Help me get them to the cabin," she instructed as Mia began administering counter-agents to the sedatives.

Miss Patterson arrived moments later, her age seemingly forgotten, as she moved to help lift Lily from the boat. Together, they carried the students one by one up the sloping bank toward the waiting cabin, leaving the luminescent water behind. However, Sam noticed traces of the blue glow seemed to cling to each teenager, like invisible threads connecting them to whatever force had guided their boat to safety.

Inside the cabin, the atmosphere was one of controlled urgency as Mia worked to stabilize the four students, administering carefully calculated doses of the counter-agents while monitoring their vital signs. "They're responding," she reported after several tense minutes. "Core temperatures rising, heart rates stabilizing. But they'll need time to fully metabolize the sedatives."

CHAPTER THIRTY SIX
THINNING VEIL

Noah remained at his monitoring station, coordinating with the FBI team, which was now converging on the east bank of the river. "They've located Dr. Rivera's GPS signal," he announced. "Moving to intercept now. Captain Harrison is personally leading the extraction team."

The news brought momentary relief, but it was tempered by the knowledge that James was still in danger, potentially recaptured by Collins and the other Guardians. And somewhere in the tunnels beneath the park, Thompson remained a prisoner or worse. The weight of those still in danger pressed heavily on Sam as he helped Mia position Aaron more comfortably on one of the cots. "What about the ritual?" he asked, turning to his mother, who was examining the stone disk with renewed intensity.

"Collins said it has to be completed by midnight when the alignment peaks. That's less than two hours away." Dr. Rivera nodded grimly, the historian in her analyzing patterns while the mother in her fighting to remain focused despite concern for her husband. "According to Dr. Blackwood and the corrected translation, the ritual doesn't require sacrifice," she explained. "The alignment creates a temporary thinning of what they call the 'veil'–a natural phenomenon that occurs every twelve years. The original purpose was to channel that energy, not feed some interdimensional entity properly."

As if in response to her words, the stone disk began to emit a faint glow similar to the luminescence they had witnessed in the river. Leila drew her grandfather's journal from her backpack, quickly finding the relevant entry. "Here," she said, pointing to a passage. "My grandfather wrote that he believed the ritual had been perverted from its original purpose. The four archetypes—mind, heart, spirit, and hand—are meant to form a circle, channeling energy back into the earth at the moment of alignment and strengthening the natural barrier between dimensions."

Noah looked up from his computer, expression troubled. "But if the ritual needs to be completed properly to maintain this barrier, and the four students are here instead of at the ritual site..."

The implication hung heavily in the air. If the Guardians' centuries-old belief contained even a kernel of truth, some kind of barrier would need maintenance during the alignment, and then preventing the ritual entirely might have consequences beyond saving four lives.

"We need to complete the ritual ourselves," Dr. Rivera concluded, the disk pulsing gently in her palm. "The correct version, based on the true translation. And we need to do it at the central chamber where the energy naturally concentrates."

Leila shook her head in disbelief. "You want to go back down there? With Collins and the others still around?"

"Not all of us," Dr. Rivera clarified. "Just those necessary for the ritual—the four students and myself to oversee it with the correct translation."

Mia looked up from where she was checking Lily's vital signs. "That's not possible," she said firmly. "They're stabilizing, but it will be hours before they're conscious enough to participate in anything, let alone something requiring focused energy or movement." Silence fell as they absorbed this setback, the clock ticking inexorably toward midnight when the alignment would peak.

The moment was broken by Noah's excited voice, "They've got him! The FBI team found Dr. Rivera and is extracting now. ETA to our location: fifteen minutes." Relief washed over the room, especially visible in Olivia's face as she absorbed the news that her husband was safe. But the problem of the ritual remained unsolved. James might have additional insights from his research in Ecuador, but would it be enough to formulate a solution before midnight?

As they debated possibilities, a new pattern appeared on Noah's thermal imaging: multiple heat signatures approaching the cabin from the direction of the river. "We've got company," he warned, switching to the exterior cameras they had positioned earlier.

The screen showed several figures moving through the trees toward the cabin, their movements deliberate and coordinated. "Guardians," Miss Patterson confirmed, recognizing how they positioned themselves to surround the building.

"They must have tracked us somehow." Dr. Rivera made an immediate assessment. "Noah, contact the FBI team. Tell them we need immediate backup. Leila and Sam, help move the students to the back room. Mia, gather only essential medical supplies. We need to be ready to evacuate if necessary."

As they rushed to comply, a voice called from outside Collins, as expected, but with the more cultured tones of Dr. Hargrove. "Dr. Rivera," he called, his voice carrying easily through the cabin's thin walls. "We know you have the selected ones inside. There's no need for further conflict. The ritual must be completed for everyone's safety."

Olivia approached the window cautiously, keeping to one side as she peered out at the surrounding woods. At least six figures were visible in the moonlight, positioned strategically around the cabin. With the river at their back and Guardians blocking the path to the road, evacuation seemed impossible. "What do you propose?" she called back, buying time while the others worked to secure the unconscious teenagers.

Hargrove stepped into a clearing where she could see him more clearly, hands raised to show he was unarmed—though the others undoubtedly weren't. "A compromise," he offered.

"Allow us to complete the ritual with the chosen ones. We can do it here, modified from the traditional setting, but still effective. Once the alignment passes, they will be returned to you unharmed."

The proposition was absurd; there was no scenario in which she would hand over four unconscious teenagers to be sacrificed, no matter how Hargrove phrased it. Yet his approach suggested the Guardians were willing to negotiate rather than attack, which meant they were operating from a position of uncertainty. "And if we refuse?" she called back, needing to understand their limits.

"Then we will be forced to take more direct action," Hargrove replied, his academic tone at odds with the threat his words conveyed. "The consequences of an uncompleted ritual extend far beyond these four individuals. The barrier must be maintained."

Inside, Noah motioned urgently to Dr. Rivera, pointing to his laptop where a message confirmed that the FBI team was ten minutes out with both James Rivera and additional agents. Just ten minutes to hold the Guardians at bay without provoking an immediate assault.

"We need more information before we can consider any arrangement," Olivia called, deliberately slowing the negotiation. "My husband has extensive research on these alignments. When he arrives, perhaps we can discuss alternatives that don't involve harm to these children."

The mention of James Rivera caused visible tension among the Guardians, their postures shifting as they conferred among themselves. "Has your husband been found?" Hargrove asked, surprise evident in his voice. The revelation that James was not only alive but free and en route unsettled the Guardians' plans considerably. Hargrove retreated to consult with the others, allowing Olivia to help move the students to the back of the cabin.

"FBI team is eight minutes out," Noah updated them. "But the Guardians seem to be preparing for something. Thermal shows them grouping for what looks like a coordinated approach from multiple sides."

CHAPTER THIRTY SEVEN
EMMINENT ALIGNMENT

Miss Patterson, who had been unusually quiet during the confrontation, suddenly straightened, her eyes widening as she stared at the four unconscious students. "Look," she whispered, pointing to the faint blue luminescence that had intensified around each teenager, no longer just clinging to their clothing but actively pulsing in rhythm with their heartbeats. The stone disk in Olivia's hand responded, its glow strengthening until it illuminated the entire room with ethereal blue light.

"It's starting," Leila realized, checking her watch. "11:30 PM—the alignment is approaching its peak."

Outside, the Guardians had noticed the growing light emanating from the cabin windows. "Dr. Rivera!" Hargrove called urgency, now evident in his voice. "You don't understand what you're interfering with. The energy must be properly channeled, or the consequences will be catastrophic!"

Inside, the glow continued to intensify, the four unconscious teenagers now floating several inches above their cots, suspended in individual cocoons of blue light. Noah stared in disbelief, his scientific mind struggling to process what he was witnessing. "This can't be happening," he muttered, recording the phenomenon on his laptop camera. "It defies all physical laws."

Miss Patterson approached the floating form of Lily Robertson, the healer, reaching out a tentative hand toward the luminescent field surrounding her. "Don't!" Mia warned, but it was too late.

Patterson's fingers had already made contact with the light. Rather than harm her, however, the energy seemed to flow through her, causing the elderly librarian to gasp as vitality visibly returned to her aged form. "The original purpose," she whispered, wonder replacing fear in her voice. "Harmony between dimensions, not separation through sacrifice. Marcus was right all along."

The phenomenon was accelerating, the cabin itself now vibrating slightly as energy built toward some unknown crescendo.

Outside, the Guardians had abandoned subtlety, now approaching the cabin with clear intent to breach the entrance. Noah's laptop chimed with an alert. The FBI team had arrived at the extraction point by the river, but would still need several minutes to reach the cabin through the woods.

"We need to buy more time," Sam insisted, moving toward the door with Thompson's switchblade still in his hand, wholly inadequate defense against whatever weapons the Guardians carried.

Before he could reach it, however, the door burst open, Collins at the front of a group of four Guardians, all armed and determined. "Step away from them," Collins ordered, weapon trained on Dr. Rivera. "The ritual will be completed as it has been for centuries." The standoff lasted only seconds before being interrupted by the most unexpected sound—coughing from one of the floating teenagers. Aaron Mitchell, the scholar, had begun to regain consciousness within his cocoon of light, eyes fluttering open to take in the extraordinary scene around him.

"What…" he managed, his brilliant mind already cataloging the impossibilities surrounding his levitation, the armed intruders, and the pulsing energy that seemed to connect him to the other three floating students. Sofia Alvarez awakened next, her artistic sensitivity immediately attuned to the visual wonder of the energy field. Then, Caleb Johnson, the natural leader, had his first instinct upon waking to reach the others despite the strange forces holding him aloft. Finally, the healer, Lily Robertson, opened her eyes, immediately concerned for her fellow captives rather than herself.

"The four aspects of humanity," Miss Patterson breathed, understanding dawning on her aged face. "Mind, heart, spirit, and hand—awakening together at the moment of alignment."

Collins appeared momentarily stunned by the teenagers' awakening, his weapon wavering slightly before he steadied it again. "This changes nothing," he insisted. "The sacrifice must be completed. The hunger must be appeased." But there was uncertainty in his voice now, the sight of four conscious teenagers suspended in luminescent energy fields clearly not part of any ritual he had been taught to execute.

Before anyone could react further, new figures appeared in the doorway behind Collins—James Rivera, supported by Captain Harrison in full tactical gear, with several FBI agents securing the perimeter outside. "Lower your weapon, Detective," Harrison ordered, his own service pistol trained steadily on Collins. "FBI. You and your associates are under arrest for kidnapping, attempted murder, and civil rights violations."

Collins didn't comply immediately; his gaze fixed on the floating teenagers as if waiting for some sign or instruction. The standoff stretched for several agonizing seconds before another voice joined the confrontation—Thompson's voice, weary but determined, as the former janitor limped into view behind Harrison. "It's over, Collins," he said simply. "The true ritual is already in progress. These children were never meant to be sacrifices; they're conduits, bridges between worlds."

At Thompson's appearance, surprise registered on the faces of everyone present, especially on Sam, who had believed the janitor had been captured or worse.

Thompson met his gaze briefly, offering a small nod of acknowledgment before focusing again on Collins. "I've called in every favor I've accumulated in fifty years," he said, gesturing to Harrison. "Your organization is being exposed globally as we speak. Every node, every member, every falsified translation."

The distraction provided by Thompson's appearance gave Harrison's team the opening they needed. In a coordinated movement, FBI agents disarmed and secured Collins and the other Guardians, efficiently removing them from the cabin despite their continued protests about the necessity of the ritual. As they were led away, James Rivera finally entered, moving immediately to embrace his wife and son with the desperate relief of someone who had feared never seeing them again.

"You did it," he murmured, holding them close. "You understood about the translation, about the true purpose." Their reunion was interrupted by a sound like crystal chimes as the energy surrounding the four teenagers intensified, the separate fields merging into a single luminescent pattern that matched the stone disk's design. The teenagers remained conscious but entranced, their expressions reflecting wonder rather than fear as they floated in formation at the cardinal points of an invisible circle.

"The alignment peaks in seven minutes," Noah reported, checking his astronomical data. "Whatever's happening is building toward that moment."

James reluctantly released his family, moving to examine the stone disk still pulsing in Olivia's hand. "The Convergence

Stone," he confirmed. "I found its twin in Ecuador, hidden in a temple with identical markings to the Whitmore Tablet. It's a key, not just a record—it activates the true ritual when the alignment approaches."

As if in response to his words, the disk began to rise from Olivia's palm, floating to position itself at the center of the pattern formed by the four teenagers. A beam of light connected each student to the stone, forming a perfect cross of energy that rotated slowly. "What's happening to them?" Sam asked, concern overriding his amazement at the spectacle before them.

James studied the pattern with academic intensity despite his obvious exhaustion. "They're becoming the conduits the original ritual intended," he explained. "The four aspects of humanity—intellect, creativity, leadership, and compassion—channel energy back into the earth rather than being taken from it. The Guardians corrupted this purpose, turning harmony into sacrifice to grant themselves power."

Aaron Mitchell's voice came from within the energy field, startlingly clear despite his suspended state. "I can see it," he said, his scientific mind seemingly able to process the information flowing through him. "The pattern's a mathematical equation balancing forces between dimensions. Perfect symmetry."

Sofia spoke next, sharing her artist's perspective and offering a different insight. "Colors I've never seen before," she whispered. "Connections between everything, seeing music or tasting light."

Caleb Johnson, the natural leader, reached out to the others within their shared energy field. "Together," he urged. "We need to be connected." Lily Robertson completed the circle, her healer's intuition guiding her as she extended her hands to Caleb and Sofia, who reached for Aaron. As their hands met within the luminescence, the energy field consolidated, no longer separating them but uniting them in a single flowing pattern. The stone disk at the center began to rotate faster, emitting pulses of light that expanded outward through the cabin walls, visible now through the windows as concentric circles rippling across the night sky above Northwest River Park.

"One minute to alignment," Noah announced, his scientific detachment momentarily overwhelmed by the wonder of what they were witnessing. Thompson moved to stand beside Miss Patterson, both of them watching with expressions that blended awe with the satisfaction of vindication after decades of helpless observation.

"Marcus would have loved to see this," Patterson murmured. "The true ritual, restored after all these years."

As the clock ticked toward midnight, the energy within the cabin reached an almost unbearable intensity, the air itself seeming to vibrate with potential. Then, precisely at the moment of peak alignment, the rotating pattern collapsed inward, energy flowing from the four teenagers into the stone disk with such force that it briefly outshone every other light source. A pulse of pure blue-white radiance expanded outward from the center, passing harmlessly through everyone present before continuing beyond the cabin, beyond the park, expanding in an invisible wave that could be felt rather than seen. In its wake, the four teenagers were gently lowered to their cots, the luminescence fading from their bodies as they blinked in confusion, fully conscious now but disoriented by their experience.

"Did we...?" Caleb began, looking to the others for confirmation of what had just happened.

Aaron nodded, his analytical mind already working to process the information download he had received during the connection. "The barrier is stabilized," he confirmed. "Not through sacrifice but through harmony. We channeled the excess energy back into the earth where it belongs."

CHAPTER THIRTY EIGHT
THE BARRIER REVEALED

James and Mia quickly checked each teenager, their limited medical training evident in their movements. "They seem unharmed," James reported with relief. "No physical damage from the energy transfer."

In the aftermath of the alignment, a profound peace settled over the cabin as if the proper completion of the ritual had restored the balance that had been missing for centuries. Outside, Harrison's team reported that the Guardians were secure, being transported to federal custody where they would face multiple charges related not just to the current kidnapping but to decades of similar crimes.

Noah's laptop chimed with incoming messages as his pre-established data uploads reached their destinations— comprehensive documentation of the Guardians' activities, membership, and global network distributed simultaneously to law enforcement agencies, media outlets, and secure servers worldwide. "It's done," he announced, satisfaction evident in his voice. "They can't hide anymore."

Thompson settled heavily into a chair, the strain of the night's events visible in his exhausted features. "Fifty years," he murmured. "Fifty years watching and doing nothing. And now, finally..."

He didn't complete the sentence, but the liberation in his expression spoke volumes. As the immediate crisis passed, attention turned to recovery and understanding. Mia continued to check each of the four teenagers, confirming that the counter-agents were successfully neutralizing the sedatives and that their participation in the energy transfer had left no apparent physical effects.

The students themselves were filled with questions, memories of their captivity fragmented by the drugs they had been given, but the experience of the ritual itself was crystal clear in their minds. "I saw... everything," Aaron attempted to explain, his considerable intellect struggling to articulate the experience. "Not just information, but connections—how all knowledge fits together like a perfect equation."

Sofia nodded eagerly, her artist's hands already sketching patterns in the air as if trying to capture what she had witnessed. "Colors beyond the spectrum," she agreed. "And shapes that shouldn't be possible in three dimensions. I need to paint this before it fades."

Caleb, ever the leader, was already thinking of broader implications. "There are others," he said, looking to James for confirmation. "Other nodes around the world where this same ritual has been corrupted. We need to reach them, show them the truth."

Lily, the healer, instinctively moved to check on Thompson, noticing the older man's obvious exhaustion and injuries from his earlier confrontation with the Guardians. "You need medical attention," she told him, examining a particularly nasty cut on his forehead with gentle fingers, "You're going to need stitches; we need to get you to the hospital," as she applied pressure to stop the bleeding.

Captain Harrison approached Dr. Rivera, his professional demeanor softened by the extraordinary events he had witnessed. "We've secured the area and have teams investigating the tunnel network for evidence," he reported. "Preliminary findings confirm everything Dr. Blackwood and your husband revealed about the Guardians' activities. This will take months to unravel fully, but their power structure is effectively dismantled."

Olivia nodded gratefully, her historian's mind already cataloging the significance of what they had discovered for the four rescued students and for understanding a pattern of corruption that had persisted across continents and centuries. "What about Thompson?" she asked, glancing toward the elderly janitor now receiving assistance from both Lily and Mia. "He was instrumental in exposing this. Without him—"

Harrison held up a hand reassuringly. "His actions have been noted. Despite some, shall we say, unorthodox methods, he'll be recognized as a key witness rather than a participant in any criminal activities. My personal recommendation will carry weight in that regard." His gaze shifted to James, who was deep in conversation with the four teenagers, explaining aspects of what they had experienced. "Tonight's events have validated your husband's work in Ecuador. The Guardians' global network is more extensive than even he realized, but with their coordination center exposed, the affiliated groups will likely collapse."

CHAPTER THIRTY NINE
BARRIER INVITATION

As the night progressed into early morning, a strange phenomenon began to manifest around Miss Patterson. The residual energy from the ritual affected her differently than the others, collecting around her in a soft luminescence that grew gradually more pronounced. "Eleanor?" Thompson questioned, noticing the change with concern.

Patterson examined her hands with wonder as the blue light suffused them, seeming to rejuvenate the aged skin before their eyes. "I can feel it," she said, her voice stronger than it had been in years. "The connection between the true purpose of the ritual. It's offering passage."

James approached cautiously, and his experience in Ecuador allowed him to recognize what was happening. "The barrier between dimensions isn't meant to be impenetrable," he explained to the others. "The original ritual established controlled points of connection—opportunities for exchange rather than separation. Miss Patterson is being offered such a connection."

The elderly librarian nodded, understanding dawning in her eyes. "I've always felt I belonged elsewhere," she admitted. "Even as a young girl, I sensed there was more beyond what we could see. That's why Marcus's research resonated so deeply with me and why I kept his work safe all these years."

The luminescence surrounding her intensified, taking on a definite shape—a doorway of light that seemed to open onto a familiar and utterly alien landscape filled with colors that shouldn't exist and structures that defied conventional geometry. "It's beautiful," she whispered, reaching a tentative hand toward the opening.

Thompson moved to her side, concern evident in his weathered features. "Eleanor, are you sure about this? We don't know what's on the other side."

Patterson smiled at him with genuine affection. "We do know, Earl. The four children saw it during the ritual. A place of knowledge and harmony, where the borders between thought and reality are fluid. A place I've dreamed of my entire life without realizing it existed."

She turned to Leila, taking the girl's hands in her own. "Your grandfather believed in connections rather than barriers. He understood that knowledge should flow freely between worlds, not be hoarded by those who would use it for power." To everyone's amazement, as Patterson continued speaking, her appearance began to change—decades melting away as her form reverted to that of a much younger woman, perhaps in her early twenties, though her eyes retained the wisdom of her seventy-six years. "I'm going to continue

Marcus's work," she announced, her voice now vibrant with youthful energy. "Just from the other side of the equation."

The transformed Patterson approached the doorway of light, pausing at its threshold to look back at the assembled group. "Don't mourn for me," she told them, her gaze particularly warm as it rested on Thompson. "This isn't an ending but a beginning—a resistance of a different kind."

With those words, she stepped through the luminescent portal, her form dissolving into the impossible landscape beyond. The doorway remained open briefly, long enough for them all to glimpse the world that had called to her. A realm of pure potential where thought and matter seemed interchangeable, where knowledge existed as tangible architecture. Then, gradually, the portal closed, the light condensing into a single point before winking out entirely, leaving them in the relative darkness of the cabin's interior lighting.

"She's gone," Leila whispered, tears streaming down her face despite Patterson's admonition not to mourn.

Thompson nodded slowly, a complex mixture of emotions passing across his weathered features: joy, loss, and understanding. "She found her home," he said, "just not the one any of us expected."

The light had barely faded when Thompson turned to James, a question in his eyes that needed no verbalization. James nodded in confirmation. "Yes," he said. "The same opportunity is being extended to you. The ritual recognized your decades of silent witness–your potential as a guardian in the true sense, not the corrupted version the organization embodied."

A similar luminescence had begun to gather around Thompson, though less intensely than it had with Patterson, as if the invitation were being offered but not insisted upon. Thompson observed it thoughtfully, watching the light play across his aged hands. "I've seen enough wonders for one lifetime," he said after a long moment of consideration. "Eleanor always dreamed of other worlds. Me, I've just been trying to make peace with this one." The light responded to his decision, receding slightly but not disappearing entirely, shifting instead into a gentler glow that seemed to comfort rather than transform. "I've got someone waiting for me on the other side," Thompson continued, smiling faintly as he glanced upward. "Not another dimension, but whatever comes after this life. Jenny's been patient long enough."

CHAPTER FORTY
FAMILIES REUNITED

As dawn approached, the practical necessities of the aftermath began to assert themselves. Harrison's team had established a secure perimeter around the cabin, and medical personnel had arrived to evaluate the rescued students more thoroughly. Parents had been notified, and their confused relief was apparent even through the phone conversations as they struggled to understand what had happened to their children.

"They'll be here within the hour," Harrison reported after coordinating the family reunions. "We've prepared a simplified explanation for now—a kidnapping plot by a criminal organization, with details to be revealed gradually as the investigation progresses."

Noah had been uploading continuous data streams, ensuring that the evidence they had gathered was secured beyond the Guardians' reach, regardless of whatever political influence they might still maintain. "Every major news outlet has the story," he confirmed, satisfaction evident in his voice. "Not the dimensional aspects—those would strain credibility—but the decades of disappearances, the cover-ups, the prominent community members involved. It's breaking globally."

Mia supervised the final medical preparations for transferring the four students. Her natural empathy was evident in how she explained each step to them, ensuring they understood what was happening despite their lingering disorientation.

As the first light of day filtered through the cabin windows, Thompson's condition began to deteriorate rapidly. The wounds from his confrontation with the Guardians, temporarily masked by adrenaline and the extraordinary events that followed, now made themselves known with a vengeance. He sat heavily in an armchair, breathing labored as Lily hovered nearby, her healer's instinct recognizing something the others hadn't yet noticed.

"Mr. Thompson?" she asked softly, concern evident in her young face.

Thompson offered her a reassuring smile, though the effort clearly cost him. "It's alright, child," he murmured. "Some journeys have to end for others to begin."

Alarmed by his tone, Sam approached, kneeling beside the chair to look into the face of the man who had finally found the courage to act after decades of silent witness. "Thompson," he began, but the elderly janitor shook his head gently. "I took a bullet meant for your father," he admitted, opening his jacket slightly to reveal a bloodstained shirt beneath, the wound he had been concealing since his miraculous reappearance at the cabin. "Managed to get the better of Collins and his men anyway—amazing what motivation can do for an old soldier. But some things can't be patched up with determination alone."

Horror spread through the group as they realized what Thompson had hidden from them: his return, his participation in the final confrontation, had come at a cost he had known he would pay. Harrison immediately called for the medical team, but Thompson waved them off with surprising strength. "Let me have these last moments with clarity," he insisted. "I've waited fifty years to see this wrong righted. Let me enjoy the victory before I rest."

James knelt on Thompson's other side, quickly assessing the wound with professional detachment that couldn't quite mask his emotional response. "Earl," he said softly, using the janitor's first name for the first time. "You saved my life. You saved all of us."

Thompson nodded slightly, his breathing growing more labored. "Finally did something right," he murmured. "Jenkins would be proud." The name of the young medic from Vietnam—the one Thompson had failed to save all those years ago—hung in the air, a ghost finally laid to rest.

Captain Harrison approached, standing at attention before Thompson in silent recognition of one soldier to another. "Staff Sergeant Thompson," he said formally, using the rank Thompson had held in Vietnam. "On behalf of a grateful nation,

I thank you for your service—both in uniform and in the decades that followed."

Thompson's eyes brightened at the acknowledgment, his gaze finding Harrison's with sudden recognition. "Captain Harrison," he said, surprise evident in his weakening voice. "You were there—Quang Ngai Province, 1970. You led the extraction after the ambush."

Harrison nodded, emotion briefly breaking through his professional demeanor. "You carried three wounded men to the extraction point under heavy fire," he confirmed. "Including a young lieutenant who would later become a CIA officer with a particular interest in unexplained phenomena around the world."

Thompson chuckled weakly, wincing at the pain the movement caused. "Small world," he managed. "You sent in the cavalry then, too." His gaze shifted to the four teenagers rescued from the Guardians' ritual: Aaron, Sofia, Caleb, and Lily. They had drawn closer as they sensed the gravity of the moment. "You four," he said, his voice gaining strength temporarily. "What you experienced during the ritual is the knowledge and the connection. Don't lose it. It was meant to be shared, not hoarded."

Aaron nodded solemnly, the scholar in him already working to preserve and understand the information that had flowed through him. Sofia's fingers continued twitching with the need to capture what she had seen, while Caleb's natural leadership had him already considering how to communicate their experience to others.

Lily, the healer, approached Thompson directly, placing her hands gently over his. "I can see it," she said softly. "Where you're going. It's peaceful there."

Thompson smiled, genuine joy transforming his pain-lined face. "I know," he whispered. "I've caught glimpses my whole life. Jenny's there, waiting. And Jenkins, too. No hard feelings after all." The light that had surrounded him earlier intensified again, but differently, not the dimensional doorway that had called to Patterson, but something warmer, more personal.

Thompson's breathing eased as the light enveloped him, his expression relaxing into one of profound peace. "It's time," he murmured, his gaze finding Sam one last time. "Remember, son—courage isn't about not being afraid. It's about being afraid and moving forward anyway."

With those words, the light surrounding him pulsed once, brilliantly, then faded along with his last breath. Earl Thompson, who had carried the burden of inaction for fifty years, had finally found redemption and, with it, release. In the silent moment that followed, even the most skeptical among them could have sworn they glimpsed something extraordinary—a young soldier in a Vietnam-era uniform, accompanied by a smiling woman and a medical orderly, briefly visible in the space where Thompson had been before fading like morning mist in sunlight.

The solemn moment was interrupted by the arrival of the first parents, Mitchell's mother and father, rushing into the cabin with expressions that cycled rapidly between fear, relief, and confusion as they embraced their son. Similar reunions followed quickly as the parents of Sofia, Caleb, and Lily arrived, their tearful joy tempered by uncertainty about what their children had experienced during their captivity.

Harrison's team managed these initial meetings with practiced efficiency, providing the simplified explanation they had prepared while promising more detailed information once the immediate medical concerns had been addressed.

Through it all, the Rivera family remained together, James holding Olivia and Sam close as if afraid they might disappear if he relaxed his embrace. "I thought I'd never see you again," James admitted quietly, his voice rough with emotion. "When they caught me in Ecuador, I realized how far their network extended... I was certain they'd eliminate me once they extracted what I knew."

Olivia pressed closer to him, professional detachment completely abandoned in the face of their reunion. "We never stopped looking," she assured him. "Even when the official search was called off, even when everyone else accepted the story that you'd been lost in a remote area... we knew."

As morning fully established itself, the cabin became a hive of activity medical evaluations, initial statements taken, and evidence cataloged and secured. The four teenagers remained the center of attention, their physical recovery progressing rapidly even as their mental and emotional processing of events would clearly take much longer.

In a quiet moment between the formal procedures, Aaron approached the Rivera family, his brilliant mind having already connected several theoretical dots. "Your father's research," he said to Sam without preamble. "It wasn't just about the ritual. It was about what happens after the correction; what we experienced during the connection."

James nodded, immediately recognizing a kindred scientific mind despite their age difference. "The knowledge transfer," he confirmed. "In Ecuador, I found evidence that previous participants in the correctly performed ritual received information insights beyond our current scientific understanding. But the Guardians suppressed this aspect, keeping the knowledge for themselves to maintain their power structure."

Sofia joined them, with a sketchbook in hand filled with drawings that shouldn't have been possible, structures, and patterns that defied conventional understanding of physics and geometry. "I can't stop drawing what I saw," she explained, her artistic passion evident in every line. "It's like... blueprints for things that don't exist yet but could."

Caleb and Lily completed their impromptu gathering, drawn by the shared experience that now connected them beyond their ordeal as captives. "We need to document everything," Caleb insisted, his leadership qualities already focusing on practical next steps. "Before it fades, before we start doubting what we experienced."

Lily nodded in agreement, her healer's perspective adding another dimension. "There were solutions there," she said quietly. "Answers to problems we haven't fully formulated yet—climate change, disease, conflict. Not complete answers, but directions, paths we could explore."

CHAPTER FORTY ONE
CLOSURE OR BEGINNING?

Captain Harrison observed the conversations from a respectful distance, his expression suggesting that this aspect of the event aligned with the intelligence he had encountered previously. "The phenomenon has been documented at other sites," he confirmed when James caught his eye questioningly. "Information transfer during moments of dimensional alignment. Most of it is dismissed as a hallucination or a religious experience, but a few cases are documented scientifically. Your research in Ecuador was getting uncomfortably close to classified material from similar incidents."

The implication was clear that the government had some awareness of these phenomena, but had approached them from a security perspective rather than a scientific one. James processed this with the practiced neutrality of an academic encountering new data. "Then you understand why this can't be suppressed again," he said, not quite a question. "Why, what these four experienced needs to be properly documented and shared."

Harrison's response was measured, balancing professional caution with personal conviction. "I understand the potential value," he acknowledged. "And after witnessing tonight's events, I'm inclined to advocate for controlled disclosure rather than suppression. The world is facing challenges that conventional approaches aren't adequately addressing."

This tacit support from an unexpected quarter shifted the atmosphere subtly, opening possibilities that might otherwise have remained closed. As the morning progressed, the four teenagers were eventually transported to a hospital for more comprehensive evaluation, though all showed remarkable physical recovery from their ordeal. Their parents accompanied them, still struggling to comprehend the abbreviated explanation they had been given but grateful beyond words to have their children back safely. Before they departed, Aaron pressed a small data card into Sam's hand containing what he described as "preliminary notes on what we experienced."

His eyes conveyed more than his words could safely express in the presence of so many official personnel. "For when you're ready to continue what your father started," he added quietly. Similar moments occurred, with each rescued student sharing selected information, Caleb arranging future meeting times, and Lily offering healing insights for Thompson's peaceful acceptance of his finality that would extend far beyond this extraordinary experience.

The Rivera family remained at the cabin after the others had departed, helping Harrison's team secure the final evidence before the site would be thoroughly investigated. James stood at the window, watching the morning sunlight filter through the trees, his expression reflective after more than six months of captivity and uncertainty.

"What happens now?" Sam asked, joining his father at the window.

James placed an arm around his son's shoulders, drawing him close in a gesture that bridged the time they had lost. "Now we continue the work," he said simply. "Not just documenting what happened here, but understanding the knowledge that was transferred during the ritual. The Guardians corrupted the original purpose to maintain their own power, but the truth was always about connection and sharing, not sacrifice and separation."

Olivia joined them, her historian's perspective already framing these events within larger human development and belief patterns. "The world isn't ready for everything at once," she observed pragmatically. "But small steps, carefully documented and verified... that's how paradigms shift." The three stood together, a family reunited against impossible odds, looking out at a world that had fundamentally changed overnight, though few people realized it.

As they prepared to leave the cabin, Sam took a moment to stand where Thompson had passed peacefully just hours earlier. The chair remained empty, but something of the old janitor's presence lingered—a sense of completion, of burdens finally set down after being carried too long. "He never did tell me exactly what happened to Jenkins," Sam remarked quietly.

James approached, placing a hand on his son's shoulder. "Some stories we don't get to hear in full," he said gently. "But I think Thompson finally finished his own story the way he needed to."

Sam nodded, understanding that redemption sometimes comes in unexpected forms and at unexpected times. What mattered was that Thompson had finally found his courage, had finally taken action when it counted most. As they stepped outside, the afternoon air carried the scent of river water and pine, the natural world seemingly unchanged by the extraordinary events that had transpired beneath the full moon. Yet for those who had witnessed the ritual, seen the true connection between dimensions, and experienced the flow of knowledge that transcended conventional understanding, nothing would ever be quite the same again.

The four missing students had been found, not only rescued from physical captivity but liberated from the corrupted ritual that had claimed so many before them. The cycle that had haunted Pinecrest for over a century had been broken, and the truth of the original purpose was restored. And in that restoration lay possibilities that extended far beyond the boundaries of Chesapeake, Virginia, connections to a deeper understanding that might, in time, address challenges humanity had struggled to solve through conventional means alone.

As Captain Harrison's team continued their documentation of the site, James Rivera embraced his family with the gratitude of someone given a second chance as the first news reports began to circulate about the exposure of a "criminal organization" operating in plain sight for generations, a subtle shift had started. The barrier between worlds remained intact, but it was no longer a wall of separation. Instead, it had become what it was meant to be: a permeable membrane allowing the exchange of knowledge and understanding between dimensions, maintained not by sacrifice but by connection. The final ritual had not ended anything; it had merely begun the next chapter in a story that stretched across worlds, across time, and across the full spectrum of human potential.

-END-

ABOUT THE AUTHOR

Ty Swartz was forged during his 20-year Navy career as a dedicated storyteller and photojournalist, documenting naval history from the decks of amphibious assault ships to Hollywood's film sets, shaping his approach as an educator. He mentors future innovators in Chesapeake, Virginia, crafting narratives, reframing classroom theories into transformative lesson plans, and creating real-world educational passports. Ty has guided over a hundred adventurous students to 13 countries through educational travel, helping them discover the world hands-on. As an award-winning master photographer, Ty owns Swartz Portraits, a fine art high school senior portrait studio focused on crafting storytelling images, in Chesapeake, Virginia.